SHADOW
OF THE
BROTHERHOOD

SHADOW
OF THE
BROTHERHOOD
THE TEMPLE BAR SHOOTINGS

BARRY KENNERK

MERCIER PRESS
IRISH PUBLISHER – IRISH STORY

MERCIER PRESS

Cork

www.mercierpress.ie

Trade enquiries to CMD BookSource,
55a Spruce Avenue, Stillorgan Industrial Park,
Blackrock, County Dublin

© Barry Kennerk, 2010

ISBN: 978 1 85635 677 0

10 9 8 7 6 5 4 3 2 1

A CIP record for this title is available from the British Library

Printed and bound in the EU.

CONTENTS

Author's Note   7

Acknowledgements   9

Dramatis Personae   11

Preface   13

Prologue   17

1   A Strange Errand   21

2   The DMP Man's Hospital   30

3   First Round of Arrests   40

4   Great Britain Street Raid   53

5   Heroic Medicine   75

6   Jack Cade O'Loughlin   79

7   Subscription Funds   89

8   The Net Tightens   99

9   Lives in the Balance   109

10   A Funeral Procession   123

11   International Connections   129

12   Rattled Nerves   142

13   Brandy and Scalpels   148

14   Raid on the Coombe   155

15   The Felon's Track   166

16   A Mock Funeral Procession   176

17   Desperado   184

18   Home for Christmas   203

19   A Discreet Arrest   215

20	Sergeant Kelly has a Visitor	232
21	A Belated Confession	243
22	Commission of 'Oyer and Terminer'	250
23	Trial	257
24	Alibi	278
25	A Plot Unmasked	289
Appendix 1		306
Appendix 2		312
Notes		315
Bibliography		338
Index		346

AUTHOR'S NOTE

None of the dialogue in this book is contrived. Where it appears, it has been taken carefully from one of several sources – newspaper articles, police accounts in the chief secretary's office registered papers (CSORP) or from court records. In some instances composite newspaper reports have been used to provide the most rounded portrayal, but the material has not been augmented for dramatic effect. References to weather conditions use hourly records taken at the Phoenix Park weather observatory. Descriptions of gas lamps, bridges, buildings and other aspects of the built environment are derived from old photographs or relevant printed material (e.g. Dublin Corporation reports) dating from the period under study. It would be impossible to annotate all of the above sources in the text.

For my parents,

whose faith in me is as big as a mustard seed.

ACKNOWLEDGEMENTS

This book would not have been possible without the assistance of many people. To begin with, I would like to thank the team at Mercier Press whose cheerful dedication shows why they are a household name in Ireland and beyond. I would like to thank John Spicer of Champion Hill Relics for his expert knowledge of the weaponry used during this period; Aoife Carroll, barrister-at-law, for her help in understanding courtroom practices and terms; Niall Bergin of Kilmainham Gaol for his enthusiastic response to my queries; Irish police historian Jim Herlihy, for taking the time to point me in some interesting directions; and Inspector Pat McGee, Donal Kivlehan and Gerry Kilgallon of the Garda Museum and Archives, Dublin Castle, for their courtesy and professionalism. Denis McCarthy of Dublin Castle also deserves a special mention.

Of no less importance was the help I received from Nuala Canny of the OPW and from photographer Tommy Nolan. Valuable assistance was also given by the staff of the Meteorological Office, Glasnevin, and by the Local Studies Department, Westmeath County Library.

I would also like to acknowledge the helpfulness of the staff at the National Archives, Bishop Street, the staff at the National Library, Kildare Street, and Mary O'Doherty and Robert Mills of the RCSI and RCPI archives respectively. Eva Ó Cathaoir, a singular authority on Patrick Lennon, was a particular inspiration and guide. She took the time to meet me and imparted some valuable insights. I would also like to thank Shane MacThomáis of Prospect Cemetery, Glasnevin, for his invaluable assistance in helping me to reconstruct a brief biography of Superintendent Daniel Ryan.

I also received some excellent help from a number of UK researchers. Peter Davis provided information about HMS *Royal George* and methods of prisoner transportation for the period and Rosalie Spires helped to research records held at the Public Record Office, London. David Cross, keeper of the West Midlands Police Museum was particularly forthcoming in helping to understand the relationship between the Dublin and Birmingham Police.

My final thanks go to Dr Marta Ramón García, Professor Vincent Comerford (NUI Maynooth) and Dr Carla King (St Patrick's College, Drumcondra). Dr King took the time to read the manuscript and offered many helpful hints and suggestions. Such altruism is in the true spirit of the *Alma Mater*.

DRAMATIS PERSONAE

Name and occupation	When arrested and where
Patrick Hayburne, barber	31 October 1867, Thomas Street
Thomas Rooney, quay porter	1 November 1867, Great Britain Street
Peter McDonnell, bootmaker	Ditto
John Dowling, casual labourer	Ditto
David Francis Murray McHale, labourer	Ditto
Jack Cade O'Loughlin (informer)	1 November 1867, Upper Abbey Street
James Dondrell (alias 'Sweeney'), bootmaker	5 November 1867, South Great Georges Street
John Walsh, pawnbroker's assistant	15 November 1867, Capel Street
Michael Feely, carpenter	17 November 1867, Mabbot Lane
Patrick McGarry, labourer	17 November 1867, Lisburn Street
William Hopper, shop assistant	23 November 1867, The Coombe
Stephen John Henrick, shop assistant	23 November 1867, The Coombe
John Keogh, shop porter	23 November 1867, The Coombe
Thomas Francis, bootmaker	25 November 1867, New Street
Patrick Lennon, cork cutter	8 January 1868, Duke Street
Denis Downey, tailor	15 January 1868, Dawson Street
Charles McNamara, bottle glass worker	17 January 1868, Londonderry
John Waters, journalist	17 January 1868, en route to *Irishman* offices
James Cooke, unknown	11 July 1868, London

INVESTIGATING OFFICERS (DUBLIN METROPOLITAN POLICE)

A Division (Chancery Lane)
Inspector William Doran

G Division (Detective Branch, Exchange Court)
Superintendent Daniel Ryan
Acting Superintendent James Ryan
Acting Inspector Mathew Carey
Acting Inspector Joseph Clarke
Acting Inspector John Egenton
Acting Inspector Rotheray
Acting Inspector William Doyle
Inspector Edward Entwhistle

TRIAL OF PATRICK LENNON (10–15 FEBRUARY 1868)

Defence Team
Theobald Andrew Purcell (Barrister)
John Ayde Curran (Barrister)
Mr Rogers (Attorney)

Crown Prosecution
Richard Warren (Attorney-General and MP)
Mr Owen (Barrister)
Dr John Thomas Ball (Barrister and MP)
Michael Harrison (Solicitor-General)
Charles Shaw (Law Advisor)
Samuel Lee Anderson (Crown Solicitor)

Judiciary
Justice John David Fitzgerald
Baron Rickard Deasy

PREFACE

Late nineteenth-century Fenian literature abounds with noble-hearted heroes who are set in contrast, both morally and physically, with the armed forces of the crown – a body of men who only find bravery *en masse*. Such accounts, written in response to public demand, were often influenced by a kind of Celtic romanticism heightened by the author's years in America or by an unashamed desire to marshal support for 'the cause'. The story of Irish nationalism is not simply some Boy's Own adventure, however. Every armed struggle incurs a cost in innocent lives.

The Irish Revolutionary (later Republican) Brotherhood or IRB was founded in 1858 by James Stephens, following the collapse of the Young Ireland movement and the disastrous rebellion of 1848. James O'Mahony formed a sister movement in America called the Fenian Brotherhood, while IRB cells were also set up in England. In an attempt to limit infiltration of the organisation by informers, the Brotherhood was divided into a number of 'circles', cells of men limited to 820 members who were under the control of one centre or leader (see Appendix 2). In theory, the members of each circle were known only to each other.

In March 1867, an IRB-led uprising in Counties Kerry, Limerick, Cork and Dublin was harshly suppressed by the British authorities. In its aftermath, the attitude of the authorities reflected the opinion that the IRB was a spent force. To some extent this view was correct, but in the months that followed, a series of incidents, such as the rescue of IRB leaders Colonel Thomas J. Kelly and Captain Deasy in Manchester, and an attack on the Middlesex House of Detention in Clerkenwell, proved that the Brotherhood was still operational on some level. Victorian Britain was appalled by these 'outrages' and they prompted the swearing in of special constables and the continuation of the Habeas Corpus Suspension (Ireland) Act, a piece of legislation that allowed citizens to be summarily arrested and detained in times of crisis. In 1868, fears of its expiration led to pressure on a minority Conservative government from a Liberal opposition, who argued for the need to grant further concessions to Ireland in the form of church disestablishment or land reform to settle the country. The debate was not easily resolved.

These 'headline' events were coupled with a wave of smaller disturbances across Ireland, England, Scotland and Wales, many of which presented a collective threat just as grave as any single 'outrage'. Unlike the events at Manchester, Clerkenwell and elsewhere, these were undoubtedly carried out with the intention of creating a general sense of panic and included assassination attempts, attacks with Greek fire (a white phosphorus incendiary device) and parcel bombs through the post. In Dublin, such guerrilla action was allegedly spearheaded by a group drawn from IRB 'circles' to form a secret assassination squad – a body whose existence was denied by some Fenian leaders, but which Superintendent Daniel Ryan of Dublin Castle's detective division maintained had been in existence since as early as 1865. When the anti-Fenian writer John Rutherford penned a book entitled *The Secret History of the Fenian Conspiracy* in 1877, it provided lurid details about the circle's activities under the leadership of Colonel Kelly, who had been 'Chief Organiser' of the IRB during the failed rising. The police had reason to believe that Kelly had established the shooting circle around 1865. Afterwards it seems to have had various leaders – each man taking the mantle of control as his predecessor was arrested.

Between November 1865 and October 1867, there were several shooting incidents, none of which showed great planning or co-ordination. After Colonel Kelly's arrest, the Irish and British administrations began to attribute overall direction of the circle to William Randall Roberts, president of the American Fenian Brotherhood's more militant 'senate wing'. In reality, it is probable that neither Kelly nor Roberts was affiliated with the circle for more than a brief period and for no longer than was politically advantageous. It was a maverick movement, operating on the fringes of IRB operations.

On 31 October 1867, Sergeant Kelly and Constable Keena became its best-documented victims. Were it not for Surgeon Richard G.H. Butcher's *On Gunshot Wounds and their Treatment* (1868), their story might never have been told. His treatise gives a day by day (sometimes hourly) account of his efforts to save their lives at Mercer's Hospital and as a result, *Shadow of the Brotherhood* presents the reader with two perspectives. On the one hand it is an investigation into the murky world of the IRB radical; on the other it is a portrayal of the suffering endured by the victims of nationalist violence. There is a kind of tragic pathos in both.

PROLOGUE

Kilmainham Gaol stood squat and impregnable in the early dawn, its strong ashlar walls slickened with dew. Suddenly, somewhere in the outside wall, a gate opened and a short, willowy figure slipped quietly into the gloom. As soon as the man appeared, two other figures – detectives from Dublin Castle – stepped quickly out of sight across the street.

Further down the mall that led from the gate, four men stood waiting for the newly released inmate. The detectives recognised two of them – Patrick Hayburne and John Clohissy. Sentenced at the special commission in 1865, they had been released from Kilmainham at the end of September. After a short greeting, which the policemen strained to overhear, the men walked off together. The detectives followed at a distance.

The freed man was Arthur Forrester, the eighteen-year-old son of a stonemason. He had come to Dublin from Lancashire in 1866 as a fiery, rather poetic young rebel. He played a key role in the attack on Chester Castle on 11 February 1867, but was arrested just a few days later, having travelled to Dublin to take part in the rising. Released due to his youth and a lack of evidence, this Fenian leader was re-arrested later that March in a Camden Street public house. When the police burst in, he drew a revolver and swore that he would kill the first policeman who laid hands on him. Afterwards his only regret was that he had been unable to shoot any of his captors. During his six-month term behind bars, Dublin Castle continued to press the English police for information about Forrester. They no longer believed him to be a mere foot soldier, recognising him to be the probable messenger between journalist John Flood, Irish-American Captain John McCafferty and other Fenians in their plans to raid Chester Castle for arms prior to the rising. He was 'smart', they believed, with 'the cunning of a fox'.

After a greeting from another early morning well-wisher, the five men took a long, meandering walk down the quays and the detectives watched as they went into 43 Essex Street – Forrester's home before his arrest. They waited nearby, informing their superintendent by dispatches that their mark would probably leave for England in the evening. Presumably he would return first to his mother's house in Salford and then go on to Manchester. In anticipation of his departure, Acting Superintendent James Ryan wrote to the police commissioners. He was confident that:

> Although the spirit of Fenianism is as buoyant as ever, still no active measures have been taken to forward the conspiracy here – at least there are no manifest signs of such activity and the whole attention of the conspirators seems directed towards England.[1]

In the short autumn evenings, bearded tradesmen huddled conspiratorially in the city's public houses, muttering about their imprisoned leaders. Such conversations were overheard and relayed by plainclothes detectives and informers to the authorities. However, as far as could be ascertained, no new IRB meeting places or drill halls were being established and its city leadership seemed disorganised or non-existent. As a result, the police glibly turned their attention towards England, especially the north, where they identified a great renewal of Fenian activity. There, the Fenian Brotherhood drew upon old working-class labour movements such as the Chartists for support. It was said that they were buying up arms in Birmingham and that Greek fire was being manufactured in Liverpool for the rescue of the Fenian leaders Colonel Kelly and Captain Timothy Deasy, who were incarcerated in Manchester in September 1867.

Back on Essex Street, the detectives shuffled impatiently in the cold outside No. 43 and waited for Arthur Forrester to leave the country. All day they watched as large numbers of radical-looking young men came and went from the house, and it was late evening before the subject of their vigil finally emerged. Before setting off in pursuit, they dispatched a constable to the Castle. From there, a telegram was relayed to the chief constable at Chester, informing him that Forrester was due to leave for England that same night.

At the North Wall, they purposely stood in full view of the *Admiral Monson*'s gangway. As Forrester prepared to embark, they were unable to resist making some sarcastic remarks that the young Fenian found it impossible to ignore. Through discoloured teeth, he replied in his very correct English accent: 'I was too well watched here to do any good.'

As the steamship pushed out into the bay towards Holyhead, it seemed as though the dangerous axis of Fenianism was shifting, obtusely and stubbornly, towards England.

1

A STRANGE ERRAND

12.30 a.m., Thursday morning, 31 October 1867

Across the dark swirl of the river mouth, the monotonous chime of a fog bell tolled purposefully, calling to unseen ships out in Dublin Bay. The sound carried under the solemn arches of the Carlisle and Metal Bridges, and up along Parliament Street where, with a dutiful tread, Constable Patrick Keena made his way towards the river, his unhurried stride dictated by official instructions. As he walked, his helmet and silver badge, number 167A, gleamed dully under the dim gaslight.

For their part in quashing the Fenian rising, the constabulary had been awarded two thousand pounds that August by a grateful parliament. Some of this was shared among the men as a reward for bravery, but associated plans to use the rest to replace the uniform with a new green one had not been passed. Thus, at nine o'clock the men, dressed in their familiar navy, had marched out on duty from Chancery Lane station, an occurrence which attracted the usual interest from those who lived in the tenement houses nearby. The public houses closed at eleven o'clock and as the last of the horse-drawn omnibuses was taken off the streets, a heavy mist began to fall. A constable's bull's-eye lantern could do little in such conditions.

Here and there, one or two people scuttled uncertainly into the dark. On Sackville Street, an upholsterer named Patrick McDonnell escorted a young lady to her lodgings and as they passed under the looming portico of the General Post Office, McDonnell noted that the time was now twenty to one. The few small reflector lamps over the post office boxes were dark. It would take him another ten minutes to get home to Dorset Street. Occasionally a cabman and his horse, starting out from the shelter under the Loopline Bridge, clipped past. Above such sights, the fog rolled, dampening the quaysides and making gloomy behemoths of the wooden-shuttered shops along its banks.

City Hall skulked unseen in the shadows behind the young constable. Keena was due to finish his shift at three o'clock that morning. Although he had only arrived from Mullingar two years before, he already had an extensive knowledge of the area's inhabitants and of the maze of alleyways and laneways that criss-crossed his beat.

It was warm for October and therefore agreeable enough for a man in uniform. Fortunately a pinch of cold air prevented the nearby drains from becoming noisome. During the summer, the beat was made unbearable by the shocking state of the sewers in Parliament Street and nearby Essex Street, not to mention the river into which they fed. The corporation had plans to lay four hundred and fifty feet of new pipes the following year.

As he walked, Keena's truncheon – the only weapon he

possessed – rested by his side. Nearby, at least four policemen from other divisions patrolled the same area, which was well known for prostitutes. One such haunt was Essex Gate, the intersection of which Keena now passed. Somewhere off to his right, an unseen cabbie and his horse waited at the stand outside the Dolphin Hotel.

There had been ominous portents earlier that evening. At eight o'clock, Constable Canning from B Division reported that while on the beat he had heard an explosion in the direction of Great Clarence Street and, in the words of his superintendent, found 'some kind of liquid composition burning on the footpath and against an old wooden gate'.[1] Having seen a demonstration of Greek fire at the Castle, Acting Sergeant Cole was sure that it was the same substance. The report reached G Division, the Castle-based detective branch of the Metropolitan Police, at half-past ten.

Officially, the administration proclaimed this to be a mere 'trifling' incident, confident that their measures were sufficient to curtail any remnants of revolutionary spirit. But despite Acting Superintendent Ryan's declaration that no Fenian meetings were being planned, a report had recently come in that one such had been held in Dorset Street on 24 October. In the event of an attempt to free Fenian prisoners, a strong force of Lancers waited near Kilmainham Gaol and a stock of hand grenades was on order for Mountjoy.

Halting for a moment at the corner of Wellington quay near Mason's opticians, Constable Keena was saluted by his division colleague Constable John Hickey, a young Meath man who had joined the force just four months after him. They possibly exchanged some banter about their respective beats. Then, remembering that the division sergeant would be around in a moment, Hickey turned and walked back in the direction of City Hall.

Left alone on the dark quay, the young policeman took note of the time. It was now a quarter to one. It would be best to stop there and wait for the sergeant to make his inspection. Across the carriageway, Essex Bridge brooded sullenly. As Keena peered into the fog, he made out the figure of a man lingering by the bridge in a dark coat. After a few minutes, the man crossed over onto Wellington Quay and walked in the direction of the Metal Bridge. The constable followed him.

As they passed the premises of Scott and Bell, silk mercers and drapers, a gas lamp afforded Keena a better view. He could see now that the man carried a white or lightish-coloured bundle under his arm. Perhaps he was a demobbed American soldier, a sight that had become almost commonplace in the city. Whatever the case, he reasoned that the man had probably committed some robbery or was about to commit one and that it would not be right to let him pass without seeing what was in the package. Reaching the doorway of James Duffy's, wholesale bookseller and publisher, Keena marshalled his authority enough to shout: 'Stand!'

It was enough to bring the man up short. Instead of turning around, however, he took a few steps forward without speaking. It was a very unnatural reaction but the constable continued to advance. Just as he caught up with the man, the stranger wheeled around, the ends of his jerry coat swishing against Keena's tunic. Everything seemed to happen in an instant. There was a flash, the sound of a report and then a cloud of blinding sulphurous smoke. Keena felt as though he had been punched hard in the chest and he fought hard to catch his breath. 'You Yankee son of a bitch,' he cursed as he watched his assailant sprint along the quay before disappearing into the mist.[2]

Constable Hickey came careening back down Parliament Street, but the Dolphin Hotel cabbie was the first to reach Essex Bridge. 'There's a house after falling,' he cried. His words echoed those of a Charles Street resident who had witnessed the shooting of Constable O'Neill the previous year. That a gunshot could evoke the fear of crumbling masonry so readily was a reminder of the state of the city's buildings. When a man staggered towards them on the footpath, they failed to realise at first that it was Constable Keena. He fell into Hickey's arms outside the Clarence Hotel, still unaware that he had been shot and wondering what ailed him.[3] When the enormity of what had happened finally dawned on him, he cried, 'I am murdered; I am shot; bring me the priest!' It was obvious that he was suffering from shock. Barking an order, Hickey sent the cabbie running back into Essex Street to untether his horse.

Just a few minutes earlier, Sergeant Kelly from College Street station had been on patrol in Temple Bar. He had a chequered police career – a long period of service, broken for a few years and then re-established two years previously. He lingered for a moment under the gas lamp framing the entrance to

Merchant's Arch. He had dark, almost Mediterranean features – a thin, small nose and a tight, wiry beard that left the cheeks over his chinstrap bare. He had been on duty for two and a half hours, and it would be a long night until he went off at six. The mist fell like a light rain on his face. He would be soaked through if he didn't get out of it soon. Once he had finished inspecting Constable Morton and the other men, he might walk as far as the cabman's shelter in Essex Street. Four years earlier, cheered on by a crowd on Eden Quay, Kelly had helped to remove an axe-wielding maniac from the rigging of the smack *Joseph and Mary*, when the old man, bent on destroying the masts, had refused to come down. He was no longer as fit as he had been then.

The GPO clock struck the quarter hour. A pair of corporation lamplighters saluted him as they went by, ladders in tow. Another few minutes and they would begin turning off the gas for the night.

When he heard the pistol report, Kelly jolted. In the silence that followed he could hear the gas hissing in the lamp beside him. Then there was a dull, scraping sound as a sash window was lifted in its frame. Collecting his thoughts, he gripped his truncheon and ran under the arch, down the steps and onto the quayside. The carriageway was empty of traffic. Looking past the abrupt end of an experimental length of tram rail, he caught sight of Constable John Morton standing near the Metal Bridge. Morton crossed over to join him and the two policemen, both over six feet tall, cut a striking appearance as they raced into the fog in the direction of the shot.

Morton, who was the younger of the two by about ten years, ran on towards Parliament Street. At eleven o'clock, he had taken a leisurely dander as far as there, but now he could not even make out City Hall. He listened, but neither heard nor saw anybody. The cabbie had already left with Constables Hickey and Keena.

Behind him, Sergeant Kelly stopped to catch his breath before turning left into Eustace Street. Morton was fitter than him and he felt thoroughly winded. Looking towards the junction of Essex Street, he could vaguely make out the shape of a gas lamp on the right-hand corner, its light thrown into an eerie dull arc by the fog. Mary Donnelly, who was one of the area's 'unfortunate females', instantly recognised the sergeant as he approached – no doubt because he had once reprimanded her for some late-night assignation. At the same time, she spotted the dark shadow of a man as it moved across the lamplight to block the policeman's advance.

'Stand back,' the man warned.

Then, without waiting for a response from Sergeant Kelly, he drew a weapon from his pocket. The sergeant appeared to pay him no heed or, at the very least, Mary Donnelly heard no reply. As she looked on, there was a report, a flash and Kelly dropped onto the footpath.

'Police! Murder!' she screamed.

The gunman turned and threw her a fierce look. For a moment she thought he would shoot her also, but he just dropped the weapon into his right coat pocket and disappeared into the fog. Left alone in the street, she stooped over the sergeant's body. He was still alive but moaning loudly. She made a vain effort to carry him to safety, but he was too heavy. In desperation she repeated her cry of 'Murder!'

Ann Clarke, who had been standing in Crown Alley when the first shot was fired, was hurrying along Fownes Street when she saw the gunman. He paid her no heed but ran down the right-hand side of the street towards the river. Hearing Donnelly's screams, she ran on until she saw Sergeant Kelly lying on the wet cobbles. A number of street children stood close by. In a blind panic, she ran for help and almost ran into the sturdy form of Constable Michael Jordan at the corner of Temple Lane. Grabbing him by the waist, she cried: 'Murder, murder; there is a policeman shot!'

With some distaste, he noted the smell of drink on her breath. At the junction of Essex Street and Eustace Street they were joined by Constable James Donnelly, who had been standing at the corner of Fleet Street. He had quickly changed his mind about the commotion being just one of the almost nightly rows among the local prostitutes. He immediately recognised Mary Donnelly, undoubtedly for the same reason that Sergeant Kelly would later claim to know Ann Clarke. Both worked in a brothel at 23 Wood Street.

The sergeant lay on his right side where the bullet had lodged. Groaning loudly from the pain, he told Constable Jordan the direction in which the gunman had gone, but before Jordan could question him any further, there was a steady clip of hooves as a second cabbie emerged through the mist, heading towards the quays. Flagging him down, Constables Jordan and

Donnelly put the stricken sergeant into the car and turned the horse back in the direction of Mercer's Hospital. Constable Morton, having heard the second shot, later reported in his beat book seeing 'a car with some persons on it ... there were policemen with the car'.[4]

2

THE DMP MAN'S HOSPITAL

The journey to Mercer's Hospital over the treacherous cobble-stone streets had been an uncomfortable one at best. Since the outside car had back-to-back bench seats facing outwards, the cabbie had been obliged to pull the hinged bar across Constable Keena to prevent him falling out. Before dismounting at City Hall, Constable Hickey asked him to go either to the hospital or to Chancery Lane station house, but using his best judgement, he decided on the former. As a reward, he was given double the usual cab fare.

The arrangements for Keena's treatment were made under the careful eye of Dr James Shaw, resident of the hospital. The young Drogheda-born apothecary had worked at Mercer's for about a year and he quickly gave instructions for Keena to be moved to an upstairs ward before sending for the surgeon, Richard Butcher. All the while, the young constable called for a priest, believing himself to be dying.[1]

The hospital, with its sixty-nine beds, was a small institution by city standards, comparable in size with Jervis Street Hospital on the north side of the city or with the Richmond, Hardwicke and Whitworth Hospitals. Tonight, being busier than usual, it was almost full. Although priority was given to surgical admissions, some of the fifty-eight in-patients were 'social' cases. One such, Teresa Cooney, had been in the hospital for some days. She had been beaten and neglected by a drunken and abusive father, and slept in a general adult ward. Another patient called Mary Hughes had been brought in the previous night with severe head wounds. She reported to a constable that her husband hit her with a hammer. He later protested that it was in self-defence.

Infectious patients who were turned away from other hospitals were admitted to Mercer's because of its daytime dispensary.[2] That put pressure on staff during outbreaks of disease. Moreover, its location in the midst of a neighbourhood of dirty, overcrowded tenements was hardly appealing. The window at the end of a central corridor dividing the wards overlooked a small garden in which a few gravestones from the churchyard of St Stephen remained. The view extended over some cattle sheds and into Andrew Moore's stables where a large, reeking manure heap stood. Depending on the prevailing wind, the smell often carried through the hospital windows.

Despite such disadvantages, the little hospital was well known as a Dublin Metropolitan Police (DMP) institution and it had served the force well in times past. In this it was comparable to the Richmond Hospital, whose handbook for resident pupils stated that 'in applications for admission as patients, members of the police force are to have a preference, and, in all present cases, vacancies must be made for them'.[3]

Ten years previously, Surgeon Butcher had treated the wounds of some of the officers involved in a serious riot at Trinity College. In more recent days, Constable Byrne had been admitted with head injuries sustained while he attempted to disperse a crowd in Thomas Street.

At other times, however, the surgeons were obliged to treat the very men whom the police sought to apprehend. Just five months earlier, Alfred Aylward, a prominent young law clerk and informer, had arrived at Mercer's by cab to receive treatment for three gunshot wounds. Constable Ryan had waited in the hall until he had his injuries dressed before arresting him. Around the same time, the hospital received a Fenian prisoner named Patrick Kearney, who was treated under guard for serious head and face wounds, his nose having been broken by the haft of Inspector Clarke's revolver. That same May, Fenian desperado James Cody was brought in for injuries he sustained during a scuffle with the police in Clarendon Street. For a small institution like Mercer's, it sometimes seemed as though it was under siege.

To Inspector William Doran of Chancery Lane station, however, the latest shootings were just two in a succession of similar incidents. He lived at nearby Usher's Quay and arrived at Mercer's at ten past one. Sleep-tousled and a little unkempt, he made his way up the gas-lit stairs and along the whitewashed corridor to the ward where Constable Keena lay. Despite efforts to brighten its appearance, the *Medical Press* had commented in 1865 that Mercer's was 'sadly out of repair'.[4] There were three floors above basement level and for convenience (and since the small two-bedded private ward was occupied) the young policeman was probably moved to the first of these. There were only eight wards, so locating him would not have been difficult.

This was the second Dublin shooting in the space of a month. Some days earlier, an unarmed plainclothes constable named John Ryan had been assigned to watch informer George Reilly as he drank with a friend in Robinson's – a public house near Blackrock hill. When the constable went outside to take some air, a shot whistled past, badly injuring a bystander. Taking cover, Ryan ran back inside and demanded that Reilly loan him his revolver. Ducking back out of doors, he took off in pursuit of his assailant. Meanwhile, a uniformed officer named Donohoe had heard the commotion and arrived on the scene. Neither was in time to stop the gunman from jumping into a waiting car and, as it sped away, its four passengers rained a deadly hail of gunshot fire onto the two officers. Both were unharmed and Constable Ryan even managed to discharge a single shot in their direction. Afterwards George Reilly was sent to the crown witness depot in Chancery Lane for his protection. Tonight's incident bore certain similarities.

There had also been another assassination attempt in September on Ormond Quay – one that left commercial agent Robert Atkinson badly wounded. This had almost certainly been a case of mistaken identity, the real target being Head Constable Thomas Talbot.[5]

Surgeon Butcher had not yet arrived. The embers of a fire sputtered in the grate at one end of the lofty, spacious ward.

Sitting by the bedside, Inspector Doran took out a pencil and some paper and prepared to take a hasty deposition. With an almost comedic pathos, the young constable told him that he was 'dying as fast as he could'. Although afraid that he would not survive long enough to give an official account to the magistrate when he arrived, Keena managed to maintain a remarkable degree of lucidity:

> I saw the man that shot me on Wellington Quay. He came from the quayside of the houses. He had a whitish-coloured bundle under his arm. I told him to wait and he at once turned around and fired at me. He was quite close to me at the time. He was low-sized, had a short black coat; I cannot say what he had on his head.[6]

As they spoke, the greying, ringlet-haired Mr Butcher was driving himself furiously by horse and car around St Stephen's Green from Herbert Street. By day, this reckless behaviour had earned him the nickname of 'Jehu', so-called after the infamous charioteer king of Israel, but thankfully the city streets were empty at night apart from the occasional cabbie and the man who sold coffee at a Grafton Street stand.

Butcher's medical casebooks reveal a man used to dealing with patients of all ages and with a broad range of complaints. Besides practising orthopaedic surgery, he treated various cancers, cleft lip and palate problems, kidney disorders, as well as trauma resulting from cases of drowning, rape, accidents and assaults – an eclectic mix. The condition of the wounded policeman evoked feelings of sympathy in him. Keena was a pitiable spectacle; in the surgeon's own words, he was:

Haggard, wild-looking, pale as death, greatly excited, tossing his hands and arms about and screaming if it was possible he could recover. The body was cold, pulse feeble and I will never forget the bewildered look of despair in which he implored to be rescued from pain; from the burning agony in which he writhed.[7]

During his examination, Butcher found a small transverse wound about three inches below the extremity of Keena's ensiform cartilage – the tip of bone below the sternum or breastbone. It looked as though it had been made by a worn shoemaker's knife, but there was very little blood.

Next, he attended to Sergeant Kelly who had just come in, supported by Constables Donnelly and Jordan. The sergeant, whose pain prevented him from stringing a sentence together, was stripped for examination by Dr Shaw and Constable Donnelly. His suffering did not seem to be as acute as the younger policeman's, but the location of his wound was similar.

Unless a shooting injury was relatively uncomplicated, most doctors adopted a conservative approach. Essentially, this entailed the daily administration of opium or its brandy-based tincture laudanum, but such remedies were often insufficient to fully deaden the sufferer's pain and many patients failed to obtain any real relief.

Mr Butcher was guided in the conduct of his examinations, as in all of his subsequent treatment, by the writings of John Hunter, whose work entitled *Treatise on the Blood, Inflammation and Gunshot Wounds* was published in 1794. The conservative Glaswegian surgeon's work was espoused by Butcher as 'a monument of his ability, his originality, and his profound thought'. Butcher also kept reference works by Guthrie, Hennen and Thompson, and, judging by his later notes, probably had a copy of Dr Thomas Longmore's *Treatise on Gunshot Wounds*.[8] This American doctor was seen as a foremost authority in Ireland, as evidenced by Dr William Stokes, a pioneer in anatomical diagnosis, who extolled him as 'one of the highest living authorities on military surgery'.[9] Longmore advocated 'the inspection of the garments worn over the part wounded … as a guide in determining whether foreign bodies have entered or not'.[10] In Sergeant Kelly's case this yielded excellent results as Mr Butcher observed that the bullet appeared to have taken an indirect course internally, glancing off one of the buttons on his tunic. Satisfied, he left the sergeant in the care of Dr Tisdall and returned to Constable Keena.

At two o'clock, some three-quarters of an hour after his arrival, Sergeant Kelly was ready to make a declaration to Inspector Doran, and a Kingstown patient called Christopher Holbrook overheard him say, 'I would not know the man again.' He watched as Kelly was turned in bed by the hospital's two porters. Before Kelly could complete his statement, he was interrupted by the arrival of Father Crotty, who had come from Whitefriar Street to administer the last rites.

Meanwhile, Constable Hickey was still on duty. After escorting Constable Keena as far as City Hall, he had jumped off the car and gone into the detective office to file a report. The room was empty apart from Sergeant Charles Smith, who was sitting behind his desk. On receipt of Hickey's news, he grabbed a revolver from the wall and ran into the fog. Twenty minutes passed before he returned empty-handed. By that time, the gunman was probably long gone and, with nothing else to be done, Hickey returned to Chancery Lane.

Shortly afterwards, Inspector Doran left the hospital. At the behest of Acting Superintendent James Ryan, he helped to organise all the available men from the four town divisions and G Division into search parties. They were ordered to search opium halls, brothels, ships in the river 'and every imaginable place where the assassin could take refuge'.[11] One such opium hall was on the very doorstep of Chancery Lane station and could only be accessed via a basement ladder.

Essex Street was in uproar for the second time that year. In January, a parcel belonging to a lodger at No. 8 had exploded in the face of his curious landlord – an event that caused the side walls and partition of the drawing-room, as well as the windows, to be blown out. Soon afterwards the street had been filled with the voices of policemen urging the crowd to keep back and the rattle of firemen's ladders. Once again, on the morning of 31 October, houses in the Temple Bar area were searched, including Arthur Forrester's last known residence at 43 Essex Street where, in the aftermath of the shooting, witnesses reported seeing two men running into the hall.

The officers involved were well aware of the dangers of making such a search. In 1855, a retired detective named Richard Doran was passing through Essex Street when he was recognised by an elderly woman, whose jeers of derision drew a crowd. Gathering around her, they knocked him to the ground and kicked him brutally, one of them stabbing him in the wrist with a knife. In 1866, Constable Penrose had a poker rammed into his eye when he peered through a Temple Bar keyhole during his hunt for a fugitive drunk. The injury kept him in hospital for six weeks. In recent years, the beating of lone officers had become so frequent that it had entered into local parlance as the 'popular amusement'. Eventually, this activity became organised around a Dublin street gang known as the 'band boys', the most notorious member of which was a powerfully built man named Francis Lacy. He served several prison terms, the longest of which lasted five years.[12]

Such hazards were undoubtedly mitigated by the size of the search party on this occasion. Chief Superintendent Campbell gave orders for his officers to take up positions on local street corners, at railway stations and points of steamship departure. They were instructed to stop and interrogate early morning loiterers. No traces of the gunman could be found, however, and their efforts were further hampered by useless but well-meaning reports from people who had heard the sound of gunfire in the night but could provide no tangible information otherwise.

Opium halls were seen as a refuge of the desperate and a hang-out of criminals and low-minded individuals. However, the drug was also used as a painkiller and at Mercer's Hospital, Mr Butcher applied it in earnest to the treatment of the policemen. He was ever watchful for what he termed its dangerous 'narcotising' effects, particularly since in June 1868 the board of Richmond Hospital had censured Dr Stokes for 'the very great amount of stimulants, so much above the average of the other surgeons which he subscribes for his patients … requesting him to diminish the amount as much as possible for the future'.[13] Whatever the outcome of the current police cases, Butcher did not want to incur the wrath of the governors by creating two new addicts.

At four in the morning, the divisional magistrate, Charles Joseph O'Donnel, finally arrived at the hospital. Distrusting the earlier deposition obtained by Inspector Doran, he set about taking the dying Keena's declaration again. By now, however, the constable had suffered for almost three hours and was exhausted. Giving a more truncated report, he asked for his father to be sent for by telegraph. Leaving him alone, the magistrate focused his attention on Sergeant Kelly.

Below on Mercer Street, reporters had already started to gather.

3

FIRST ROUND OF ARRESTS

By eight o'clock on Thursday morning, a light breeze had risen from the west, dispersing much of the previous night's fog. As rain spat against the window pane, Acting Superintendent James Ryan sat behind his desk and completed a rather hurried, terse account of the night's events.

Exchange Court, a blind, urine-soaked alley off Dame Street, was the site of the headquarters of the detective division. The entrance to the lane was restricted by an archway built just wide enough to allow access to horse-drawn traffic. It was bounded on the right by the imposing bulk of City Hall, at the end by the G Division mess hall and on the left by the carriage office and the detective offices. Inside the police complex a long corridor led past the waiting-room and onto a small interior courtyard, the sky over which was frequently filled with the raucous cries of seagulls. At its far end, there was an ash shed, a urinal and some wooden-seated lavatories. A passageway led past the courtyard, through a large kitchen and out by the Palace Street Gate. During a period of eighteenth-century prosperity the superintendent's rooms had housed one of the city's best taverns, where weekly wine banquets had been held.

In his report, James Ryan admitted to the police commissioners that the identity of the attacker was unknown to either of his victims. Some hours later, taking more care with his handwriting, he compiled a fuller version of the night's events, concluding stoutly that:

> The person who fired is hardly a thief, because thieves are not known to carry such weapons, therefore there is no reason to doubt he is a Fenian, and it is by no means improbable he is a hired assassin as he seemed to know well the use of his revolver.[1]

In writing, he was mindful of the attack that had left commercial agent Robert Atkinson severely wounded that September near Water Row Market. Constable Charles O'Neill had been shot near the same location in 1866. These and several other similar incidents were enough to arouse suspicion that the latest shootings were something more than the work of a mere footpad. Moreover, the acting superintendent knew that the attack on O'Neill had been a blunder, the original target being John Smollen, a seasoned acting inspector from his division who was due to take retirement on disability grounds. Described by former Fenian recruiter John Devoy as one of the smartest policemen in G Division, the King's County detective was watched for three days and nights as he made his way to and from his lodgings near Ganley's wool stores on Usher's Quay. On the designated evening, the gunman, Richard Kearney, had got drunk and missed the rendezvous. Some time after this attack, an informer reported that 'in three different places, he heard it said that more policemen would be shot'.[2] In a Bride Street beer shop, the informer saw one would-be assassin carrying a revolver and a bowie knife. Many Fenians kept blades because they were not proscribed under the terms of the Arms (Ireland) Act 1843. After Atkinson's shooting, a writer for *The Irish Times* had lamented that:

> One of the most dangerous results of the Fenian Movement is the introduction of the American practice of discharging loaded revolvers at obnoxious persons in the streets. This reckless method of revenge is of recent importation and is more dangerous than the hedge-firing which has now happily ceased in Ireland.[3]

Since his shooting in September, Atkinson had again twice been mistaken for a detective and was in fear of his life:

> The last time was Saturday in Church Street as far as which I took a short walk, my back not being yet healed and was resting in the shop of a customer. The other occurred in North King Street. In both cases, the parties were plundering hay from carts openly in the streets.[4]

Although he felt sure that the latest attack was Fenian in origin, James Ryan resolved to wait until nightfall before making a final pronouncement. He still expected reports from each of the police districts and since it was still early, there was a chance (however unlikely) that some family had not yet awoken to the theft of their goods and property.

The city's journalists had no such scruples. All of the day's daily newspapers carried reports about the shooting, epitomised by the *Irish Times'* headline which read, 'Murderous Attempt to Shoot Two Policemen'. The newspaper speculated that the gunmen were most likely young Americans who had come across the Atlantic to join a fresh Fenian insurrection. In 1866, several hundred of these men, many of whom were demobbed Civil War soldiers, were arrested in Ireland under the terms of the Habeas Corpus Suspension Act. Aside from their characteristic square-toed boots and slouch hats, it was their lack of deference towards the 'quality' and proud bearing that made it easy for the police to pick them out.

At ten o'clock that morning, Ryan's brother, Superintendent Daniel Ryan, arrived from Blackrock to resume command of G Division. Before joining the DMP, he had been a carpenter. It was a background to which Frederick Bussy Moir alluded when he wrote that while he was undoubtedly resolute with a keen sense of morality, Dan Ryan was not particularly well-educated.[5] Like most of his peers, his rise in the force was attributed to hard work and he had built his career on some key cases. One of these was the infamous 'Jack in the Box' affair, solved while he was still an inspector. His investigation led to the arrest of the perpetrator of a series of larcenies at the Steam Packet and Railway stores and in its aftermath, Magistrate Joseph William O'Donnell wrote a glowing report, extolling his 'foresight and intelligence'.[6]

Despite this, he was not always so successful. One of his first acts as superintendent was to lead an investigation into the death of Mr Little, a Midland and Great Western Railway cashier whose throat was cut as he counted company money. Since the contents of the office were left untouched, it was initially presumed that this was a case of suicide, but the coroner's inquest returned a verdict of wilful murder. A local woman named Mrs Spollen laid the finger of blame on her husband. In an attempt to find the murder weapon Police Magistrate Thorpe Porter asked for a section of the Royal Canal to be drained, but when the search began Ryan announced:

> Whoever found the razor should receive a guinea. A razor was accordingly found in the mud almost immediately, but it was manifest that it had not been there until the search was directed, for it was perfectly free from rust or corrosion.[7]

It was not a promising start to his career as superintendent and Porter levelled a charge of incompetence against Ryan and his department. In the years that followed, the superintendent continued to investigate murders amid a plethora of more mundane matters such as the regulation of hackney carriage licences, identification of missing persons, the recovery of stolen property and investigations into gambling rackets. One of the more colourful arrests made by him and his men was reported in the *Freeman's Journal* on 23 April 1859. In spectacular fashion, Ryan managed to disrupt a Sunday morning cock-fighting circle in West Essex Street:

> The entire of the G Division became suddenly most devout and proceeded under his [Dan Ryan's] orders to twelve o'clock mass … When mass had terminated, the gimlets who were in coloured clothes came out of the church in the midst of the congregation and, making a short turn, presented themselves in front of the

Olympic circus. Before any alarm could be given, Superintendent Ryan and his men had gained admission and, in a few minutes stood in the centre of the lists, where 37 individuals and Mr Ruth were enjoying a hard-fought rubber of 5s 10d. Nothing could exceed the consternation of the proprietor and the devoted 37 and, finding themselves trapped, various attempts were made at a cut and run, but escape was hopeless and they had to submit.

When he alighted from the train at Westland Row on Thursday 31 October, Dan Ryan made his way directly to Exchange Court. He normally entered by a special doorway just inside the gate, from which a narrow hallway led past the downstairs detective offices and up a narrow stairwell to his apartment. There, James informed him of the night's events. By now, the news was all over the city and a crowd had gathered on Wellington Quay to gawk at the blood-stained wall next to Duffy's bookshop.

The brothers settled on a plan of action. James, who was in charge of the College Street station, would take a cab over there to view the occurrence books – volumes in which all of the previous night's beat information was kept. Dan would remain behind to brief his team, gather intelligence from known informants and consult with the under-secretary.

Sandwiched between the Provincial Bank of Ireland and the College Hotel, the College Street headquarters resembled a large, rather nondescript townhouse. It was home to what John Devoy described as the 'grenadiers' of the DMP. The constables, most of whom were six feet tall or more, lent muscle to house raids organised by Dublin Castle, interrogated witnesses and patrolled the heart of the old city. Two doorways with rounded pediments and anthemion motifs flanked three ground-floor windows. Five glaze-barred casements on each upper storey looked out onto a truculent city below. Inside, it was rather cramped – an impression belied by first appearances. A wide polygonal hallway ushered visitors into a large reception room on the left. There were some further quarters behind – a kitchen with a copper range and a mess area. A corridor led to another narrow hallway and a single wooden staircase beyond which a small yard opened to the sky. At the far end, there was a urinal for the use of the officers as well as five roof-vented cells.

When he arrived from Exchange Court, James Ryan asked to speak to Constables Morton, Jordan and Donnelly. He was particularly interested in Ann Clarke, whose reported drunkenness would not, he hoped, prejudice her value as a witness. He decided to take her and Mary Donnelly into protective custody for a few weeks. Upstairs was a hodge-podge of rooms fitted out for that purpose, as well as a dormitory for the younger officers who lived in the station. Such lodgings were far from ideal and, from a practical point of view, College Street was vulnerable to attack. One of its walls bordered on Fleet Street and another abutted a public house. The Chief Secretary, the Earl of Mayo, Richard Southwell Burke, felt that an unoccupied building in Green Street – formerly the North Dublin Union Cholera Hospital – would be a more suitable headquarters, but until this could be arranged, Ryan had to make do with the facilities at College Street.

Meanwhile, Constable James Dillon was assigned by Dan

Ryan to post proclamations throughout the metropolitan area and all officers were given a description of the attacker.

Around midday, Sergeant Shaw and Constable Kelly from Drumcondra barracks went out on the beat. Drumcondra was a little market-garden hamlet nestled around the Tolka Bridge, beyond which the scenery gave way to a rural landscape dotted with cottages, hedgerows and wheel-rutted laneways. The only large buildings of note were All Hallows College and Belvedere House, a stately mansion owned by the Coffey family. The community was close-knit and outsiders were comparatively easy to identify.

Unlike their metropolitan counterparts, Shaw and Kelly were members of the RIC – a semi-militarised force that wore a distinctive dark green uniform and carried loaded carbines with saw-backed bayonets on patrol. Due to a delay in posting the attacker's description to the outlying districts, they were forced to rely on the report in that day's *Irish Times*. Based on the details it contained, they stopped two furtive, unkempt men near the barracks.

'What brings you up this back road?' Shaw asked.

'We're going for a walk,' answered the first, a florid-faced man with lank brown hair.

The sergeant was sure that he answered the description of the gunman, but on searching him found only one shilling and three pence in his pockets. He gave his name as Patrick Deegan and said both he and his older brother Michael, the second man, were unemployed machine sawyers. They lived in a row of small, ramshackle cottages near the docks, called Sheriff Place.

Despite their protests, the officers hauled them both over to Summerhill Station. From there they were taken by cab to the Lower Castle Yard in Dublin Castle. After a short interval, Chief Superintendent Campbell arranged to accompany them to College Street.

Their interrogation was conducted by Sergeant Charles Smith as well as by Detectives Joseph Clarke and William Doyle, who had been assigned since 1866 to break up subversive Fenian activity in the city. Earlier that same morning, Doyle had supervised the arrest of the barber Patrick J. Hayburne. He had been under surveillance since the beginning of October due to his friendship with Arthur Forrester. The police immediately suspected him of complicity in the latest shooting and he was picked up quietly around midday. While he waited in custody, the police searched his Thomas Street home and found two documents in his bedroom, both signed 'Dad'. The first, written from Kilmainham Gaol on 5 October was a simple letter of introduction, intended to recommend an unnamed *émigré* to the Fenian Brotherhood upon his arrival in New York. The second ran as follows:

> If you go out as soon as you get out and by Liverpool, you can take the letter with you but if you go by Queenstown you are sure to be searched. Liverpool however in any event is the best way because you cannot miss a passage on any Wednesday and Saturday … In any event, I wish you to call on McBride and Co. as they are the publishers of the *Irish People*. See Mr O'Sullivan and tell John O'Mahony and say that I sent you to tell them how we are here.[8]

Although the content of the letters was highly suspicious, there was nothing specifically incriminating in them and it was obvious that Hayburne had been planning to leave Dublin long before the shooting. Nevertheless, he was immediately delivered to Mountjoy Gaol under the terms of the Habeas Corpus Suspension Act. By now, this Act had been in force for twenty-one months in Ireland.[9] Two days later, *Saunders' Newsletter* and the *Daily Express* carried a small report about the arrest, but did not connect it to the police investigation into the shootings.

A search of the prisoners at College Street yielded little apart from a pound note concealed in a songbook. The prostitutes Mary Donnelly and Ann Clarke were brought down to see whether they could identify either of the Deegans as the assailant. Clarke said that Patrick was very like him, except that the gunman had whiskers around his jaw. When one of the policemen scrutinised his face, he noticed signs of recent shaving and as a result, both men were kept in custody. Despite the circumstantial nature of the evidence, they were charged on suspicion of involvement in the attack and the police informed curious reporters that they had received 'some confirmatory evidence'.[10]

Hoping to take the brothers to be identified by the wounded constables, the detectives dispatched a messenger to Mercer's Hospital. Hardly having slept, Mr Butcher wrote in the strongest terms that 'the excitement consequent on such a course would be attended with great danger to Keena and Kelly in their present deplorable state' and he gave no hope of their recovery. The same message was delivered to the waiting reporters and as a result, the coverage in the evening papers was rather sparse. One notable exception was the *Freeman's Journal*, which bragged that it 'had the opportunity ... of seeing and speaking to both the wounded policemen', confirming that the bullet that injured Keena had entered 'below the xyphoid cartilage at the end of the sternum, by which it passed into the stomach'.[11]

The likely source of this inside information was Sir John Gray, MP for Kilkenny and chairman of the Dublin Corporation waterworks committee. Significantly, he was also the proprietor of the *Freeman's Journal*. His newspaper connections were not as important to the governors of the hospital as his influence with the corporation, however, and because of this they were probably prepared to divulge whatever information he wanted. Gray spent a little time by the bedsides of the two policemen before speaking to the hospital's governor, Dr John Morgan. The hospital board hoped to obtain a £100 increase in its annual government grant and although Morgan worried that the due date had passed, Gray reassured him that he would support a late application. With a new sense of resolve, Morgan wrote to the lord mayor to inform him that:

> The funds are so constantly and severely called on by such cases as are brought in extreme danger and distress to the hospital – for example the two policemen who have been shot.[12]

He went on to praise the porter's assistant – a mere boy called John Halligan who had only recently been taken on as an assistant. Reflecting afterwards on the night's events, Morgan wrote of him that 'he could hardly be done without lately, owing to those police cases'.[13]

On Thursday evening, Constable Edward Wall stood in Thurles Station and watched for the arrival of the Dublin train. Equipped with an *Irish Times* description of the gunman, he paid particular attention to a passenger who carried a lightish-coloured bundle. He arrested him and took him to the station where he informed the sergeant in charge that his name was Michael Jordan – a native of Carrigaholt, County Clare. He said that he had been out of work for some time and that he was 'on tramp', moving from town to town in search of employment. Regardless of the fact that his bag contained nothing more sinister than six pence and a bundle of clothes, the resident magistrate signed a transmission warrant and returned him to Dublin via Kingsbridge. There he was bustled into a police cab and brought to Chancery Lane station.

That Thursday night, the constables going on duty were furnished with loaded revolvers and pistols seized from Fenian detainees. Many were old, of uncertain quality and had a potential to backfire. Each was checked as it left the station and, knowing that many Irish-American Fenians were trained in swordsmanship, the constables were also given cutlasses for close-quarter combat. On entering the dark network of alleys in which Constable O'Neill had been shot in 1866, one of the officers accidentally fired a bullet into a ships' chandlery at 24 Mary's Abbey. It pierced the wooden shutter and plate glass window and woke a number of the area's residents.[14]

Meanwhile Superintendent Ryan was pursuing his own line of enquiry. Before leaving Exchange Court, he instructed Constable Smyth to dispatch a telegram to Captain W.H. Palin, the son of an East India Company officer who had returned to Manchester to take up a post as chief constable. He wanted to know where Arthur Forrester was.

4

GREAT BRITAIN STREET RAID

By the time the morning newspapers hit the streets on All Souls' Day, Friday 1 November, they all carried news of the shooting. *Saunders' Newsletter*, perhaps the most sensational, ran with the headline: 'Murderous Outrage this Morning – Two Policemen Shot'. The general assumption was that the gunman had been a Fenian and *The Irish Times* commented on the fact that the city was swarming with demobbed American soldiers. To others, capture of the assailant seemed an unlikely prospect. The *Freeman's Journal* noted rather eloquently that 'rumour with her thousand tongues has been busy everywhere but it is greatly to be feared that the perpetrator of this terrible outrage will evade his pursuers'. The twice-weekly police gazette *Hue & Cry* came out that morning, as it did every Friday, and was circulated to every police station in the country. Among its list of army deserters and notices of prominent crimes was a new proclamation:

> The Lord Lieutenant is pleased hereby to offer a reward of £1,000 to any person who shall, within one month from this date, give such information as shall lead to the conviction of

the person who committed the said outrages or either of them and a further reward of £300 to any person ... as shall lead to the arrest.

At two-thirds the amount offered for the capture of Fenian leader James Stephens in 1865, the sum was impressive. Joseph Sheridan le Fanu's *Warder*, a conservative Tory publication, remained pessimistic, however. Such gestures would need to be backed by real action on the part of the government.[1]

The shootings were directly responsible for an urgent spate of reorganisation within the detective division. That morning Sergeant John Egenton, who left for Millbank prison in charge of a convict, was appointed *in absentia* as acting inspector. Sergeant Thomas Rotheray, who had proved his worth in 1865 when the division was on the hunt for James Stephens, was also promoted to the same rank.[2] Acting Sergeants Philip Mathews and John Kelly were put forward as full sergeants to replace them and Edward Cullen was elevated from constable to the rank of acting sergeant. The divisional rank and file was similarly reinforced. Constables John Bride and Peter Priestly were transferred from C and D divisions, and officers Patrick Ennis and Patrick Doyle, both of whom had seen previous service with the detective branch, were re-employed.[3]

The previous day's interrogation in College Street had been unsuccessful, but Acting Inspectors Doyle and Clarke hoped to gather new evidence by speaking with the Deegan brothers' former employers, Messrs Walpole, Webb and Bewley. The detectives arrived at the yard to find it bustling with activity.

The city's shipbuilding trade was enjoying a new lease of life after a long period of depression. That summer the company had launched the iron steamship *Dublin*, the third of a fleet of screw colliers, as well as a lifeboat named the *GV Brooke*. Now, the *Mullingar* – on order by the City of Dublin Steam Packet Company – was due for completion.

The yard hands were either unable or unwilling to provide any information about the Deegans. Leaving empty-handed, the detectives walked to Mr Martin's nearby cabinet works where another of the Deegan brothers had recently been employed. It comprised a wood mill, joinery, wagon works and timber merchants and occupied an extensive lot at the intersection of Fish Street and Mayor Street. The previous evening, fire brigade chief Captain Ingram had received an anonymous warning that a blaze was going to break out in a moulding room of this premises and he arrived to find it in flames. His men were able to use a water tank to put it out, but several hours later most of the hands were still involved in the clean-up operation, which consisted of removing the charred and soaking wood to one end of the yard.[4]

The shipyard and nearby cabinet works were reputed to be something of a Fenian hotbed. Belfast man Terence McClelland, who was arrested for activities associated with the Brotherhood in 1866, had once worked in the shipyard and the current foreman of the works was a tall, full-bearded man called McEvoy, who was named by the informer Alfred Aylward as a possible Fenian 'centre' or chief in charge of two hundred men. The detectives learned nothing.

Aylward was a pale youth with lank black hair. By his own admission he was of 'melancholic temperament' with some old injuries that included 'broken teeth' and a badly healed 'left collar bone and three ribs'. He was accustomed to sending his information through Crown Solicitor George Bolton in Nenagh – a man whose office he had once managed as law clerk. He was possibly a member of the IRB, but his letters to Bolton suggested an antipathy for physical force nationalism. He had picked up the information about McEvoy from one of his 'pets' – a man whom he believed to be in regular communication with one of John Devoy's adherents. They usually met in the front drawing-room of a house in Castle Street. As was often the case with his dispatches, the evidence was circumstantial.[5]

Before midday, Constable Morton and Mary Donnelly went to Capel Street and gave their accounts of the shooting to Charles J. O'Donnel, the divisional magistrate who had taken the wounded officers' declarations. The previous month he had tried a number of women for prostitution – a crime that carried a sentence of forty-eight hours imprisonment and a fine of five shillings. Discreetly ignoring Donnelly's profession and making allowances for her illiteracy, he read her statement aloud and then asked her to make her mark.

Despite the previous day's arrests, there was still no hard information apart from a statement taken that morning from Professor Hugh Ferguson, the rather mercurial head of Dublin Castle's veterinary department. Well known for his cattle plague committee work, he worked at 14 Pitt Street where there was a dissecting room. Evidently, he had been *en route* from nearby Dublin Castle and he gave a description of a man whose appearance resembled that of the assailant.[6]

Dan Ryan needed something more substantive, however. During the day, he put a car on special hire for a guinea, took an A Division constable with him and went to meet one of his informants.[7] He knew he was putting his own safety at risk, but the danger was reduced somewhat by an informant vetting process that involved correspondence between many sections of the Irish administration as well as the English police divisions. As a result, leeches, drunks and IRB men hoping to learn the habits of the police were routinely filtered out.

Ryan's informers were a wretched lot who had a thorough dread of being exposed and were liable to melt into the shadows if anyone else was assigned to meet them. Such personal trust had been engendered by a courtroom revelation from the informer Pierce Nagle in 1865 that he had been in communication with the superintendent for two years without a 'shadow of suspicion' falling on him. Nagle was employed as a 'paper folder' in the offices of the Parliament Street-based Fenian newspaper, the *Irish People*, from whence he had been able to report on the activities of the Brotherhood and supply Ryan with an 'action this year' message intended for the Tipperary IRB. The inference was that here was a man who would not betray an informer's confidence until absolutely necessary. Ryan's feelings were ambivalent, however, and he disliked the eagerness with which Nagle was prepared to inform on people to earn money.

After the *Irish People* trials, the Tipperary police had been instructed to place Nagle's family under protection in Fethard.

Soon after this, rumours circulated that his brother, who lived in New York, had been assassinated by some vengeful Irish-Americans and when Nagle read about this in *The Irish Times*, he had good cause to believe it. He wrote a frantic letter to the Home Office, but the allegation was disproved by the British consul, Edward Archibald. Afterwards, his brother and his wife were unwilling to admit any familial connection for fear of their lives. Being an informer was a dangerous occupation that destroyed bonds of family and friendship.

The superintendent was accustomed to meeting his informants in isolated places or late at night. It often occurred to him that a trap could be waiting, and his family also feared for his safety:

> As a matter of course, my return home would be looked for at the usual hour but in the meantime I received word to be at a certain place and should go there, consequently my family would be disappointed – even their meals would be irregular and of little use to them and after having watched for my arrival until far into the night, they would conclude that I was assassinated, such alarming summons having been in circulation.[8]

Ryan's fears were not without justification. A threatening letter delivered to Sackville Place station after the murder of an IRB man named George Clarke had promised the police that 'it won't be long before you get what you want ... and that will be a few pills that won't degest [*sic*]'.[9] On 12 February 1866, another letter to Exchange Court warned of a threat on Superintendent Ryan's life, as well as on those of Judge Keogh and Inspector Launcelot Dawson. According to the writer, a party of IRB men had watched the superintendent's movements as he came and went from the 1865 commission – a court established to prosecute those arrested in the *Irish People* newspaper offices – but they were unable to find an opportunity to shoot him:

> Those vile Dupes always was at me to join them as the trout I did so. One of them shewed the revolver and bullets prepared for that purpose and two of them, upon their oath for that awful Deed. Dear sir, for your own sake be careful and causious as would such to Protect life … the foolish class has laid me unto the knowledge of their secret and I did not want that knowledge so they are forcing me to have some money from them as I know something about arms. I never took one scent from them altho' very poor in pocket. Belive me sincerely, a Connaught man. For Christianity's sake, I done my own Part.[10]

Some IRB members were opposed to the scheme of shooting Dan Ryan or his men on the grounds that killing policemen was futile, but others were willing to do the job. The more radical among them insisted that Ryan should be dispatched, since it was through his statements to the government that the Arms Act had come into force. Of late, Acting Inspector Edward Hughes had informed the superintendent that a young *émigré* home from America had been quite surprised to hear that he was still alive because:

> … in New York it was commonly declared that Hughes and Ryan … ought not be allowed to live … and if a man could not be found here [Ireland] to shoot them, a man would be sent from New York for the purpose.[11]

Hughes was shot in November 1865, possibly in reprisal for James Stephens' arrest, as he made his way into the detective offices with Acting Inspector William Doyle. On that occasion, Superintendent Ryan discreetly omitted to inform the commissioners that Hughes had lain on the deserted pavement for a number of minutes before he was dragged to safety. Fortunately, he and Doyle sustained little but bruises, the bullets lacking the power even to tear their clothes.

Although the detectives had a specially designated, if somewhat obscure, entrance to Exchange Court through the stables in the Lower Castle Yard, it was not always used.[12] As a result, two known IRB men, Thomas Brady and John Reilly, were able to observe and trail various officers from a Dame Street location in 1866.

Operating in this *milieu*, Superintendent Ryan's fears and those of his family seemed reasonable. However, on this occasion, his fortitude was rewarded when he learned of something he had long suspected – that an IRB assassination circle or 'vigilance committee' was at work in the city. Comprising thirty men, its duty was to watch the movements of police officers and informers, and to shoot them if possible. The name bore some resemblance to the San Francisco Committee of Vigilance, a vigilante group formed in 1851 which targeted criminals and government corruption. Each member on patrol was assigned 'his particular beat and … a certain number of hours every night'.[13] On an ideological level, the existence of the circle hinted at a refusal to engage with the civil authority whose power it probably did not accept as lawful. The members of the Brotherhood had taken an oath calling on them to accept the notion of a 'republic virtually established', thus promoting a belief in the primacy of their own rudimentary justice system – one that defied the existence of an 'alien' court system and police service.

Some days after the meeting with his informant, Ryan compiled a report for the police commissioners, taking care to mention that:

> Some members of this circle are regularly appointed in their turn for duty by night. Each man so appointed is armed with a revolver and paid 6s 6d per night for each night they are out and on the night the policemen were shot, eight of those men were out on duty.[14]

He further discovered that the initial purpose of the gang, which he believed had been set up as early as 1865, had been to protect the IRB from men such as Pierce Nagle as it became aware of their activities, and that its members were mainly shoemakers who had spent some years 'on tramp' in the United Kingdom and America. He informed the police commissioners that it was led by Colonel Thomas J. Kelly – an Irish-American soldier who had directed the IRB as its 'Chief Organiser' during the abortive rising in 1867. Kelly and his companion Timothy Deasy had been arrested in Manchester for loitering in September 1867, but later that month Acting Inspector John Mallon was informed that a plan was in train to rescue both men from their prison van. His warning went largely unheeded by the Manchester police.

On 18 September 1867, the two Fenians, both of whom

had been charged under the terms of the Vagrancy Act, left Manchester courthouse en route to Bellevue prison some two miles away. They travelled handcuffed in separate compartments in a prison van known as a 'Black Maria', along with four other occupants. They were guarded by a middle-aged police sergeant named Charles Brett, whose job it was to ferry prisoners to and from the courthouse. In addition to the normal complement of officers, there were five policemen on the outside box seat, two on the rear step and four following behind in a cab.

As the van passed under the heavy arch of the Hyde Road railway bridge, a man ran into the middle of the carriageway and levelled a pistol at the driver. His initial reaction was to attempt to pass, but before he had time to do anything, a rescue party of about thirty to forty Fenians leaped over an adjacent wall and surrounded the convoy. Finding themselves outnumbered, the ten guards, all of whom were unarmed, quickly abandoned their charges. Some of the rescuers grabbed the horses' reins and tried to turn the prison van back towards Manchester, but when one of the animals attempted to lunge forward in its harness, a pistol was fired into its nostrils, killing it instantly. A crowd began to gather. Some of the attackers tried to move the corpse out of the way, while others began to shout at passers-by to keep back and threatened to shoot any who dared to interfere. The scene grew increasingly chaotic.

At the same time, some of the rescue party had begun to make a concerted attempt to break open the Black Maria with a motley assortment of crowbars, hatchets and sledgehammers. One of them called on Sergeant Brett to unlock the door but he refused. In the confusion, a revolver was levelled at the key hole and Brett, who happened to be peering through the opening, took the full brunt of the shot in the head. As he slumped back onto the gangway floor, one of the other prisoners, a prostitute, cried out, 'He's killed.' In response to a hurried request from the gunman, she took the keys from his pocket and passed them through the ventilator.

Kelly and Deasy were spirited away under darkening afternoon skies. The IRB later castigated the colonel 'for his carelessness in permitting himself to be arrested and his reck-lessness of the safety of others in allowing the rescue'.[15] As a fugitive, Kelly was no longer in charge of the Brotherhood or the assassination circle he had allegedly established and Dan Ryan was hard-pressed to provide answers about his whereabouts.

The Dublin IRB was decimated by arrests in the aftermath of the failed rising, but the increasing severity of gun attacks, although random, suggested a new source of funding. In such an atmosphere, the proprietor of the pro-Fenian *Irishman*, Richard Pigott, argued that Constable Keena's shooting 'could not have been designed by any combination or conspiracy, since it was clearly not premeditated'.[16] The members of the assassination circle also belonged to their own IRB circles and in an organisation infiltrated by informers, it would have been extremely difficult to assemble the thirty men on a regular basis. As a result, many of their attacks, aided by a small corps of Irish-Americans who, in implicit recognition of the ballad written by 'Fenian' poet John Keegan Leo Casey had come over to take up arms at the 'Rising of the Moon', bore the hallmarks of personal revenge attacks or minor power struggles. By his own admission, Ryan's informant was often barred from assassination circle meetings and could only glean their proceedings at second hand but, despite that, the superintendent was able to make a reasonable guess about the gang's activities. Meanwhile a miasma of apprehension descended over the city.

On Friday afternoon, Superintendent Ryan assembled Inspectors Darcy, Freeney, Burke and Mulholland in his office. He briefed them about the whereabouts of some alleged Fenian desperadoes and sent them to meet Richard Corr, the portly, full-bearded superintendent of C Division who would take charge of the arrests. Corr was disliked by many Dubliners on account of his heavy-handed approach, but he had a reputation for getting results. In February, he had commandeered his entire division in a dawn interception of the Holyhead steamer, *Alexandra*, which had resulted in the capture of a large number of Fenian suspects trying to enter the country.

At three o'clock, Corr stood and waited in his position opposite Ryan's wine and spirit stores, 94 Great Britain Street. Unable to join the raid because of his clubbed foot, he relied on his men to make the arrests. A light rain was falling onto the muddy street – this was a poorer part of the city remarkable for the absence of the taffeta-clad ladies so commonly seen in the smarter areas of town. Outside cars, their jarveys dressed for the weather, jostled alongside flat carts hauled by plodding dray horses. When Corr gave the signal, Acting Inspector Mulholland crossed the street and entered the premises. His brief was to check on the locations of the suspects and to ensure that none of them managed to give the raiding party the slip. There was plenty of room for escape through two side entrances into Marlborough Street, both of which would require manning from the outside by police constables picked for the task.

According to a later police report, Mulholland loitered casually at the bar and located three of the men sitting together in the snug. The first was Thomas Rooney, a stout, fair-haired quay porter who looked older than his years. He was the only reasonably well-dressed man among the group. His brother John had joined the ill-fated *Jacmel* (also known as the *Erin's Hope*) expedition which reached Ireland from New York in May 1867. This brigantine had landed him in Waterford with Colonel Warren and many others before rounding the coast and sailing into Sligo Bay with 5,000 stands of arms originally intended for the rising. With no one available there to unload them, however, the ship had then sailed up and down the coast of Sligo and Donegal for a week before returning to New York without unloading its cargo. The informer John Joseph Corydon had identified John Rooney as one of those present at Fenian Brotherhood meetings in New York and he was arrested with the other *Jacmel* passengers when they disembarked. For the past two months, Thomas had anxiously awaited news of his brother through the American Consul William West. He hoped to see him released on grounds of his American citizenship.[17]

A small beardless man with lank, tousled hair sat beside Rooney. This was Peter McDonnell, a bootmaker from Kennedy's

Lane, who was in close conversation with the third suspect, Francis David Murray. He seemed savvier than the boyish-looking McDonnell and regarded the policeman carefully with heavy, dark eyes. Murray was possibly an opium addict and his clothes, greasy from the rain, looked as though they had been slept in. Before he left the premises, Mulholland marked the position of a fourth suspect – John Dowling. He was a rather stout individual who stood at the opposite end of the bar. It seemed as though he had been a past employee, since he was speaking desperately to the barman about getting more work.[18] He looked about twenty years older than the others.

When the police burst in, there was a sudden commotion and chairs were knocked onto the sawdust floor. Murray grabbed his hat and started for a side entrance, but it was already covered. Superintendent Corr ordered his men to draw their revolvers. Acting Inspector Mulholland seized Murray by the elbows, drew his arms back and pushed him up against Thomas Rooney. 'Don't attempt to put your hands towards your pockets,' he cautioned. Murray struggled violently until the inspector put a revolver to his head. Turning him round to face him, he managed to retrieve a needle pistol and a six-chambered revolver from his clothing. 'I'm disarmed and will surrender,' Murray spat, 'I may as well throw you this as well.' He attempted to put his hand into his back pocket, but Mulholland grabbed it. 'Only for the grip you have of me, I would have shown you some sport with the revolver,' he added. On searching with his free hand, Mulholland found six rounds of ball cartridge and a small box of percussion caps.

Meanwhile, Acting Inspector Freeney had Rooney pinned to the floor. 'What was that for?' he protested. A revolver was pressed against his forehead. Freeney searched him, shouting triumphantly when he found a green-baize pistol cover.

A large crowd of onlookers gathered on the street outside and gawked with evident interest as Mulholland, Freeney and the rest of the police party manhandled their prisoners towards the waiting cabs. Some were deliberately obstructive and ignored Superintendent Corr's order to disperse. It was only with some difficulty that they managed to leave the scene. As the guarded car jostled past the Metropolitan church, Acting Inspector Mulholland turned awkwardly to Murray. 'You bastard,' he said, 'would you have used that thing?'

'I don't know what I might have done,' Murray answered, 'when I had to fight for freedom.'

After a few minutes, the cabs rattled into the Lower Castle Yard. This accommodated the military aide-de-camps' quarters, extensive stables with a forge and riding school, the office of arms, the headquarters of the metropolitan police commissioners, and the office of the prisons' inspector. Earlier that March, it had borne witness to the bedraggled presence of almost two hundred prisoners, fresh from the doomed insurrection. Without doubt, it was an intimidating place for any suspect – IRB or otherwise – to be held.

The four men were led through a back entrance into Exchange Court. Murray claimed that he had been thrown about violently in the cab and that the police had torn his clothes. Superintendent Corr began by informing him that he intended to put him on a charge sheet for shooting Sergeant Kelly of the B Division and a constable of the A division.

'What is your name?' he asked.

'McHale.'

'Oh, is your name not Murray?'

'Who's after giving my name to you?

'No matter. Is it not Murray?'

Settling on 'Murray McHale', he admitted that three of his revolver chambers were empty, but refused to admit that he had shot the policemen. His needle pistol, despite being empty, still contained the paper canister that would normally remain after the charge. That suggested it had also been fired. 'I have already proved that I am a man,' he snapped defiantly. 'I can shoot with both hands and I would still be a man only that you came so suddenly.' He had made similar statements during the short cab journey. When questioned about his colleagues, he insisted that Peter McDonnell had only called into the shop for a drink and he felt certain that there was 'a traitor in the camp'.

For Superintendent Ryan, the brief interview was enough to identify young Murray as a likely assassin. Alfred Aylward had already described him as a dangerous character, before supplying further details of his whereabouts – in particular that he was a 'shoemaker who lives in a backroom, opposite gate, Ship Street barrack, drawing-room floor'.[19] The police called to the house where his father, a wire worker named Peter Murray, confirmed that his son was a shoemaker by trade. He was a most 'incorrigible' character whom he had not seen for two months. He had no idea how his son was living, but could confirm that he was constantly in the company of the other two men – Rooney and McDonnell. The old man's sense of annoyance was almost palpable. Wire workers were highly versatile craftsmen who could turn their hand to items as diverse as fire-screens, birdcages and pinion wire for clocks and watches. Ship Street was a centre for the trade and Murray had worked there for many years. Unwelcome attention from the Castle authorities was the last thing he needed.

Rooney and McDonnell were also interviewed before being removed to Sackville Place police station. John Dowling (perhaps the 'traitor in the camp' to whom Murray had referred) remained behind in a cell in the Lower Castle Yard. Ryan's strategy for handling him thus came down to the simple fact that this man, already known to the police, was more likely to talk when removed from his colleagues.

Dowling protested that of the four, he knew only Murray. He claimed that he had taken a glass of porter from him and that as they chatted, he noticed a gun in one of his pockets. Evidently, Dowling somehow managed to spirit the gun away from the table to show it to the proprietor, whom he hoped would contact the police. He returned it afterwards to Murray's pocket, citing the whole incident as an example of his loyalty, since 'if I were in any way connected with them, I would not tell of his having the firearms'.[20]

The Irish Times grossly exaggerated the details of Murray's arrest, writing that he had the American eagle on his coat buttons. To the two handguns found with him was added a fictitious arsenal including sixteen rounds of ammunition and a quantity of detonating caps. If the police hoped for a breakthrough in Keena and Kelly's shootings, they were to be sorely disappointed, however. Apart from his initial statement, Dowling remained sullen and tight-lipped. The official police report listed several broken teeth and a cut to his left hand, but whether or not this happened in custody was not recorded. Attempts to elicit new information revealed very little apart from some silent nods which were taken by the fact-starved detectives to signal assent in response to the question of whether they were holding the right man in Sackville Place.

By now, evening had fallen. Completing the work that his brother had begun that morning, Dan Ryan marked his report on the arrests 'Confidential' and entrusted it to John Mallon who made a copy for the Home Office. The original was submitted to Police Commissioner Lake.

Lake, who was a soldier by background, had been roused from sleep just hours after the shootings. With military attentiveness, he stayed awake into Thursday morning, writing to the under-secretary, Sir Thomas Aiskew Larcom, with whom he was on friendly terms, and pressing the detective office for further details. Lake had formerly been an officer in the Madras engineers and was later nominated a Companion of the Order of the Bath for his part in the defence of Kars. His governorship of the Phoenix Park Royal Hibernian Military School demonstrated a continued interest in military affairs – a focus which he had brought to all his police work since joining the force in 1858.

The professions were not necessarily mutually exclusive and

the commissioner's military experience had acquainted him with French and Russian secret service methods. He abhorred the *agent provocateur* system and similarly disapproved of disguises, 'holding that a police officer with ordinary intelligence and good character ought to be a match for any ordinary conspirator. It was simply a conflict of intellects, in which all the advantages were with the police ... the best armaments for a detective were to prove himself truthful, sober and zealous'.[21]

However, it was subterfuge that characterised the threat from the assassination circle, and the 'sober and zealous approach' of two unarmed policemen had failed to counteract it, so Lake reluctantly agreed to an order for two hundred police revolvers from Messrs Webley and Son. This was handled by Sir Thomas Larcom, who headed the police in the chief secretary's absence. Larcom contacted the Home Office and secretary of state for war, and awaited word that the weapons were ready for viewing at the small arms office or 'Proof House' in Banbury Street, Birmingham.[22] It would take over a week to organise the shipment.

The Earl of Mayo had been fifteen miles away at his home in Naas, County Kildare, when the shooting took place. His father had died that June, raising him to the peerage at a point in his career when he already had onerous responsibilities as chief secretary of Ireland and a Member of Parliament. He had substantial authority over Irish affairs – far more than the lord lieutenant, the Marquis of Abercorn, whose post was something of a sinecure. Of late, Mayo had had little opportunity for recreation and this latest incident meant an urgent recall to the city. Once he had dealt with his affairs at Dublin Castle, he planned to travel across the water to visit Lord Leconfield and his constituents at Cockermouth, before attending the first cabinet meeting of the session at Downing Street on Tuesday 7 November.

Direct questions were bound to be asked of Mayo about the police shooting in Westminster and, as if that were not enough, he had a myriad of other issues to contend with. Among a stack of petitions was one from Robert Atkinson, who was lobbying him for an accountancy position at Dublin Castle. Mayo refused to commit but agreed to compensate him for his loss of business and to pay any medical expenses arising from his shooting.

On Friday 1 November, he had also received a letter from the shrewd and meticulous home secretary, Lord Gathorne Hardy. Although Hardy had not followed his father into the legal profession, he debated at least as well as a trained barrister. Having assumed the post just six months earlier, at the age of fifty-three, he quickly discovered that his tenure was a demanding one. Now he turned the screw with subtle force:

> I have a letter to the Queen already written … the use of firearms in the streets is becoming a formidable evil but if it cannot be checked in Ireland where you have more stringent laws, what are we to do here?[23]

Considering the September prison van escape in Manchester, Tuesday's cabinet meeting was likely to be fraught and Mayo might need to remain at the Irish Office in London for some time. After he departed for England, Larcom sent a reply to Hardy's letter through the latter's permanent under-secretary, Adolphus Frederick Octavius Liddell. He made sure to attach a copy of Superintendent Ryan's full report, writing that 'there are this day some faint hopes of recovery of these two men'.[24] The lord lieutenant was similarly briefed.

Although Superintendent Ryan may not yet have had the details of exactly who was involved in the shooting, he now knew the whereabouts of some of the city's principal IRB men – individuals whose arrest could help to add some substance to his new information.

Ironically (considering the IRB's public repudiation of assassination), it seemed as though the shooting circle drew its normal *modus operandi* from an overall Fenian strategy in which members were encouraged to avoid 'direct confrontation with the forces of the crown except where superiority of numbers absolutely assured victory'.[25] The effectiveness of the gang had begun to produce a commensurate weakness in the information-gathering potential of Dublin Castle and needed to be curbed. In Ryan's own words, it had a 'very bad effect on the exertions that are being made to trace out suspicious, dangerous characters'.[26]

On Friday night the constables went on their respective beats in pairs, but that left some districts virtually unpoliced. The same arrangement had been enforced during the spring and summer. As darkness fell, they spread out into the streets. A lone policeman, separated from his colleague, encountered a disorderly crowd on Victoria Quay. Singling out a prostitute as the ringleader, he managed to make an arrest with the help of two passing soldiers but as he escorted her away, he was knocked over by a drunk who drew a glittering object from his pocket. Failing to realise that it was nothing more than an empty whiskey bottle, the policeman recoiled. Grasping the bottle, the drunk laughed. 'If it were a revolver,' he sneered, 'I would have blown your brains out.'[27]

5

HEROIC MEDICINE

As the interrogations at Dublin Castle continued into the night, Surgeon Butcher made unrelenting efforts to save the lives of the two policemen. Earlier that Friday, Superintendent Ryan had requested that he and his colleagues consult the army surgeons for their advice. At that time, there were several such men in the city, some of whom were attached to Dublin Castle.

. When Butcher made his ward round just after breakfast at nine o'clock, he found that Constable Keena had begun to vomit bile. He could not help but notice his 'same wretched countenance and a constant craving to cool his throat and the rasping feel in it'.[1] As he checked his pulse, Keena dozed, but then started up again alarmed, asking whether it was possible to save his life. The surgeon provided some immediate relief by drawing off a pint of urine with a silver catheter before arranging for his belly to be stuped with laudanum-sprinkled flannels wrung out in boiling water. The mixture was allowed to soak right through the cloth. Next, he ordered a grain of calomel and opium with twenty shots of laudanum to be given every second hour. The treatment was similar to that advocated by Dr Longmore.[2]

Recent wars had allowed military surgeons, some of whom had been personally instructed by Richard Butcher, to obtain first-hand knowledge of gunshot wounds in the field. In his *Notes on the Surgery of the War of the Crimea*, George McLeod wrote about how his Mercer's Hospital training helped him to save a young soldier's life, and by the early 1860s such information was being included in updated textbooks.[3] Civil surgeons still had much to contribute, however, and Butcher was used to dealing with trauma cases on an almost daily basis.

Despite the limited facilities available to him, Richard Butcher kept abreast of the most current scientific thought of his time. He was best known for his modification to the common surgical saw, having written in the 1851 *Dublin Journal of Medical Science* that it was inspired by the bow-saw used by cabinet makers to cut curves. He was also prepared to try improvements made by others and when a woman called Ellen Robinson was fished out of the Liffey, he treated her successfully with a new and novel technique of ventilation called Hall's Method.[4]

'Heroic medicine' continued to operate alongside such advances. It was an aggressive brand of treatment that had been *de rigueur* for over half a century when Butcher received his training. It included practices such as intestinal purging (with calomel), blood-letting (venesection), vomiting (tartar emetic), profuse sweating (diaphoretics) and blistering. In fact, some doctors had so much faith in blood-letting that they were prepared to draw off almost four-fifths of a patient's blood. By 1867, however, attitudes were changing. Although the Richmond Hospital minutes show that tartar emetic was still to be used as part of a list of 'such medicines and appliances as ... should be kept supplied to the resident pupils for cases of emergency', Longmore showed how other practices such as blood-letting had fallen out of favour and were only practised on rare occasions.[5]

Mr Butcher took a similar stance and treated the two policemen using the best medicinal means available. Before leaving Keena's bedside, he ordered a dietary list to be hung up, detailing his food requirements – cold chicken jelly and beef tea jelly in occasional spoonfuls.

At midday, he attended to Sergeant Kelly, who lay just a few beds away. The use of stimulants continued, together with mercurial ointment smeared over his belly. According to a lecture given by Dr Moore at the hospital on 28 October, mercury had an observable effect on bile production and thereby on digestion, and it may also have found use as an antiseptic.[6]

At three o'clock, Butcher returned to the bedside of the young constable. Finding him restless, he fetched an amber vial containing some medical hydrocyanic acid. He ordered it to be added to each dose of laudanum, two drops every second hour. When largely diluted at about two per cent, it subdued the constable's spasms and nervous irritability. At the very least, it might stop him from trying to leave his bed again – something he had attempted that morning.

Between times, the hospital was besieged by a throng of well-wishers. One of the more distinguished was the lord mayor, William Lane Joynt, whom the *Irishman* of 2 November described as 'portly enough for a burgomaster and magnificent enough in all his belongings to have been painted by Rubens'. He arrived at the hospital that evening accompanied by the mayor-elect, Dr William Carroll. Their visit was intended as a civic gesture, but in practice it was a little intrusive. Joynt, who was also a magistrate, was politely informed that Sergeant Kelly's condition was less critical than that of the young constable but that it would be impossible to give a prognosis. Since neither officer was well enough to receive them, he and Carroll simply offered their hopes that both would be returned to their families.

By midnight, Constable Keena had grown quieter and more restful. Afraid to relieve himself because of agonising pain, he asked for help and another catheter was inserted. A few beds away, Sergeant Kelly lay watchful and silent with a half-scared look in his eyes.

6

JACK CADE O'LOUGHLIN

On Friday night, Inspector William Burke and a party of constables stood waiting in the shadows near the junction of Upper Abbey Street and Capel Street. The evening was clear and starlit and much colder than it had been in previous days. At eleven o'clock, the nearby public houses would begin to disgorge their drunken patrons onto the streets.

Shortly after midnight, a tall, dark-haired, athletic-looking man of about thirty years of age wheeled into Abbey Street from the direction of Capel Street Bridge and strode down the centre of the carriageway. His beard, absent from his face and lip, ran from sideburns to meet under his chin. He was obviously drunk. 'Stop him,' Inspector Burke cried. Constable 42C grabbed his right arm and recognised the hard bulk of a revolver through his grey frieze coat. 'What have you got there?' he asked.

'What's that to you?' the man leered, his face pitted with smallpox scars.

With the aid of a colleague, the officer wrestled him onto the cold flagstones and held him by the arms. He loosed a six-chambered Colt revolver, loaded and capped, from around the man's waist. A further search yielded eighty-six percussion caps.

To Jack Cade O'Loughlin, the indignity of such a police search was not new. Superintendent Ryan had raided his lodgings before and as recently as 25 October he had been named by Alfred Aylward as an active member of the Brotherhood. He was known to have been a non-commissioned officer in a Fenian guerrilla regiment in America and Ryan later asserted that 'he set no value on human life'.[1] As the policemen grappled with him, a tall, brown-haired man walked past, going in the direction of Capel Street. He slowed enough to attract Inspector Burke's notice, but when questioned by one of the constables, he was allowed to go on his way.

Meanwhile, O'Loughlin was taken to join Rooney, McDonnell and Murray at Sackville Place while the police searched his mother's lodgings at 20 Jervis Street. There they found a small single-barrelled pistol and a photograph of him in the uniform of an American Union Army corporal.

Next, they raided the Capel Street home of Daniel O'Connell Considine – the stroller they had stopped. Standing in his night-shirt, he told them that he was a labourer from Ticknock, County Dublin. He had been in a house in George's Street that evening but couldn't remember the number. Although his illiteracy ensured that there was no correspondence to incriminate him, one of the constables discovered a small pistol in a drawer. He claimed that it belonged to an amateur actor who used it in theatricals, but he had no licence for it and was placed under arrest.

At noon on Saturday, a convoy of prison vans rolled up Stafford Street towards Capel Street police court. Armed constables were assigned to guard the men inside, since the drivers could only be held responsible for the welfare of their horses. In the first van, the now tattered-looking Thomas Rooney sat handcuffed to Daniel O'Connell Considine with a constable facing them, while Jack O'Loughlin and Francis Murray were handcuffed in the vehicle behind. Peter McDonnell, whose van brought up the rear, was unshackled. John Dowling was noticeably absent.

After spending some time in the cells, the men were taken upstairs. The ramshackle courtroom was packed with curious reporters and onlookers as well as by the two prostitutes, Mary Donnelly and Ann Clarke, who had been escorted there by Acting Inspector Doyle. A journalist from the *Irishman* noted that Rooney appeared 'to have been in great poverty' and similar observations were made about the other men.[2] As they waited, Francis Murray suddenly recognised Michael Hayden, the grocery assistant from Ryan's, who had come to give evidence.

'Don't be turning around giggling at me or I'll give you a belt in the neck, you bloody bastard you. What are you grinning at me for?'

When Magistrate Charles J. O'Donnel arrived, he instructed the prisoners to line up in front of the two female witnesses. He began by questioning Mary Donnelly: 'You swore an information before me yesterday?'

'I did.'

'In that information you stated that you were present when

Sergeant Kelly was shot in Eustace Street at the corner of Essex Street.'

'Yes, your worship.'

'Look around and see if you saw the face of anyone in the dock before.'

She looked along the line and then back towards the magistrate.

'No, your worship, only I have seen the second man [Considine] doing business in Capel Street putting up shutters.'

Pausing to consider this, the magistrate continued: 'You stated to me that after the man fired at Sergeant Kelly, you screamed. He turned around and looked at you and you saw his face distinctly?'

'So I did, your worship.'

'Now, look at these five men and see if you know any one of them to be him.'

Both women now took a cautious look towards the dock. They agreed that the gunman was not among the prisoners, but that Francis Murray was most like him.

Next, the detectives gave their statements. Thomas Rooney objected to Acting Inspector Freeney's evidence about the baize revolver cover and was allowed to cross-examine him at length. Could he, Rooney argued, swear that it belonged to a pistol or might it not be used as a purse? A demonstration of how well Murray's revolver fit inside the so-called 'purse' infuriated him and, with curses, he was manhandled to the back of the court by the police attendants.

When order was restored, the barman from Ryan's wine

and spirit stores took the stand. He confirmed that he had not heard any of the men talk about the shooting of Kelly and Keena, but that he had seen them come into Ryan's two or three times before.

As the prisoners left the court, Francis Murray and Jack O'Loughlin were bundled into a van which veered away up Capel Street and across the river towards Parliament Street. It arrived at Mercer's Hospital shortly after Mr Butcher's three o'clock ward round. In the presence of Magistrate O'Donnel, the handcuffed men were confronted first with Constable Keena and then with Sergeant Kelly.

The young policeman was quite uncomfortable. Having slept very little during the night, he had started to vomit and complained of a tearing feeling in his throat. Despite his falling temperature, Mr Butcher wrote rather despairingly that his arms were frequently 'thrown across the chest and seeking for aid to the internal feeling, deep in [sic] that he cannot describe'.[3] Iced champagne was occasionally given to assuage his thirst. He was in no condition to identify either prisoner. When it came to Sergeant Kelly's turn, he looked at Murray and said, 'if that was the man who fired, he must have changed his clothes'. Once again, fellow patient Christopher Holbrook overheard him say that he would not know the gunman again.

Afterwards, the prisoners were returned to Capel Street police court. When the magistrate entered the courtroom, Rooney, who had been in the cells below, thrust his arms forward: 'Before the proceedings commence, your worship, might these darbies be taken off us?'

'Oh, I should say so. I did not know they were on.'

When the handcuffs were removed, the men threw their arms about, laughed and congratulated each other. Then they watched as Superintendent Corr stoutly defended the conduct of his colleagues during the Great Britain Street arrest: 'We were all armed and I directed the officers to draw their revolvers.'

'You directed the officers to do so?'

'Yes, your worship.'

This prompted Rooney to cry, 'You didn't order us to do it, you may depend!' Remembering how heavily armed they had been, the men laughed heartily. The magistrate was sympathetic: 'I think the only charge that can be maintained is that of having the arms. As to the other charge against Murray, I will simply dismiss it without prejudice. Have you, the prisoners, any questions to put to this witness [Corr]?'

There was a sudden flurry of voices. Rooney complained that the police had a 'happy knack of tearing clothes' while Murray was eager to show the magistrate the state in which his tie had been left.

'I do not doubt at all your having been treated roughly.'

'Well, I daresay it was necessary,' Rooney replied sarcastically.

When the magistrate came to handle the charge against Jack O'Loughlin he was anxious to settle the question as to why he had been found with a Colt revolver in a proclaimed district: 'It is loaded about six months, your worship.'

'But there were eighty-six percussion caps,' Inspector Burke persisted.

The prisoner fixed him with a glance: 'Wasn't I very much intoxicated at the time?'

'Yes.'

'And that's my personal property, your worship,' O'Loughlin continued, pointing at the weapon.

'Do you have a licence to carry arms?'

'No, your worship. I carry it to defend my life. My life has been threatened since I came to this city. It belonged to me in the army of the United States.'

'Then you should have got a licence for it.'

'I didn't know I could get one, sir, and I didn't like to lose the revolver. I carry it for a perfectly innocent purpose. I don't belong to any illegal society – never did.'

The Arms Act allowed for certain districts to be 'proclaimed'. Within these areas, all weapons were expected to be surrendered and the constabulary was empowered to search for hidden caches of armaments. In addition, anyone who was caught with a weapon was liable to face imprisonment. Thus, O'Loughlin faced considerable risk. By itself, however, the fact that he was arrested with a 'loaded' revolver was not particularly remarkable. It took over five minutes to arm a percussion weapon like a Colt. First, it had to be half-cocked so that the barrel could revolve freely. Next (the chamber having been inspected for cleanliness) a horn was used to insert the powder. A metal ball of ammunition was pushed into place and rammed into the barrel with the weapon's loading rod. A small amount of grease was then smeared onto the opening to prevent water ingress. Finally, the projecting 'nipple' at the rear of the chamber was capped. If he wanted to protect himself, he needed to keep it permanently primed

By the time the court adjourned, the men's treatment at the hands of the magistrate had been nothing less than amiable. Having taken an interest in their weapons and ammunition, he remanded them on a week's bail, pointing out that the case involving at least two of them was very weak. This news came as a disappointment to Superintendent Ryan who had hoped to detain them on the lord lieutenant's warrant. Later, he admitted to Commissioner Lake that no positive identification had been made by any of the witnesses and that they may not have had the 'real' men. In rather woolly terms, he ventured that there was a sort of 'moral conviction' for Murray's culpability.

Such quasi-religious language was not at all unusual in Irish police reports. The force was guided by the founding principles of Sir Robert Peel and Patrick Colquhoun. Both believed that it was the policeman's responsibility to act as a kind of guardian of the poor by ensuring that public house licensing laws were observed and that working-class activities and gatherings were strictly supervised. The clergyman, teacher and charity worker occupied the same moral platform. That might help to explain why, for instance, G Division was responsible for the regulation of the city's pawnbrokers. The downside of such thinking was that it granted implicit permission to make arrests on scant evidence in the interests of protecting society.

Ryan hurriedly considered how potential informers among the men might be treated. John Dowling was a likely candidate, as was Jack O'Loughlin, although admittedly the latter had not yet made any formal statement in that regard. An informant newly arrived from England had reported a difference in feeling between the Irish and British IRB. In England, no notice was taken if a man was seen speaking to a policeman since it was generally assumed that the British constabulary had been infiltrated by the Brotherhood. In Ireland, however, such an encounter would result in the man being 'brought before a council of his fellow conspirators' where he was liable to be 'condemned as an informer'.[4] One particular example of this was seen in the case of James McCabe, who was arrested on 23 October 1867. Upon his discharge that same evening, he was immediately suspected of having given information. Allegedly, the IRB council who sat to consider his case resolved to assassinate him and his life was only spared when the centre who was elected to fill his place refused to sanction it.

Superintendent Ryan instructed Acting Inspector Carey to escort O'Loughlin to the Richmond Bridewell by cab for his safety. Infamous in nationalist circles, the prison was located just off the South Circular Road. Daniel O'Connell had once been imprisoned behind its 18-foot high walls. While figures of national prominence were still likely to be housed in the governor's apartments, the introduction of the 1865 Prisons Act meant tighter security measures for ordinary criminals, particularly in the wake of James Stephens' embarrassing escape from Richmond Gaol in 1865. Lumped together with the other inmates, the Fenian prisoners found that they were obliged to sleep on hard plank beds rather than hammocks and they were introduced to mindless, repetitive tasks such as oakum picking and walking on treadmills. Friends and relatives were forbidden to visit, and letters were kept from inmates. If O'Loughlin expected special treatment, he was sorely disappointed. He was immediately put onto hard labour.[5] John Dowling, who had hinted that he might be induced to make 'extraordinary revelations', was delivered to Kilmainham along with Murray, Rooney, McDonnell and Considine.

7

SUBSCRIPTION FUNDS

On Friday evening, as the city's Catholic families prepared their usual fish supper, a messenger from the governors of Mercer's Hospital made his way to the Mansion House and waited for the lord mayor to finish his dinner. Sir John Gray had already spoken to him and the governors' letter was expected. It outlined a request on behalf of the hospital to increase its annual budget in the aftermath of the recent police shootings and Gray had promised to remain in the city until Saturday morning to vote on it.

When the chamber convened that Saturday, it was relatively easy for the Liberal aldermen to muster *en masse*, confident that their impromptu hospital motion could not easily be withstood by the few Tory members present. This was due to the fact that at that time, Dublin Corporation was composed almost entirely of Liberal members with a Conservative minority.[1]

Shortly after the proceedings began, the governors' letter requesting a grant increase was read. Immediately, Councillor Byrne stood up to protest that such business was inappropriate for the chamber. He accused the Liberals of using it as a pretext for introducing an unrelated motion – namely the appointment of Dr Quinlan as city prisons' physician. For several minutes, Byrne continued to argue successfully against the shoehorning of this Liberal favourite, berating the lord mayor and accusing him of impetuosity. As matters became more heated, Joynt was forced to accept that it was not the proper time for Mercer's Hospital to apply for a grant increase and the item was temporarily struck off the agenda.

The next motion was hardly less contentious. No. 3 committee was asked to consider whether a sum should be drawn from borough funds to assist the Kelly and Keena families or whether it should be raised through private subscription by the aldermen themselves.[2] In defence of the first proposal, A.M. Sullivan made a lengthy speech in which he described the corporation as the 'real government of the city' and called on the citizens to do all they could to assist in bringing the assassin to justice.

The subject of assassination was one about which Sullivan could speak with some authority. As a constitutional nationalist he had often been at odds with the IRB; in February 1864, his denunciation of a proposal to erect a monument to Prince Albert in College Green had put him on a collision course with James Stephens and the staff of the *Irish People*. Despite Sullivan's patriotic stance, the IRB seemed to believe that it alone reserved the right to conduct a campaign of popular agitation. Sullivan was, however, willing to accept that despite their differing methodologies, Fenianism was 'the natural product of the long … and heartless misgovernment of the country'. He also repudiated the *Irish People* trials of 1865, when a number of prominent Fenians, including James Stephens, Jeremiah O'Donovan Rossa, Charles Kickham, Thomas Clarke Luby and John O'Leary were arrested and the crown implied that their proposed insurrection was to have involved a wholesale massacre of landlords and Catholic priests.

Despite such occasional support, Sullivan's refusal to join the IRB in 1858 and his continued disapproval of its methods brought him to the attention of more radically minded members. According to his brother Timothy, his death was decreed in the early part of 1866:

> His residence ... was about three miles outside the city, in an unfrequented district; a great part of the road was dark and narrow, and at one side were the ruins of some old houses. It would seem an ideal place for an ambush.

Fortunately for him, the journalist had many friends in the Brotherhood, one of whom slipped into the *Nation* offices to warn him soon after an assassination plot was hatched. Allegedly, he refused to believe that any Irishman would murder him and continued to walk home unaccompanied. In the summer of 1866, James Stephens was questioned twice about this threat on the journalist's life. Speaking at a conference in Brooklyn, he flatly denied that he had taken part in a tribunal to pronounce judgement either on him or the editor of the *Irish American*, P.J. Meehan – rather the opposite. When grilled about Meehan by a member of the Corcoran circle at the New York Cooper Institute, he claimed that by his order 'that man's life was saved'.[3]

Thus, when Sullivan stood in the council chamber to denounce the shooting of the constables as something 'odious and horrible', it was as a man who spoke from experience. By the time that the lord mayor rose to speak, the aldermen were receptive and hushed. Fresh from Friday's visit to Mercer's Hospital, Joynt believed that he voiced the feelings of every Dublin citizen:

> ... in denouncing as strongly as he could this base, cowardly, and un-Irish crime. Until the end of the lamentable war in America no one ever heard of persons carrying loaded revolvers through the streets. It was thought such a system would never exist here.[4]

When he informed them that he intended to use the borough fund to make a donation to the officers' families, the chamber burst into applause. Mr Casson, who represented a 'very respectable ward', lent his support, as did some of the other aldermen, but there were also those who opposed it just as strongly. In particular, Messrs Devitt, Manning, Plunkett, Dennehy and French, all of whom were Tories, dissented on the grounds that it was an illegitimate use of corporation funds and might set a precedent. They reminded the chamber about a recently defeated cattle show motion which, if accepted, would have signified a similar case of misappropriation. It seemed as though the Tory minority might win out until Alderman Manning suddenly withdrew his objection, swinging the vote in favour of its Liberal proponents, five against four. No. 3 committee was then charged with drawing a cheque for £100, made out in favour of the lord mayor, a suggestion calculated to avoid the onus of liability falling on any individual alderman, should public discontent stem from such use of corporation funds.

Some Dubliners grumbled that they were already overtaxed, but Richard Pigott's *Irishman* noted with sardonic zeal on 9 November that the corporation's gesture was an example of 'true philanthropy'. However, elsewhere in the same issue, a more critical headline ran: 'The Way the Money Goes' with the strap-line: 'The funds of the City of Dublin voted away for the benefit of the families of Government Officers'.[5] The obvious way to stifle such anger, it seemed, was to call upon the generosity of the general public rather than that of the corporation. *Irish Times* letter-writers began to call for an organised subscription for the families of the two policemen so that citizens could mark their disgust at the crime. One of these appeared in the 15 November edition:

> I, as a large rate payer, was proud to see that the members of the Corporation took the initiative in the good cause by acknowledging their services, rendered at all times to the citizens, by voting £100 for the use of the sorrowing families of those brave men who fell by the hand of a demon in human shape.

The readers of *The Irish Times* had good cause to expect that such a fund would be instigated because that was precisely what had happened in 1866, when a fund with the rather long-winded title of 'The Murder of Constable O'Neill Fund for the Relief of His Widow and Five Orphans' was set up. It was widely subscribed to, with an *Irish Times* address set up to receive the monies and a published list of contributors.

Although many citizens eagerly awaited an opportunity to 'hand in their mite' a second time, no such formal arrangement was made this time around.

Despite some inaccuracies, the 9 November edition of the *Irishman* made some very interesting points. In one article, its readers were reminded of a recent violent attack in the Phoenix Park and the fact that when Pigott had called on the corporation publicly to denounce the incident – an attack on the son of Dr Shannon by two soldiers with their belts – he went unheeded. When it came to the shooting incident, the victims were liveried policemen. 'Uniform,' he argued, 'in the eyes of the corporation, alters everything.' It was this same disproportionate attention that Robert Atkinson railed against in his letter to Crown Solicitor Samuel Lee Anderson later that month, when he wrote that had he been a wounded policeman, public sympathy would have been with him and perhaps a large subscription raised. 'Surely,' he wrote, 'the life of a citizen is as valuable as that of a policeman?'[6]

An accusation of gross partiality and pro-government sentiment was levelled at the corporation, which the *Irishman* claimed was prepared to act in a biased manner at the expense of civil rights. The comparison between Shannon's beating and the recent shooting was a misleading one, however. The *Irishman* inaccurately described Kelly and Keena as having been 'armed on the watch, looking out to arrest desperate characters'.[7] Not only were the two officers unarmed, they were ordinary members of their division. In this, the *Irishman* was not the only offender, however, since the *Daily Express* was guilty of similar misreporting.

On Saturday 2 November, British Under-Secretary of State James Fergusson wrote from Whitehall to Acting Superintendent James Ryan:

> I have laid before Mr Secretary Hardy your letter of the 1st instant and I am to express his deep regret at receiving the report of the shooting of Constable Patrick Keana [*sic*] and Sergeant Stephen Kelly of the Dublin Metropolitan Police.[9]

The London *Times* made it abundantly clear that the Dublin 'outrage' represented an attack on the English crown, and Fergusson's letter conveyed a subtle governmental pressure to bring the attacker to justice.

While the newspaper debate raged, the police continued to search for the gunman. In response to his query of 31 October about Arthur Forrester's whereabouts, Captain Palin replied to Superintendent Ryan by telegraph. He informed him that the young Fenian had left Manchester on Monday or Tuesday morning, perhaps for Sheffield. This eliminated Forrester as a suspect, since he could hardly have returned to Dublin in time for the shootings.

During the course of Saturday morning, a portion of the Liffey was dragged between the Essex and Metal Bridges at low water. Although Constable Keena had reported that the gunman was carrying a bundle, it seemed as though he had discarded it by the time he met Sergeant Kelly. On the night of the shooting, the river had been unusually low as a consequence of the spring tide, and any bundle thrown over the wall would have thudded into a bank of soft mud.[9] Acting Inspector Rotheray and the constable assigned to the task hired a boat for 10s.[10] Finding nothing in the Liffey itself, they swung their lanterns over the opening of the new iron grill barring the end of the River Poddle – an underground route to the Castle – where it merged with the Liffey, but it seemed unlikely to either of them that anything could have been thrown past the robust metal bars, particularly given the angle it was at from the bridge. Ultimately, their investigations yielded nothing.

That night, in an attempt to replicate their efforts in Great Britain Street, twelve-man police patrols from each of the Dublin police divisions were assigned to search public houses in their respective districts for suspicious characters. They stopped people in the streets and catalogued names, occupations and residences for future reference.

Out of sight of the raiding parties, a carefully guarded meeting of IRB centres and sub-centres was held, this being one of those rare occasions on which the Brotherhood made some attempt to follow its own rigid regulations. The most important of these was the concept of secret cells or circles. Each 'A' or head centre elected nine 'B's, who in turn elected nine 'C's. The 'C's, none of whom were supposed to know any of the hierarchy apart from their own 'B', elected nine 'D's each. In theory, this resulted in a total of 820 men. Although Superintendent Ryan's informant (a rank and file 'C') was denied admission to the meeting, it did not stop him from speculating that the gathering represented a possible attempt to reform the Dublin circles; the centreships of which had been decimated after the rising.[11] By the autumn of 1867, there were at least fifteen circles in

Dublin comprising over 4,635 men. Despite this, only three were led by centres who had been in charge prior to the rising. The remainder were under new leadership.

In a strange parody of the corporation fund for the wounded policemen, a collection was started at the meeting by James Dondrell for the benefit of the shooting circle. Dondrell, a Leitrim man, was second in command to the infamous Fenian Thomas Francis, a centre with sixty-five men under his control. Some members of the circle had gone into hiding and would most likely need financial support, but there was also the more immediate plight of the arrested men to consider:

> Subscriptions were collected for the defence of Thomas Rooney and Peter McDonnell. The Head Centres reasoned that a collection for the defence of Francis Murray McHale would be a waste of money, since the case of him having been found having arms without a licence was a clear one.[12]

A similar subscription had been instigated a week earlier for the benefit of the man who had been arrested for shooting at the crown witness George Reilly, but not for Jack O'Loughlin, who was suspected of being an informer. Such collections were deemed more necessary than ever, since one of the letters found in Patrick Hayburne's room complained that ordinary IRB members were lacking even essential commodities such as clothes and food.

Despite accumulating evidence about the urgency of the threat posed by the shooting circle, there was a delay in obtaining warrants for the detentions of Thomas Rooney, Peter

McDonnell and John Dowling. Only Francis Murray had been arrested with arms and Rooney's possession of a baize pistol cover amounted to very little. As a result, Superintendent Ryan struggled to advise the lord lieutenant as to what the warrants were for and they were scribbled upon and bandied about for a number of days. He was eventually forced to concede that in fact, they were 'for the detention of those who had not arms but are nevertheless considered dangerous'.[13] Although his opinion was ultimately endorsed by Commissioner Lake, such indecision wasted valuable time and it was 8 November before any sort of consensus on the wording of the warrants was reached.

8

THE NET TIGHTENS

On Sunday 3 November, Sir Hugh Rose, Baron Strathnairn, wrote a letter from the Bessborough Estate in Tralee:

> My dear Lord Mayo, I must sincerely hope you may have caught the assassin of the two poor policemen of which you tell me in your letter of 1st, for which I am much obliged.

The word 'sincerely', with its veiled threat of repercussions, could not have been lost on the chief secretary. A man with a reputation for arrogance and imperiousness, Strathnairn had dealt with the Indian Mutiny in 1857 and knew how to handle such things. At Sehore, he had presided over the courts martial of 140 sepoys, all of whom were convicted in a single day and led blindfolded, arms tied, to be shot in the head by British infantrymen. It was rumoured among Fenian circles that he had personally commanded sepoy mutineers to be shackled to the mouths of cannons before the weapons were fired. When he arrived in Ireland fresh from the subcontinent in 1865, he found that the previous commander of the Irish forces had under-estimated the Irish Republican Brotherhood – a mistake he vowed not to repeat. If Mayo's politics were Liberal at heart, Strathnairn's were most decidedly Tory. As he wrote that November, his part of the country appeared to be in a state of unrest. Not only did he have to contend with repeated requests from the Killarney magistrates for troops, but he had personally observed IRB agents collecting funds at the local regatta whose 'appearance and manner towards the notabilities of the county were unfavourable. Four men, two of whom were around with rifles, were in panic [*sic*] by a keeper cutting up a deer. They pointed their rifles at him and threatened to shoot him.'[1]

Perhaps the Prussian-born commander was a little edgier than usual. He was contemplating making a trip to England and in his absence he would need to leave the forces under the stewardship of Major General Cunningham. The several points of security that concerned him would need to wait until his return. Unfortunately, neither he, nor his chief military investigator, Lieutenant Colonel Percy Feilding, trusted the detective office to any great degree. In particular, Strathnairn felt that Superintendent Ryan lacked enthusiasm and he suspected (correctly) that there were informers within his division.

By Monday 4 November, Dublin Castle had collated some reliable intelligence about the shooting circle's activities as well as general Fenian movements, but there were still significant shortcomings. To bridge this gap, the administration began to pay about £63 per week (approximately £2,730 in today's terms) for information to informants.[2] Such efforts to destroy the IRB would be pointless, however, if official communication channels could not be secured against leaks. That same day, the

Freeman's Journal astounded Castle authorities by reporting on the contents of Superintendent Ryan's confidential dispatch to Captain Palin. It informed the general public that Arthur Forrester was a suspect, misspelling his name as Forrestal. The Earl of Mayo wrote immediately from the Irish Office to Sir James Fergusson. Insisting on greater caution in the handling of the case, he remarked that:

> If it had turned out that the Dublin Police were right in their signal suspicions, the publication of such intelligence would have inevitably defeated the ends of justice ... it is impossible to communicate with safety, any important information by telegraph or otherwise to the police authorities in any part of England if the information is to be immediately made public in the manner which it has been on this occasion.[3]

Besides leaked information, the police had other more immediate concerns to deal with. That Monday morning, an anonymous letter was posted to Superintendent Corr's Buckingham Street home. On opening it, he discovered a blue watermarked scrap of paper with the outline of a coffin drawn in thick black ink. Evidently, somebody wanted to give him their opinion about Friday's raid.[4] Unknown to Corr, the assassination circle had already assigned one of its members to trail Inspector Burke and watch his movements. In the afternoon, a second anonymous letter was delivered to the *Irish Times* offices. Written in a disguised hand, it purported to give a true account of the police shooting:

> There was on that evening a meeting of the Fenian officers for the purpose of closing up the month of October accounts. I

was deputed by my superior officer to deliver up the papers and accounts to the branch office, South city, with instructions not to surrender the documents to anyone. When on my way, and in performance of my duty, I was rudely interrupted by a constable at the corner of Blessington Street. After crossing the water, I was about turning up Eustace Street when another policeman had the audacity to interfere with me doing what is called by the enemy, 'his duty'. I was on duty and did my duty. In a few seconds after, I was again interfered with by another constable. In obedience with my orders, I did my duty and trust I always do so whenever so importantly engaged.[5]

Although its veracity still needed to be confirmed, this was the first public explanation of events on the night of the shooting. The writer, who claimed to be a non-commissioned officer of the 'Fenian army', entreated the Blessington Street constable to come forward. As a witness, he might help to dispel the notion that the gunman had acted out of sheer bloody-mindedness – portraying him instead as a courier who was on a mission. Perhaps due to fear of IRB recrimination, he had not done so.

Meanwhile, Superintendent Ryan delegated some responsibility for the case to Inspector Doran, who had taken the statements from the wounded policemen. He briefed him about the whereabouts of James Dondrell or 'Sweeney', who was allegedly planning to shoot Acting Inspectors Doyle and Clarke – the detectives whom Ryan had recently assigned to break up the assassination circle. Clarke was already well known to the city's IRB radicals, some of whom still bore him a grudge for breaking the nose of a Fenian named Patrick Kearney.

On Tuesday night, Inspector Doran made his way to South

Great George's Street with three constables from A Division. The gas lamps had just been extinguished when Dondrell, an athletic, sallow-faced man dressed like a 'Yankee' stepped furtively into view, linked at the arm by a prostitute named Anne Bradshaw. She was known to the police and the inspector felt that they were trying 'to shun observation'.[6] As the couple approached the corner of Fade Street, opposite Pim's department store, one of the waiting policemen slipped out of the shadows and tackled him to the ground. It took two officers to hold him and during the ensuing scuffle the prostitute was arrested for obstruction. With the aid of the light from a kerosene bullseye lantern, Constable Fox noticed that the man was armed. Inspector Doran reached his hand over to Dondrell's left side and, feeling the haft of a weapon in his inside vest pocket, attempted to seize it. After a violent struggle, Doran recovered a fully loaded six-chambered revolver. Having satisfied himself that there was no accompanying arms licence, he bundled Dondrell into a cab and took him to Chancery Lane station.

Dondrell arrived there to find himself standing next to the hated informer, John J. Corydon. For a moment, the two were tantalisingly close and a brief exchange ensued: 'Ha, here you are John Joseph,' the Fenian cried. 'I believe I know you.'

'Yes, and I know you. I suppose that's enough for the present,' Corydon said. 'I'm not dead yet.'

'More's the pity,' Dondrell replied.

Inspector Doran ordered Constable McDonnell to search the prisoner in a separate room. Noticing a hole between the lining of his vest and the cloth, he put his finger in and found a portion of a letter. It had something about the 'Saxon foe' written on it and an English address: 'Thomas Sweeney, Blackrod Post Office, Chorley, Lancashire.' Arthur Forrester hailed from near there. 'If you hadn't taken me so short, I'd have dropped a few of you,' Dondrell taunted in his Irish-American accent.

The constable was undeterred: 'What was the revolver for?' he asked. 'Was it for shooting sparrows?'

Later, Corydon confirmed the identity of the man in custody. He had seen him frequently in Clinch's public house in Camden Street – the same premises in which Forrester had been arrested the previous May. A more significant location was 43 West Essex Street, where Dondrell, Forrester and Peter McDonnell had all been employed as bootmakers. This time, no forced entry was necessary; Inspector Doran simply used the suspect's house key, discovering that he had been living in one of the upper rooms for the past two years. The next morning, James Dondrell was remanded to the Richmond Bridewell for a few days where he joined the informer Jack O'Loughlin, who had been kept in the prison for his protection.

Events continued to unfold in the city. On Monday 4 November, a Sackville Street jeweller named James Mayfield bartered with a young customer named Denton White, accepting a new pin-fire percussion revolver in exchange for a ring. Two days later, needing ammunition, Mayfield decided to visit James Calderwood's gun shop, which was some doors away on the same street. In the early years of the nineteenth century, the company had done a brisk trade in duelling pistols. Inside, a number of imported European weapons were displayed in the window, beyond which a number of old brass-barrel flintlock blunderbusses, on repair for provincial customers, vied for space with newer items. Calderwood's son immediately recognised the weapon as one that had been stolen from his father's window display and decided to impound it.

Bereft of his revolver, Mayfield stormed out of the shop and went to find young White who, despite his thievery had been honest enough to give the jeweller his address as a surety. Mayfield demanded that he return the ring and White, despite his protests, had no choice but to hand it over. Later, the young man paid a visit to Calderwood's shop and angrily tried to persuade the gunmaker to hand back the revolver. By then, however, Calderwood's son had convinced his father of White's theft and the old man refused to budge. Sensing perhaps that he was losing ground, White pleaded that he was willing to pay if the gunmaker would only allow the matter to drop. It had been a mistake to steal the weapon from such a prestigious establishment. There were of number of armouries in side streets and alleys all over the city, but Calderwood was 'Gun manufacturer to the Lord Lieutenant and armourer to the Constabulary'.[7] When White ran off, Calderwood contacted Dublin Castle.

Acting Inspectors Doyle and Clarke set off for Manor Street. Three months before, some revolvers had been stolen from Kavanagh's gun shop on Dame Street and it was possible that the two events might be related. The door was answered by William Frederick White. He said that his brother Denton was out and that he had no firearms except that which he had a licence to keep. When White fetched his revolver, Acting

Inspector Doyle immediately recognised it as one of those stolen from Dame Street, due to its unusual Italian patent and Belgian manufacture. Such guns were relatively common in Liverpool and London, but extremely rare in Dublin.

Alarmed, White admitted that the weapon had originally belonged to his brother who got it from a friend named William Hopper. He had a hundred cartridges which he had bought in Mary's Abbey off Capel Street, but the ammunition had not been used and the box was still unbroken. The detectives escorted him by cab to Sackville Place station and Inspectors Mathews and Ronan succeeded in rounding up his brother. They charged him on suspicion of revolver theft. Although a member of the IRB, Denton White was not involved with the assassination circle. Despite that, he was able to give Acting Inspectors Clarke and Doyle the name of a new and potentially interesting suspect – William Hopper, a gun thief who masqueraded as a DMP constable.

That night, there was some further drama on the south quays. Sergeant Dagg of A Division was on duty opposite Nicholas Walsh's public house, a garrison music saloon known as 'The Two Soldiers', when a local prostitute called Margaret Murphy attracted his attention: 'Sergeant, come here. Listen and you will hear something about revolvers and something else.'

She had been standing near the open hall door of 49 Usher's Quay when she overheard a man say that on the night the constables were shot, he and a man named Mullen were standing on Capel Street Bridge. Mullen urged him to keep 'dark' so that it would not be found out. When Dagg went to investigate, he walked into the hall of the wrong house, but realised his mistake and pressed his ear to the wall. He only managed to pick out the words, 'twas a splendid revolver' before a curious crowd gathered outside and forced him to return to the street corner. After a moment, he retraced his steps – this time to the right house. Inside the open hall door, a drunk stood talking to two women and he greeted the policeman in friendly terms: 'You must take a treat, sergeant. All you have to do is to go to Walsh's and order the drink.' It was a foolhardy gesture.

'How is it that you want to treat me?' Dagg asked gruffly. 'I don't know you, nor do you know me. If I want a treat I can treat myself.'

'Bessy, go and get us a half pint,' the man insisted.

Obediently, she slipped off in the direction of Walsh's. The drunk followed. The saloon had closed a half-hour earlier but in answer to the drunk's insistent knocking, Connor the barman opened the door a sliver. Having received advance warning that the police were about, he refused to let him in. His prudence was rewarded when Sergeant Dagg knocked a few moments later. Connor informed him that the latecomer was Thomas Hemingway and that his brother had gone home in the early part of the night. Certain that he was implicated in the police shooting, Dagg followed him as far as Queen Street Bridge and arrested him with the help of two colleagues.

Banding together for protection, the three officers frog-marched Hemingway to Newmarket station. Attacks on prisoner escorts were commonplace and stone-throwing mobs, keen to participate in the 'popular amusement', often fell upon the police, sometimes in gangs of 300 or more. Sticks and stones were used and, on extreme occasions, bricks, kettles, old basins and other objects were flung out of tenement windows. In 1854, Dagg had been brutally set upon when he attempted to break up a gang of street fighters at Islandbridge. When he followed them to a nearby house they dragged him into the hall and gave him a vicious beating, leaving his uniform in shreds.[8]

The journey to Newmarket was mercifully uneventful. The prisoner gave his full name as Thomas Alexander Hemingway, a journeyman cooper with an address at 26 Ellis Quay. He had no weapons, but during the interrogation he attempted to throw two pieces of paper into the fire. The first was addressed to J.J. Mansfield, a widower who owned two sets of coffee rooms in London – one in Bishopsgate and the other in Union Street.[9] Business there was difficult and the note probably related to some troubled financial transaction. The second, which could not be so easily explained read, 'all cash; all right; rest easy'. It seemed that the man Hemingway had met on the night of the shooting was Peter Mullen, a Drogheda Fenian whom Alfred Aylward had identified as a likely assassin, but without further evidence, the magistrate was obliged to accept Hemingway's innocence.

There was more bad news waiting for the police at College Street station where the Deegan brothers had been discharged along with the bewildered Clare man, Michael Jordan, due to lack of evidence of their involvement in the shootings. When Acting Inspector Rotheray hauled Jordan before Mary Donnelly and Ann Clarke, both women denied that he was the gunman. Before being released, he raised some laughter in court by asking the magistrate for his return train fare to Ennis.

9

LIVES IN THE BALANCE

Four days after the shooting, John Keena arrived in Dublin by train from Mullingar. According to Thomas Larcom, he was a poor man who depended greatly on his son for material support. He made his way directly to Mercer's Hospital, where he was introduced to Mr Butcher. The policeman's 'bewildered look of despair' made a deep impression on his father, particularly since before being shot he had been in the prime of life.[1]

Opening a glass container under the old man's gaze, Butcher carefully dislodged half a dozen leeches and applied them to an area just above the constable's injury. The treatment lasted about forty minutes, the leeches' saliva working to anaesthetise his wound and prevent his blood from clotting. Afterwards, calomel or 'mercury chloride' was administered to aid laxation or purging of the bowels.

By nightfall, the young policeman was more restful and, having taken *Cannabis Indica* and opium, he slept fitfully under his father's concerned vigil. Unfortunately, his vomiting had returned by morning and with dismay, Mr Butcher noted that he was 'sometimes harassed with the most violent straining without ejection of any fluid … when the sensation was fully upon him, I have seen him grip the throat and, as he expressed himself when the paroxysm had passed, he could tear out the piece.'

By now it was evident that Constable Keena was dying, and Sergeant Kelly was moved to the next ward so that he did not have to witness his suffering. Before the shooting they had been virtual strangers and the sergeant had not even known his first name. Now he was keenly aware of the young man's plight and it affected him deeply.

When Mr Butcher returned to the ward on Tuesday 5 November, Kelly's spirits were still subdued. However, as his pain was almost gone, Butcher stopped the calomel. He continued to administer opium in grain doses of powder every third hour, and for the first time, there was some hope that Kelly might recover. Then, early on Wednesday morning, his condition worsened. His nurse helped him to void two and a half ounces of pure arterial blood, after which he almost fainted.

Once again, the sergeant's life hung in the balance. Butcher prescribed *Digitalis Purpurea* – a sedative poison known for its effects on the heart. Only a tiny dose could be given, however, and its diuretic effects partially explained his flushed face and subsequent thirst, which the nurses attempted to slake with ice.

For his part, Constable Keena had long since ceased to obtain any relief from ice, either on the tongue or in packs applied to his spine. He lay completely exhausted and emaciated, his face continually displaying 'the same ghastly stare'. His death was hourly expected and Father Crotty came over from Whitefriar Street to give the last rites. Later that afternoon, he made occasional attempts to vomit, suddenly rolling from side to side in an effort to rid himself of the feeling in his throat. He grabbed anyone who was within reach but eventually slumped back onto his pillow. Eventually, at half-past two on Thursday afternoon, he feebly asked his father to help to turn him over in the bed and the old man called for a nurse. Together they gingerly turned him on his side. Given the violence of his week-long suffering, his sudden repose seemed strange and remarkable. A change came over his face and he slipped away without the slightest appearance of pain. Throwing himself onto the bedside, his father cried out, 'Oh that I should rear my fine boy to that age, to be assassinated!'[2]

The inquest into his death was held twenty-two hours afterwards. Dublin hospitals were still responsible for all of the city's judicial post-mortem inquiries, despite the corporation's motion in 1864 to erect one or two mortuary houses with adjoining jury rooms for 'the bodies of those persons who unhappily meet with death suddenly and violently'. By 8 January 1866, premises had been built in a corporation yard in Fishamble Street, but it was only open a month when employees from a neighbouring firm complained about the 'annoyance being occasioned by the removal of bodies and from inquests held therein'. Despite some hopes that a back entrance could be knocked through into Winetavern Street, the building was closed and the situation was not resolved until the city morgue was constructed in the early 1870s.[3] In the meantime, the theatre at Mercer's Hospital continued to be pressed into use as a *de facto* coroners' court.

Outside, the street was thronged with people, anxious to hear news of the proceedings. Constable Keena was the seventh patient to die that month but his passing was by far the most public. The inquest reminded City Coroner Dr William White of that of Constable O'Neill which had been held in Jervis Street Hospital the previous May. In its aftermath, he had lobbied the government to suitably equip officers who patrolled dangerous parts of the city; the police commissioners had eventually agreed to armed parties of two. It was a short-lived measure. In the main, DMP constables were issued only with truncheons 'because of the rarity of homicides and serious personal violence in Dublin'.[4] In response to the Fenian threat of the late 1860s, an 18¼-inch, 10-ounce truncheon appeared on the streets. It could not deflect a bullet, however, and the coroner's point was not lost on the public. Moreover, as the *Freeman's Journal* had pointed out just days before Keena's inquest, not only was O'Neill's assailant still at large, but so too was the assassin of George Clarke, who had been shot on the banks of the Royal Canal in February 1866.[5]

Clarke, who was suspected of being an informer, had been on the premises of an IRB weapons factory when it was raided by the police. On 9 February, he was hailed by an acquaintance on the corner of Abbey Street and from there the pair went to Dorset Street where they joined two men who said they needed help moving boxes from a house on the North Circular Road. Travelling via the canal, they walked along the side of

Mallot's Mill, but as they stood arguing about the directions, Clarke heard the sound of feet running behind him. According to *The Irish Times* of 12 February 1866, he was hit on the head by something hard before being shot. He died two days later.[6]

Recalling the incident, the *Daily Express* of 1 November took a strong line about these men – described sarcastically by Alfred Aylward as the 'Canal Heroes' – insisting that they 'must be taught that it is as least as dangerous to resist the police here as it would be in New York'. Such polemics were of no help to Constable Keena, whose body now lay in a hospital theatre.

Before the proceedings commenced, the fifteen jurors were addressed by the coroner: 'I think you are all pretty familiar with the circumstances that have rendered this inquiry necessary. The deceased constable when on duty at night, was met in the street by an assassin, fired at, and wounded. It is certainly much to be deplored that our city should become the scene of these assassinations. It is to be hoped that they were not committed by our people – that they must be perpetrated rather by those foreigners who are amongst us and whose presence must be the cause of much mischief to the country.'

Nineteenth-century post-mortems could often be highly public affairs and beneath its dust-catching ledges and buttresses, the theatre was packed, not just with jurors and policemen, but also with medical students who jostled for position in the gallery. Immediately prior to his arrival, Mr Butcher had checked on Sergeant Kelly, informing an *Irish Times* reporter that he was now much improved, being a much more powerfully built man than the deceased constable.

Since the instigation of the 1836 Medical Witness Act, coroners had had the authority to compel appropriately qualified medical practitioners to conduct post-mortems and testify at inquests. Those who refused were liable to be held in contempt of court. It had taken some years for the procedure to become widespread, despite the efforts of its most tireless advocate – surgeon, MP and founder of the *Lancet*, Thomas Wakley. This was partly because of memories of the 'Resurrectionists' – men who robbed and sold corpses for medical dissection before the 1832 Anatomy Act. The practice had caused public outrage, particularly after the revelation that William Burke and William Hare had been killing people 'to order' in Edinburgh in 1827–8. Fortunately by the 1860s, the public had begun to accept the need for post-mortem examinations in cases of suspicious death, thus opening the way for the development of forensics.

Mr Butcher stood immersed in the dusty sunlight and rolled up his sleeves. He liked to show off his muscular forearms to his students. No doubt they had been strengthened in the boxing ring, where he had once given a good account of himself against the English champion, Jem Mace. He was joined by the rather more placid Dr Edward Ledwich, a burly man with a florid, gentleman farmer's appearance, and by Dr William Moore, who had been with Mercer's for six years.

A recent lecture by Dr Moore, delivered on 29 October, had reminded students of the necessity of approaching the human organism in 'an enlarged and philosophical spirit'.[7] When combined with an outpouring of public sympathy, the tragic circumstances of the young constable's death called for something more than a disinterested post-mortem, however, and under the gaze of those in the gallery, that 'enlarged' spirit was put to the test.

Butcher gently removed the sheet covering the body. With the aid of his colleagues, he endeavoured first to pass a bougie (a slender, flexible, cylindrical instrument) through the track of the wound in an effort to locate the bullet, but its progress was quickly arrested. To begin the pathological examination, he cut a slit up the constable's abdominal wall, through the *linea alba* – a central line that is often visible in muscular individuals and runs from the ensiform cartilage or breastbone, down to the pubis. Each lateral portion was then divided and the flaps thrown back.

It was immediately evident that Keena's organs were clumped together in a heavy mass of blood and that the solar plexus had been completely broken up. The violent diaphragmatic spasms caused by its destruction must have been excruciating.

Next, he lifted up the omentum, a fatty organ close to the stomach, noting as he did so that the under-surface of the liver had been torn for about an inch by the passage of the ball. From there, the shot was deflected to the right kidney and part of the diaphragm was split vertically. The edge of the pancreas was also cut, as was the inferior *vena cava* – a vein that returns unoxygenated blood to the heart. It was this injury that had caused much of the policeman's internal bleeding.

To locate the position of the ball, Mr Butcher used a

Nelaton probe, an instrument that was fast gaining popularity in gunshot cases. It consisted of a small knob of biscuit china placed at the end of a slender metal stem, the purpose of which was to take an impression of a leaden bullet or rusty iron projectile when it was placed directly against it. Moving the *post magnus* muscle aside, he inserted the probe, detected the roughened bone of the fourth lumbar vertebrae and discovered the location of the bullet. It was remarkable that the injury had not resulted in paralysis – up until Keena's death, Butcher had routinely asked him to move his legs.

The doctor who treated Constable O'Neill in 1866 found that the ball had also entered through his liver, passing out by the spine and breaking a portion of his vertebrae. Such injuries were normally fatal, as Dr Longmore observed, since haemorrhage was 'likely to follow quickly'.[8] Although Constable Keena's injuries were markedly similar, his life was probably prolonged by the fact that the ball had torn only the under-surface of the right lobe of the liver 'close to its longitudinal fissure' rather than going right through it. But it would have been no small mercy for Keena if he had died a quick death like O'Neill.

Before concluding the post-mortem, Mr Butcher extracted the bullet, noting that it was of the 'minnie [*sic*]' form, three-quarters of an inch long and nearly half an inch in width and height. The body was then covered and the inquest commenced.

Inspector Doran confirmed that he was attached to Chancery Lane station and that he had taken a statement from Constable Keena on the morning of 31 October. It read as follows:

I saw the man that shot me on Wellington Quay. He came from the quayside of the houses. He had a whitish-coloured bundle under his arm. I thought that this man wanted to evade me; that perhaps he had something stolen and I did not think it would be right to let him pass without seeing what it was. I told him to wait and he at once turned around and fired at me. He was quite close to me at the time. He was low-sized, had a short black coat; I cannot say what he had on his head.[9]

While he accepted that this preliminary statement might be valuable, Magistrate O'Donnel argued that his later account was the more accurate of the two:

I, Patrick Kenna [*sic*], Police Constable of the Dublin Police, believing myself to be in immediate danger of death, make this, my dying declaration as to the cause of the condition in which I am now in – that at about a quarter to one o'clock this morning, I was standing at the corner of Essex Quay near Mason's Shop when I saw a man on the opposite side near the bridge and as he seemed desirous to avoid me, he attracted my attention. He passed across on the flagway of Wellington Quay. He had a whitish-coloured bundle under his arm. I called after him to wait and he said, 'I won't' and I followed quickly after him and when [at] about Duffy's Shop I overtook him, I said, 'I will make you wait' when he turned around and when about a yard from me, he presented a pistol and shot me in the belly. I wheeled back towards the bridge and shouted and met a constable named John Hickey who put me on a car and brought me here.[10]

Although it was difficult at first glance to appreciate the differences between the statements, there were in fact two. The first concerned the distances over which the shots had been fired. The second related to motives and attributes which were ascribed to the gunman in the first account, but conspicuously absent from the second. This was most likely due to Constable Keena's marked deterioration in the hours between Doran's arrival and the magistrate's.

Mr Butcher confirmed that the policeman's death had been caused by internal injuries rendered by the grey, bloodied bullet that lay in a tray beside him. Dr White, the city coroner, continued: 'There is one thing we are all perfectly satisfied with. That this poor man in his misfortune fell into the best hands he possibly could (Applause). In this case, I was particularly struck with the skilful treatment that the man received from Dr Butcher and the post-mortem examination satisfied me that nothing could save the man's life whilst everything was done to alleviate his sufferings.'

The coroner summed up for the jury: 'Gentlemen, you have only to enquire as to the cause of the deceased's death. As to that, you have chiefly the dying declaration of the man himself which is of the strongest evidence.'

The fifteen men found no difficulty in reaching a unanimous verdict. Foreman John Keane stood to speak: 'We find that the said Patrick Keena died in Mercer's Hospital from the effects of a certain pistol or gunshot wound, inflicted on him at Wellington Quay in the City of Dublin on the morning of 31 October in said year when in discharge of his duty as a Police Constable by a person at present unknown.'

Before the inquest could conclude, there was a slight murmur in the gallery. 'Will the verdict not also contain a finding of wilful murder?' one of the jurors asked.

'Gentlemen,' the coroner answered, 'the best way is not to define the crime but merely the facts and leave the verdict open to the law officers of the crown to deal with.' This was more than fair. Too often, a finding of murder or manslaughter by a coroner's jury had the effect of indicting the accused before a case even came to trial.[11] Although not a lawyer (as the majority of his British counterparts were), Dr White displayed a remarkable understanding of the judicial system.

In due course, the results of the post-mortem were sent to the metropolitan police medical attendant, Dr Thomas Nedley. Besides being personal physician to the lord lieutenant, he was responsible for overseeing the condition of prisoners who were due to stand trial. In 1866, he had petitioned in favour of IRB prisoner Edward Duffy on the grounds of his ill-health, but this was overturned by the attorney-general and Dr William Stokes. His report on Constable Keena's death was similarly unbiased.

The inquest gave the police a lot to consider. Had the murder weapon been recovered, they could have conducted some limited analysis to examine its staining as they had done in previous cases. The standard chemical test involved the application of a mixture of sulphuric acid and potash to a surface on the basis that blood turned black when exposed to it.[12] Without it, the solitary, hard-won piece of evidence – the bullet which Butcher had extracted from the body – was a small, if hopeful clue. The distinctive groove in its base did not match American Civil War Miníe design. It seemed similar in shape to the French-designed, single-ringed .69 calibre bullet, yet smaller. Now they waited anxiously for the removal of the second bullet from Sergeant Kelly as this would allow them to compare the ammunition and discover whether the same weapon had wounded both constables. Was it possible that there had been two gunmen?

Ordnance normally lodged in the body when its velocity was almost spent before entry.[13] That could only happen if the weapon was discharged at a distance or if it had little firing power in the first place. Bullets fired from Enfield rifles were known to become distorted at the apex, which then became compressed and turned back from the force of the impact. The bullet taken from the constable was indeed flattened, but not severely so. In addition, judging by the amount of gun smoke reported by some of the witnesses to the shooting, it was possible that a single-shot muzzle-loading pistol had been used, since such weapons required a larger black powder charge than their more modern chamber-loaded counterparts. On the other hand, neither of the injured officers bore signs of powder grain impaction on the skin – a common injury that resulted from the discharging of such weapons at close quarters.

The evidence suggested that the 'assassin's' weapon – for he was now described as such by the newspapers – had come from England or the Continent. It was equally possible that it had come from one of the small arms factories sourced by the Fenian Colonel Ricard O'Sullivan Burke in Birmingham before the March 1867 rising. Too few weapons – probably not more than a couple of thousand – had come into Ireland before the rising and there had been even less ammunition available with which to load them. In an effort to solve the problem, the IRB established a number of 'factories' in Dublin. One of these was located at Loftus Lane – a two-storey former stable leased by Colonel Kelly. Its proprietor, Thomas Barry, later told how Kelly had been with him on the day he went to see the building with a view to purchasing it. He felt it might be too expensive but the colonel pledged to put up the remainder of the money. It produced so many bullets that by 7 February 1866, the furnaces were burnt out and needed to be reconstructed. The front entrance and windows were blocked up and it could only be approached through a narrow passageway, barred by a heavy iron door.[14]

Dubliners had vivid imaginations. People still recalled Kelly's Loftus Lane exploits and the newspapers were quick to pick up on rumours that he had returned to the city. 'It has been stated that Colonel Kelly is at present in Dublin and that the authorities are aware of the fact,' the *Nation* of 9 November gossiped. During Friday's cabinet session in London, the Earl of Mayo reminded Home Secretary Gathorne Hardy that an assassination society had been formed under the colonel's guidance and that 'much blood will be shed unless some of the leaders are taken'. The Duke of Cambridge added fuel to the fire when he sent Hardy a private paper suggesting there was an alliance between the gang and the 'Rouge abroad' (French republicans). 'He too warns that assassination and burning are to be the weapons of warfare ... certainly the continual shootings corroborate [it],' Hardy added. Later that evening, he privately admitted that it would be terrible to live under the kind of apprehension that Judge William Keogh faced on a daily basis. Spurned by nationalists as an oath-breaker for accepting public office in 1855, he enthusiastically sentenced leading Fenians to imprisonment in 1865 and had been the subject of death threats ever since.[15]

The Castle authorities had a clearer picture of Fenian movements than the government in London, facilitated in part by correspondence sent through sessional crown solicitor for Nenagh, George Bolton, and his informer, George Black.[16] They were aware, for instance, that some Irish-American delegates had held a meeting with the remaining Dublin centres on Sunday 3 November in an attempt to rebuild the IRB in that city. Another was planned for Sunday 10 November and would be held somewhere not far outside the city. Colonel Thomas J. Kelly's name was no longer as potent as it had been within the IRB and in the months after his prison van escape, he had managed to flee to New York. Displaced by President William Randall Roberts, who led the senate wing of the American Fenian Brotherhood, his period of influence in Irish affairs had come to an end.

Before the close of Friday 8 November, there was another important piece of news. Jack O'Loughlin wrote to Crown Solicitor Matthew Anderson from the Richmond Bridewell.[17] He claimed that the man who shot the police officers was a Fenian – a man whom Alfred Aylward claimed held sole charge of the Dublin IRB's remaining arms for assassination purposes.[18] His name was Patrick Lennon.

10

A FUNERAL PROCESSION

At eleven o'clock on Saturday morning, 9 November, a solitary coffin covered with a black cloth and decorated with jet mountings was removed from Mercer's Hospital, carried on the shoulders of four A Division policemen. The day was fine and sunny with blue skies and occasional clouds. While the hearse waited with its white-plumed horses, about six hundred policemen from the various divisions lined up along South William Street under their respective superintendents and inspectors.

As soon as the coffin appeared, every head in the large crowd was uncovered and prayers for the repose of the soul went up along the street. As a show of respect, an honour guard of horse police dismounted under the orders of Inspector Ward and Sergeant Connolly. After a respectful interval, they set off slowly down the street. Behind them came the first mourning coach carrying Constable Keena's parents, sister and aunt. For them, the loss was doubly acute. Not alone had the young man died, but the regular remittances he sent home were now gone and they faced an uncertain future.

Members of the various divisions marched solemnly behind in procession. The officers of A Division, to which Constable Keena belonged, came first, under the commands of Superintendent Fitzpatrick and Inspectors Doran and Bennett. Behind them marched the men of B Division, headed by Chief Superintendent Campbell and Inspectors Devon, Cunningham and Harrington. There were over one hundred C Division men under the command of Superintendent Corr and Inspectors O'Connor and Freeney. D Division was supervised by Mr Masterson and the remainder of the procession was brought up respectively by E Division under Mr Gaffney and by Inspector Fitzpatrick and the men of F Division. Police Commissioners Henry Atwell Lake and John Lewis O'Ferrall followed behind in closed cabs. Together, the marching policemen formed a cortège several hundred strong.

For about an hour and a half, the funeral wound its stately way through the streets – first along South King Street, then down Grafton Street, Westmoreland Street and Sackville Street. That day's *Westmeath Guardian and Longford Newsletter* reported that the procession was so long that 'when the hearse was turning into Britain Street, the carriages at the end were coming over Carlisle Bridge'. The lord mayor, William Lane Joynt, and town clerk, John Norwood, distinguished themselves by walking the route on foot, a gesture that was not lost on Constable Keena's father.

The Irish administration intended to make a statement – a show of civic strength to defy the IRB gunmen. Apart from a small piece that appeared in the *Daily Express*, Superintendent

Ryan had managed to keep the details of the removal secret. Saturday was an ordinary working day for most Dubliners, a circumstance that reduced the numbers of bystanders on the streets. The reporters grumbled, but it was a small price to pay if further opportunistic attacks were to be avoided. Overall, the atmosphere at Dublin Castle was tense. With most of the force taking part in the procession, there were precious few officers left to oversee public order, so Superintendent Corr assigned Acting Inspector Gorman to organise the reserve constables.

Onlookers continued to gather as the cortège wound its way up the broad expanse of Dominick Street towards the Broadstone railway terminus. There, the escort of policemen formed a double line through which some officers from G Division bore the coffin towards the platform. They were relieved after a short interval by constables from other divisions, a pattern that was repeated so that each man could take his turn. As they approached the colonnade, swept clear of its usual throng of cars outside, they passed a distinguished group of railway and government magnates who held their hats by their sides. They included the chairman, Mr Cusack, the manager, Mr Skipworth, and the attorney-general for Ireland, Robert Warren. The government had pledged to cover the cost of the funeral.

Six officers from each division – thirty-six in all – were detailed to accompany Constable Keena's remains to Mullingar. They filed solemnly into an oil-lit carriage, but the coffin was assigned to the unfurnished guard's van, a decision that drew some murmurs of discontent from the waiting reporters.

When the engine pulled into Mullingar station that evening, it was met by a large number of townspeople and local policemen. Under dense and heavy skies, they helped bear the coffin past the crêpe-decked shops of the town. Reaching the constable's home place at Ballyglass, the procession halted and a crowd of neighbouring people gathered to pay their respects. Later, the casket was carried into the house and as night fell, a dense fog settled.

By the following afternoon, the weather showed no improvement. Sunday 10 November was the feast of the Blessed Virgin. That, and the two-day fair which was due to begin the following morning, had swelled the population of Mullingar considerably. The town was crowded with hawkers, farmers and buyers. Mingling among them were people who had walked ten or fifteen miles to hear Constable Keena's funeral mass.

The fair was second only to the annual event in Ballinasloe and a large additional police force had been drafted in to assist the town's usual complement of twenty-one. So many came to pay their respects that by the time the funeral began, the grounds of the little church were packed to capacity. When the aging Catholic curate, Fr John Kelly, ascended the pulpit to deliver a powerfully worded homily, the few reporters present were careful to note the empathy he showed for the suffering of Keena's family. The Church had been careful to condemn the recent assassinations, followed by the Dublin-based *Saunders' Newsletter* – a conservative, anti-Catholic daily – but when the *Newsletter* sarcastically complimented the IRB for its 'fine Sardinian spirit', A.M. Sullivan cleverly exploited the comment to his own advantage. Choosing not to acknowledge its true connotation, he criticised the publication for its 'bloodthirsty' standpoint, describing it as nothing more than an organ of Lord Mayo.[1]

When the service ended at half-past four, a great swell of people, many of whom could not find room in the church, followed the remains over the three miles to the Church of Ireland cemetery at Lynn.[2] The coffin was flanked by a number of parish curates who recited the *Te Deum*. Alongside the fair-goers and constabulary, many of the town commissioners, poor law guardians and merchant traders also came to pay their respects. A reporter from *Saunders' Newsletter* remarked that had more people been aware of the funeral in advance, many more would have come from Dublin.[3] Even so, there were several thousand in attendance.

Darkness had fallen by the time the cortège reached the graveyard. Just off the high road to Mullingar near the north-eastern bank of Lough Ennell, it was clustered around the ruins of an ancient church. This had once been the site of Saint Cormac's seventh-century cell foundation, Lann Meic Luchain. An aged alder tree overhung the high altar and stone font, filling the place with a quiet sense of reverence.

As the coffin entered the cemetery, Constable Keena's mother Margaret, not having had the heart to look on the face of her son the previous evening, began to cry out. She had arrived too late to Mercer's Hospital to witness his final moments so the bearers relented and laid their charge on the grass in front of the open grave. A dense fog hid the light of the moon. Several matches were struck and the casket lid was raised with some difficulty. By this light, she looked upon his shrouded features. After a few moments, the lid was replaced and the coffin eventually lowered into the ground.

Not all of the remains were interred at Lynn, however. Shortly after the post-mortem, Mr Butcher had discreetly removed and cleaned the constable's lumbar spine. He intended to display it in his widely acclaimed private museum with 'the bullet that did the damage'.

11

INTERNATIONAL CONNECTIONS

On Monday 11 November, Dubliners awoke to a light fog. By the afternoon, it had thickened into a dense blanket that heralded an early nightfall. Although Londoners consumed more coal per capita, the second city of the empire was still burdened with at least fifty days of charcoal-smelling fog each winter. Immortalised in the shanties of sailors who lay at berth, it could be more than just a nuisance and during heavy spells the newspapers were peppered with reports of tragic drowning accidents in the Royal or Grand Canals. In some ways perhaps, it matched the sombre mood of the administration, whose failure to protect its constabulary was belied by the praise heaped upon it by John Keena, the father of the murdered policeman. That day, a glowing letter appeared in *The Irish Times*:

> Sir, with your usual good feeling towards the afflicted, I trust you will kindly … allow me to return my sincere thanks and those of my family to His Excellency, to the Commissioners of the Police, and the officers and men under their command, for having paid all the expenses relative to the death and removal of the remains of my son.

As the paper went to print, the 'Ryan's gang' returned to face Magistrates O'Donnell and O'Donnel at Capel Street court. The notable exception was John Dowling, who it seemed was now turning queen's evidence. Jack O'Loughlin and Daniel O'Connell Considine appeared separately, but for the same charge. The collective charge against all five was for possession of unlicensed arms in a proclaimed district.

Undoubtedly, the police had charged the men in a hurry, giving them little time to prepare their defence. The American Secretary of State, William H. Seward, proposed his own theory for this. Having just received word that Constable Keena had died, he wrote to the US minister for England, Charles Francis Adams. He was sure that nothing other than public panic was responsible for such expeditious justice, understandable when according to an enclosed *Evening Mail* clipping of 9 November, 'almost every day has its story of a fresh street assassination; the work of the same conspiracy'.[1]

As a result of James Dondrell's collection for the incarcerated members of the shooting circle, Thomas Rooney and Peter McDonnell were able to hire a Stafford Street solicitor named Charles Fitzgerald. Francis Murray, Jack O'Loughlin and Daniel O'Connell Considine were a different matter altogether. Due to the *in flagrante* nature of their arrests, and in particular O'Loughlin's alleged willingness to turn informer, the IRB leadership decided that it would be a waste of money to arrange representation for them.

The remainder of the assassination circle continued with its reprisals, however. On the morning of the Capel Street examination, Inspector Burke received a threatening letter at his Marlborough Street home. The correspondent, who signed himself 'P.J.J.' or 'J.P.P.', included enough details to let the detective know that he had been trailing him for two weeks. Besides his participation in the Great Britain Street raid, Burke was also responsible for arresting Jack O'Loughlin, and his earlier appearance at Capel Street police court made him a key target. The letter contained a crudely drawn picture of an assassin firing at his intended victim. The wording was ominous and laced with invective:

> The Contents of a good Fenian Revolver … will not give you time to repent you disgrase to sweet Tiperary it is a lover of the green flag that sends you this … remember your goings you cur you Saxon spy of Danish Blood you cur you Peirse Nagle. You should like to no who sent you this but you will Not till you get the Contents of my Revolver.[2]

When the proceedings opened at Capel Street, Burke was noticeably absent, but Superintendent Corr signed a deposition on his behalf. Having waited for the gas lamps to be lit, the chief clerk read over the circumstances of the Great Britain Street raid. Anxious to get to the nub of the issue, Fitzgerald began by questioning Acting Inspector Mulholland: 'Did you find any arms or ammunition on the prisoners Rooney or McDonnell?'

'No, I did not,' Mulholland replied.

The magistrate was surprised. He agreed with the solicitor that the Arms Act did not legislate for items such as the pistol-case that was found with Rooney. Although the case against him was more clear-cut, Francis Murray, who had listened with interest to Fitzgerald's defence, sensed an opportunity to win ground: 'When this man [Mulholland] swore his information on Saturday week last, there was nothing said by him about my having sworn an oath, or made any effort to draw a pistol: how could I have done so when he admitted that his first act was to pinion my hands behind my back?'

Acting Inspector Mulholland repeated his original statement. Unfortunately for Murray, it referred to him having threatened the police. 'I never made any statement to the effect that I would *use* the pistol,' Murray protested, 'but I was surprised. The inspector said to me: "You're a terrible fellow, would you have used that thing", the pistol, and I said I didn't know what I might do.'

'I never said a word to him in the coach,' Mulholland replied.

In summary, the solicitor believed that the charges against his clients Rooney and McDonnell should 'fall to the ground'. To his satisfaction they were acquitted, but Superintendent Ryan, who had anticipated this outcome, had obtained the necessary Habeas Corpus Suspension Act warrants and promptly removed them to Dublin Castle.

Just as the IRB leadership feared, no legal side-stepping was possible in Murray's case since he had been arrested with firearms – a clear violation of the Arms Act. His case would be tried at the next commission with Jack O'Loughlin, Daniel O'Connell Considine and James Dondrell. Dondrell continued to assert that his revolver belonged to a brother who had recently returned from America and reasoned that if he had applied for a licence it would have been taken away, leaving him temporarily defenceless. None of these arguments were taken seriously, however, since unknown to him, the chief secretary had become particularly interested in the firearm and its provenance.

After the inquest, Thomas Larcom informed Mayo that the bullet recovered from Constable Keena matched Dondrell's weapon. It was an interesting coincidence, and one that he felt would pay dividends if a knowledgeable informer was to place Dondrell at the scene of the crime. When Police Magistrate William Allen called to see Larcom, he informed him that, according to Kavanagh the gunmaker, the weapon came from Sligo and was a modification of 'what in Yankeedom they call the Needham pistol'.[3] It was also a breech-loader which set it apart from the more primitive front or muzzle-loading weapons which up until then had been the hallmark of the assassin.

In the days that followed Keena's funeral, Larcom sent the revolver over to the police office for further examination and Superintendent Ryan would not allow it out of his sight. He ventured a different theory about its history. He believed the weapon was one of a number that had been manufactured in Belgium by Eugene Lefaucheux. It featured a popular pin-fire mechanism, one of the main innovations of which lay in its use of cartridges which dispensed with the need for black powder, percussion caps and bullets. A metal spur protruded from the bottom of each cartridge to catch the hammer. Thus, the problem of gas freely escaping inside the chamber was overcome. As an added bonus, the weapons were also much more likely to fire when wet. In 1861, Colonel George Schuyler had purchased ten thousand for Lincoln's Union Army. However, they were less powerful than the popular Colt revolver and after the war the soldiers were allowed to keep them as souvenirs. This was one explanation for the appearance of the revolvers in Ireland, but Ryan believed that they had been imported by William James Hill of St Mary's Square, Birmingham, who sold them on as his own patent.[4]

Hill was a weapons finisher who had an interest in the 'improvement of breech-loading guns'. Having been approached in 1865 by Fenian arms agent Ricard O'Sullivan Burke, who haggled over the purchase of arms for the Brotherhood under the alias of 'Edward C. Winslow', Hill renewed his patent for their modification in January 1867, presumably in an attempt to fulfil the order.[5]

The chief secretary noticed that both Dondrell's weapon and another – possibly the one taken from Murray – had the same maker's mark, but were of different construction, and he was eager to pursue the source of the distribution network further.[6] Writing to the permanent Home Office under-secretary, Adolphus Liddell, on Monday 11 November, he enclosed a description of the recovered weapon, stating that it had been 'taken from the man suspected to be a party in the assassination of the two policemen in Dublin a short time ago'.[7] Some days later, the mayor of Birmingham confirmed that it had come from Mr Hill.

Meanwhile, Superintendent Ryan continued to gather information about the assassination circle. As the Capel Street proceedings wound to a close, he wrote to Commissioner Lake to inform him that although John O'Mahony's New York Fenian Brotherhood continued to maintain tentative links with Colonel Kelly's followers in Ireland, there had been a split in the American Brotherhood, the greater part of which was now led by a Brooklyn dry goods merchant named William Randall Roberts. His faction, called the 'senate wing', was more militant that O'Mahony's supporters and it was Roberts who had planned the Fenian Brotherhood's failed attack on Canada in 1866. Roberts did not believe armed insurrection would succeed in Ireland and according to some, his *modus operandi* was subterfuge and 'plots and plans of all kinds', hatched against Great Britain from New York.[8] To Superintendent Ryan, it seemed plausible that Roberts had made a connection with the assassination circle in Dublin.

Roberts' London arms agent was James Cooke. He first came to police attention during the summer of 1864 when he left gainful employment to gather curiosities from donors who were sympathetic to the Fenian cause. These were then sold at the Chicago Fair – an attempt by then IRB leader James Stephens to raise the finances needed to stage an Irish rebellion. However, Cooke's work was easily traced by Acting Inspector Hughes through advertisements in the *Irish People* newspaper and he was arrested when he arrived in Drogheda in November 1866. The books he was carrying, one of which was an eighty-two page volume entitled *To the State Centres, Centres and*

Members of the Fenian Brotherhood of North America, left the police in little doubt about who they were dealing with.

When Cooke was committed to Mountjoy on 28 November 1866, his wife Sarah wrote to the governor. She pleaded that her husband had only returned to Ireland to dispose of a small property and that he was planning to take his family to the United States. She claimed that his identity had been mistaken.[9] The government conceded and he was released on condition of his going to America. He sailed from Queenstown just a few weeks before the rising and shortly after his arrival in New York, he and a man named Maurice O'Donoghue met William Roberts to discuss a way to reunite the disparate parts of the Brotherhood.[10] Settling on a plan, they appointed Daniel O'Sullivan, a man with a strong Kerry accent, as secretary for civil affairs.

A key part of their strategy was to install O'Sullivan as their financial agent in Paris. From that city he would pass American remittances to the IRB. O'Sullivan sailed from Quebec on 10 May and arrived in Liverpool two weeks later, travelling on from there to London and later to Cork. Using some addresses he had been given, he called on some of the IRB centres in Ireland there, but found that in practically every case they had fled or were in prison. The circles in Belfast also lacked leadership and were in disarray. His first-hand experience convinced him that the existence of large circles prior to the rising had compromised the security of the Brotherhood and that the presence of half a dozen reliable men in each parish would have been more effective. Everywhere he went he found that the circles were scattered and demoralised. He then made his way to Dublin where he managed to persuade some of the more influential centres to travel to France to meet with Roberts. Soon afterwards, he steamed back across the channel towards England.

When Roberts arrived in Europe, his initial impressions of the IRB's fortunes were discouraging. Like O'Sullivan, he met with a profound sense of disillusionment everywhere. On 1 July, he convened a meeting in the French capital and it continued in session until the fourth. His aim in so doing was to unite the Irish Republican and Fenian Brotherhoods under the common banner of a new constitution. In this, he was almost wholly unsuccessful.

One of the delegates at the Paris meeting was John Walsh, a pawnbroker's assistant and committed assassin. Although known to the police for over two years, he had managed to maintain a rather shadowy presence until 16 October 1867, at which point the police commissioners asked Matthew Anderson to search the newly organised Fenian files at Dublin Castle for any mention of him relative to the purchase of arms.[11] Up until then, he had made no efforts to conceal himself, even marrying a sister of Mrs Thomas Clarke Luby.[12] There was a sudden turn in his fortunes when a revolver was traced to his possession.[13] Based on a description given by Constable Matthew Donohoe, Superintendent Ryan suspected that Walsh was involved in the attempted shooting of the informer George Reilly in Blackrock on 20 October.

Before leaving Paris, Walsh and the others tried to persuade

President Roberts to stage another Irish rising the following January, but Roberts urged them to postpone it until the summer of 1868. In the meantime, he would plan seven district conventions with the aim of electing a 'Supreme Council' to keep the IRB under control in Ireland and England.[14] Two members were elected almost immediately – one for southern England and another for Leinster. According to Daniel O'Sullivan, other regional elections were deferred on the basis that for the most part, the post-rising IRB leadership was moribund and once new centres friendly to the senate wing had been installed, it would take some time for their members to become acquainted with Roberts' vision.

Walsh, along with two other IRB men based in Ireland, John Murphy and Michael Feely, left Paris with a promise of 30,000 rifles and ammunition, but in the context of existing resources, it could not have been more than an empty promise. Nevertheless, it was enough to enforce a proviso that any intended rising in Ireland would need to occur simultaneously with another planned raid on Canada, and the delegates were sworn to do everything in their power to prevent any premature call to arms in Ireland.

Afterwards, Daniel O'Sullivan made a second visit to Cork where he appointed a representative with the authority to bring all the Munster circles into communication with the senate wing. He also appointed travelling organisers to work in areas where the Brotherhood was weak such as Kerry, Clare and rural Cork. O'Sullivan and Roberts then returned to America to continue their efforts to unite the Brotherhood there.

Some IRB rank and file members had already begun to look to the senate wing for material support. When Patrick Hayburne revealed his plans to travel to America, an unnamed correspondent had advised him to seek out Daniel O'Sullivan to inform him that:

> The men here are sadly in want of shoes and clothes. Some money should be sent them at once. It can be sent to some friend in Dublin who can send in the sum appropriated to each one. By having their names sent to him, there is no trouble in the matter and money is better spent in that way than on damned conventions and such foolish proceedings.[15]

At a meeting which convened on 3 September in Cleveland, Roberts claimed that he had reunited the Fenian and Irish Republican Brotherhoods and he disclosed expansionist plans. Meanwhile, John Murphy, Michael Feely and John Walsh had begun the task of forming an Irish Directory in Dublin. It was sanctioned by some of the centres, who included Thomas Francis, William Brophy and Patrick McGarry. It aimed to introduce a new tier of middle management to the IRB and countervailed James Stephens' original dictatorial model which had produced an unwieldy, sometimes uncontrollable organisation. One of its regular duties was to communicate directly with James Cooke in London, and through this liaison the Directory would guide the operations of the assassination circle. On 11 November, Superintendent Ryan reported that:

> Recently twenty revolvers have been received from Cooke in London and placed in the hands of the greatest desperadoes that

could be selected from among the conspirators with instructions to shoot down detectives, Crown witnesses and everyone else they suspect of being opposed to their views.[16]

Ryan suspected that Cooke's opposite number in Dublin was Denis Downey – an arms agent who had imported weapons in 1866.[17] Besides his regular business as a tailor, Downey made IRB uniforms, and during a raid on his house in Trinity Street, a quantity of guns, moulds and bullet caps had been seized. A shipment of phosphorus was also received by Downey, evidently for the manufacture of Greek fire. The prospect of such incendiary devices being in the hands of a gang of subversives was truly frightening. According to Ryan's informant, Cooke's revolvers were just an initial instalment, but Thomas Larcom later wrote that they were 'the only supplies ever advanced'.[18] Nevertheless, even twenty revolvers in the hands of 'desperadoes' could be extremely dangerous and Superintendent Ryan appealed to the government through Commissioner Lake for warrants to arrest all the men named in his report. These comprised the IRB Directory of three (John Walsh, Michael Feely, John Murphy), the shoemaker Thomas Francis, William Brophy, who had been accidentally shot in Lynch's public house the previous year, Patrick Lennon, who led the rebels during the rising, James Byrne, who was allegedly at the attempted shooting of George Reilly, and Patrick McGarry. He was certain that by so doing, it would considerably upset the IRB 'programme' and disrupt the movements of the assassination circle.[19]

The impetus for taking such action was a report that the circle had renewed its plans under Patrick McGarry and Michael Feely to assassinate Head Constable Thomas Talbot. The last ham-fisted attempt on his life had left commercial agent Robert Atkinson wounded and temporarily bedridden.

In official correspondence concerning the assassination circle, William Roberts was portrayed as a shadowy mastermind. An 'outrage' policy would have been relatively inexpensive to maintain since, judging by recent events, it seemed that all that was required was a small cache of arms, some ammunition and phosphorus. *The Irish Times* of 4 October 1867 pointed out that the strategy employed by some subversives was clearly to create an impression that Fenianism was still a vibrant force in Britain and Ireland, thus bringing into the pockets of the American leaders 'some eight or ten thousand pounds'.

If there was any element of truth in this, Roberts gave no outward show. His diplomacy at the Paris meeting had succeeded in suspending attempts to stage a repeat rising but it was certainly not enough to interrupt small-scale incendiary attacks; if anything, they actually intensified after September 1867. Perhaps, like James Stephens in 1861, he was trying to take charge 'of what he could not suppress'.[20]

12

RATTLED NERVES

Shortly before nine o'clock on 14 November, a servant woman at Green Street courthouse made her way to the clerk of the peace's office. It was used by the attorney- and solicitor-generals for the duration of the special commission trials and was not part of her usual cleaning round. In return, she could expect a gratuity. In the corridor, she passed a stream of people going to that morning's session. Among them was Augustine E. Costello, the infamous Fenian captain who was on trial for his alleged complicity in the ill-fated *Erin's Hope* expedition. He had slept at the courthouse overnight along with the jurors and crown witnesses for the trial. She would clean those quarters next.

Bustling quietly into the room, she attended to the empty grate. A moment later, the office exploded, smashing the furniture to pieces and destroying the roof and windows. The doors of a set of rooms along the corridor outside the office were wrenched open and windows on the opposite side of the street shattered instantly. With the destruction of the north wing's ceilings, the damaged portion of the courthouse filled with dust which made it hard to breathe and see. At Linenhall

Barracks the garrison mobilised, assuming they had heard a discharge of artillery.

Superintendent Ryan dispatched Acting Inspector Entwhistle and Sergeant Ennis to investigate. By the time they arrived, the foggy morning had begun to clear to a wet mist and firemen were busy picking through the worst of the damage. They took particular note of rumours that some attributed the explosion 'to other than escaped gas and ... that Fenianism has something to do with it'.[1] In the hours that followed, the lord mayor, lord mayor-elect and city engineer also attended the scene. By some miracle, there were no fatalities. The servant had been knocked unconscious, but apart from having her hair singed was otherwise uninjured. Thomas Larcom, who well understood the potential for unfounded gossip, dispatched an immediate telegram to the chief secretary who was still in London:

> Explosion of gas at courthouse, Green Street. Some injury to the building. No person injured. You may hear this attributed to other causes for which there is no foundation.[2]

For the second time that month, the message was intercepted and read by eager journalists who reported its full contents in the following day's London *Times*. After Mayo's recent letter to the Home Office regarding the Arthur Forrester leak, this new disclosure was extremely irksome. Rumours were rife. To many, the explosion seemed deliberate, particularly since it was recalled that there had been a threat to disrupt the city's gas supply prior to the March insurrection. Was this an attempt by the authorities to cover up the work of Fenian incendiaries?

Mr Stephens, secretary of the Alliance Gas Company, put a stop to such idle speculation. He asserted that the blast had been caused by nothing more than evaporation from a patent slide gasolier during the night. A lack of water in the pipe had allowed gas to fill the damaged office, but revealingly the police report added:

> We overheard some of the jurors say that, on returning to bed, they noticed a very strong smell of gas, and one said he changed into another room the smell being so strong in that which he originally slept in.[3]

The *Daily Express* commented that the supply had not been turned off fully at the meter in case the resident jurors needed a night light. The court keeper stoutly denied this, informing reporters that the cocks had all been turned off, apart from a small jet of flame that was kept lighting the corridor for the convenience of the policemen on duty.[4]

Nevertheless, Dublin Castle took the incident as a warning of what might happen if the republican threat went unchecked and in private they were at least willing to consider the possibility that the explosion was the product of some kind of sabotage. They were well aware that the IRB had its eye on larger armaments than mere pistols and rifles, and for this reason, the Ballincollig powder mill in County Cork was a key concern. The Green Street explosion may well have been an innocent (if expensive) coincidence, but it was loaded with significance. It was a reminder that death at the hands of renegades might also come by fire.

Baron Strathnairn, who was most concerned about this threat, received a request from the prime minister, Lord Derby, to come to London. He went, but refused to consider an invitation to second Her Majesty's speech. He knew it was going to favour the government Reform Bill which, if passed, would enfranchise the urban working classes in England and Wales, so he tactfully accepted a dinner invitation instead. A rather more liberally disposed chief secretary joined the queen and her cabinet on 18 November amid rumours of threats on the monarch's life.

The fate of the three men who had been accused of involvement in the Manchester prison van escape needed to be discussed. The lord president of the council, the Duke of Marlborough, believed that an example should be made. When canvassed for his opinion, Mayo felt that it was necessary to come to the defence of the Irish administration. Despite recent events, he emphasised that Fenianism was far less troublesome in Ireland and that no man of 'good character or property ... or any Protestant Irish' belonged to it. It would nevertheless 'take long to put things right'.[5]

The same day, Gathorne Hardy, who had received some threatening letters, wrote to his son Stewart about the matter of his personal safety. 'That is in God's hands,' he admitted. 'Threats are not always realised, although I believe in this instance there are desperate hands engaged ready for any bad work. I hope I may be spared to live long among you all.'[6]

The House of Lords convened the following day. Speaking about the impotence of the English police in the wake of the

Manchester rescue and of Superintendent Ryan's attempt to warn them, the Earl of Russell went on the offensive: 'They had a telegram from Dublin, had they not?'

The prime minister robustly challenged the imputation. 'No doubt there was a telegram from Dublin,' he answered, 'but those precautions were taken in a very large increase of police in attendance on the van.' He explained that no further measures had been taken because the authorities had not expected so bloody an attack.

Lord Derby refused to see the latest wave of outrages as anything other than simple thuggery. He loathed the idea of an independent Irish Republic, since its own people were clearly not up to the task of ruling themselves. If the British Empire relinquished its hold on Ireland, the country would surely degenerate into anarchy. (Such rhetoric was not new. Indeed, it was strikingly similar to the wording of a speech given by John Fitzgibbon, Earl of Clare, when he introduced the Act of Union to the Irish House of Lords in 1800.) What the prime minister detested most was the brand of Fenianism that had left one constable dead in Dublin and another fighting for his life. He railed against their 'secret incendiarisms, attacks on unprotected houses, murders of single and unarmed policemen, [and] attacks on police barracks which are known not to be defended, attempts to fire houses by men who have not courage to show themselves'.[7]

His one concession was to those who rose openly in rebellion 'by force of arms to establish their principles and views'. These men alone could claim status as revolutionaries. With the governments of America and France, two nations with strong republican traditions, keeping an eye on Irish affairs, it was perhaps politic to display at least some magnanimity.

13

BRANDY AND SCALPELS

Sergeant Kelly lay uneasily in his hospital bed. He had not been insensible to Constable Keena's pain or to the anguish of his father, but his spirits were sorely shaken when he realised why he was being moved. In the days that followed Keena's death, Mr Butcher reported that he lay 'perfectly restless, staring at the ceiling and scarcely can be induced to take the trouble of speaking'.[1] Although the indomitable surgeon had little time to attend to him, he redoubled his efforts after the inquest. Treatment with opium and ice applied to his abdomen continued. Eventually, his bleeding stopped and his condition stabilised. Once he had achieved a better frame of mind, he told the surgeon: 'You have been too kind to me.'

The consulting army surgeons still looked upon his death as inevitable, however. Having dealt with gunshot wounds in tented hospitals in the Crimea and elsewhere, they knew that when a Minie ball struck a bone, it usually shattered and caused untold internal damage. A round perforation the size of a bullet only occurred in certain rare cases. Superintendent Ryan cautioned the hospital staff not to discuss this information with the press since one policeman was already dead and it would not do to create further panic.

Sepsis was the 'pestilence that walketh in darkness' in the dingy, overcrowded wards of large hospitals and four illnesses flared up with such frequency that they came to be known collectively as 'hospital disease' – erysipelas, septicemia, pyaemia and acute gangrene.[2] There were several factors in Sergeant Kelly's favour, however. To begin with, sanitary conditions at Mercer's, although not great, were still marginally better than those in the field. Secondly, Mr Butcher had been using silver catheters which were naturally sterile and, having resolved to wait until his patient had recovered his strength, he had not yet actually performed any invasive surgery.

On 10 November, his patience was rewarded when for the first time he noticed a slight purplish discoloration on the right side of the sergeant's chest. There was no pain on deep breathing and on percussion he felt 'a slight fullness'. Although he concluded that this was nothing more than a natural murmur, he later doubted himself and wondered whether it might also mark the bullet's exact location.

The next few days were uneventful enough. The nurses continued to administer opium judiciously, taking care to ensure that the patient was not becoming addicted. Twice in two days, a dozen leeches were applied to the area around his wound. By now, his pain had entirely abated and he was beginning to get a reasonable amount of sleep. After several further examinations, Mr Butcher had begun to suspect that the bullet lay between the eighth and ninth ribs on Kelly's right side, a guess that was seconded by Dr Moore. He returned later and wrote in his clinical notes:

> I thought I could discover within the chest, a solid body. Twice, I got the slight shock to my finger so as to make me certain that the foreign body was within; small, weighty and moveable. After these gentle efforts, the foreign body eluded me altogether and the best directed touch could not discover its presence.[3]

Doctors William Moore and Edward Ledwich followed Mr Butcher's lead by attempting to feel for the bullet themselves before it 'hid itself'. There could be no better men to verify the location. Ledwich, a doctor of many years' standing, had been the joint author of *A Treatise on Practical Anatomy*. Complementary to this volume was Moore's *Paralysis and Atrophy from Lead Poisoning* – a useful text considering the bullet's composition.

Caution prevailed, however, and it was several days before the doctors could be sure of its location and attempt an operation. An 1859 edition of the *Lancet* had described Mr Butcher as one of the most conservative of surgeons – a laudable characteristic – but by now, Sergeant Kelly had been in hospital for over two weeks with little offered to him other than analgesia and beef tea. As a result, tension reigned at Mercer's and extended to the medical staff upon whose shoulders so much public expectation now rested. The operation would be difficult and uncertain and there were few who were willing to perform it. Dr Ledwich harboured an aversion to performing major surgical operations, preferring instead to give lectures on the subject and Dr Moore's forte was more clinical than surgical.

Inevitably, the task fell to Richard Butcher. On the morning of 16 November, sensing that Sergeant Kelly could not be stirred without a fatal risk, he dragged his wooden bed away from the wall with the help of some orderlies and turned his affected side towards the window.

Sometimes, gunshot cases were taken to theatre, not necessarily to ensure a sterile environment, but to throw more light on the wounds. The lord lieutenant had commented favourably on the new Mercer's theatre during a tour of the hospital in 1855. In Sergeant Kelly's case its use was deemed unnecessary, since Mr Butcher was able to gain a good degree of illumination from the winter sun. There were windows on one side of the ward only and they looked out onto the passing traffic of Mercer Street. The sergeant was laid in position facing the glass but after a moment, was turned towards his left side to maximise the light – a movement that obscured the location of the bullet.

Mr Butcher left the ward and returned at midday. Despite Governor John Morgan's advocacy of general anaesthesia (he had invented the ether inhaler), Butcher was reluctant to use it and stoutly defended this position, despite Sergeant Kelly's evident terror at the prospect of an operation. Butcher believed that anaesthesia meant nothing less than 'sporting with life beneath the sagacity of a medical practitioner' and that it left the limbs, organs and muscles in a flaccid, almost inoperable condition.[4] It would be better for Kelly to have a hot dose of brandy and rest until his pulse was stronger.

The bed had been placed square against the window and

Butcher was obliged to sit on the covers in rather cramped quarters. Two orderlies held the policeman, who tensed his muscles in anticipation. Despite the brandy, he was sensible to the first cut. The surgeon made a 3½-inch deep incision along the course of his ribs. When the second one was made, Kelly cried out in agony as a tablespoonful of purulent matter escaped along with some coagulated blood.

Removal of the ball demanded great care. For some time, the medical profession had observed the change from musket balls to long, coned bullets with dismay. When fired, the conical end acted like a wedge, driving through tendons and other soft tissues that together might have slowed a more primitive projectile. It was a simple design innovation but one that entailed more complex extraction. It was important to ensure that the long axis of the bullet was removed in line with the track of the wound. Otherwise, there was a risk that its tip might tear some internal structure on its way out and cause further complications. Mr Butcher pressed steadily upon the site of the incision and satisfyingly the bullet presented its convex end and was drawn out. Sergeant Kelly was overjoyed, but suddenly felt quite faint. He was given as much brandy as he wanted. As he lay there exhausted, the surgeon quietly examined the bullet in the light from the window. It was stamped with the first two letters of the word 'police' where it had struck the sergeant's tunic button. A small piece of cloth was compressed into a deep groove on its flattened edge. Compared with Longmore's treatise, it was a textbook example:

A gunshot wound, whether received from a direct or indirect projectile, may be complicated by the entrance of extraneous bodies of various kinds, most commonly portions of the cloth or buttons ... such foreign substances ... often have a special bearing on the progress of its cure.[5]

Despite his prodigious strength, Mr Butcher's hands were small and delicate. Before stitching the wound up, he put his index finger into it and moved it around gently to ensure that another piece of tunic had not also gone in with the bullet. The practice was a common one among pre-Listerian surgeons, particularly those who worked in the field. Indeed, Dr Longmore described the finger as perhaps the most effective implement at the surgeon's disposal. On the other hand, many army doctors had witnessed soldiers die within two days of such probing.

When he had finished, Butcher pressed a few shreds of oil-soaked lint into the track of the wound and placed a small lint compress on either side, held together with some strips of adhesive plaster. Due to its similar shape and size, he was sure that the bullet had been fired from the same pistol as the one that killed Constable Keena. Up until now, the detectives could not rule out the possibility that there might have been two gunmen. Now they knew that they were searching for just one man.

In the meantime, money continued to pour in for the deceased constable's family. It prompted another acknowledgment from John Keena to *The Irish Times*. He was particularly grateful for £5 sent from the military secretary, Colonel Leicester Curzon Smyth. On 19 November, a requiem mass was held for his son in St Andrew's Church, Westland Row. It was attended by all of the city's confraternities and held in front of a catafalque surrounded by candles.

News of Sergeant Kelly's operation was fast becoming the talk of the city. Despite their previous misgivings, the city's army surgeons spoke of it with wonderment and on 17 November, the *Freeman's Journal* boasted that Mr Butcher had cared for the sergeant with 'all the tenderness of a woman', proclaiming him a 'world-famed citizen' and that his recent *chirurgie* would 'rank amongst the most remarkable on record'.

The next day, the sergeant needed to be propped up in bed due to some fluid retention. Quinine was prescribed to alleviate his leg cramps and to help wean him off the opium and he was given brandy and eggs for the first time. Later, he was moved to a fresh bed. On 18 November, Mr Butcher noticed that his bowels had 'moved too freely' so he prescribed a number of astringent treatments over a two-day period.

By 22 November, Sergeant Kelly was sleeping uninterruptedly without pain, even on deep breathing. Although his voice was barely audible, his oedema had disappeared and it was clear that he was on the mend. That evening, reports about his favourable recovery appeared in *Saunders' Newsletter* and *The Irish Times*, the latter commenting quite sensationally that, had it not been for the button on his tunic, the bullet would almost certainly have pierced his heart.

14

RAID ON THE COOMBE

The assassination circle had always been a maverick gang, probably as far back as 1865 when Tom Frith, fresh from shooting Acting Inspector Edward Hughes, asked General Francis Millen, a former Mexican army officer and key figure in the American Fenian Brotherhood, to lead them. Millen dismissed him and there was no reason to believe that the attitude of the leaders – some of whom were prepared to lend material support to the gang in secret while refusing to admit to doing so in public – had suddenly changed. Had affiliations with Colonel Thomas J. Kelly and William R. Roberts been more than nominal, its activities would undoubtedly have been more structured, giving some outward indication that it was subject to control. Instead, it was reactionary and unpredictable.

Suppressing it was easier said than done, however. While on the one hand, loose organisation allowed regular infiltration by informers, it also meant there was a propensity for subversives to appear sporadically from any quarter. A new sense of fear began to take root among the city's business community who were afraid to be seen dealing with the police in case their premises were blown up or burned by members of the shooting circle and cases of larceny began to go unreported. 'We would tell you anything,' an informer told Superintendent Ryan, 'but really the times are such that we don't want to see you at all as we don't know where one of those vagabonds is lurking, and may destroy us before morning.'[1]

On 15 November, a document written in cipher was left in the hallway of the Grafton Street photographer, James Robinson. He showed it to a friend, but both agreed that it was not the Pitman system of shorthand. It was quickly decoded by the police:

> We, the directors of the Irish Republic hereby order that all members ... hold themselves in readiness in order to back up any rising which there will surely be and on the said day [22 December] to arm themselves and meet at Ballsbridge ... and drive the Sassanach into the sea and establish the Irish Republic ... we can easily ... cut off the gas and sack the city at our ease, murder the citizens and take the city.[2]

The document, signed by James Stephens and 'J.K.' Roberts, was a risible attempt at forgery. If the mere content was not enough to persuade the police that it was a hoax, the signatures were a sure indication – James Stephens was no longer in control of the IRB and in any case its counter-signatory should have been 'W.R.' and not 'J.K.' Roberts. Regardless, the writers hoped to play on a sense of public panic. Superintendent Ryan captured this sense of unease when he drafted a report about the number of foreign men 'of the artisan class' who were now in Dublin. They appeared to be stout, well-fed and comfortably but not extravagantly dressed. They hung around the city's public houses during the day and took particular notice of its most prominent buildings.[3] The police had been encouraged by their superiors to interpret all such working-class gatherings as 'Fenian' and for this reason kept careful watch on the Abbey Street Mechanics Institute. This only served to generate a atmosphere of Castle-fuelled fear and suspicion, however – one that hindered rather than aided real investigation work. Since early 1866, twenty constables had been temporarily assigned to G Division to watch the movements of such characters and their reports helped to persuade an alarmed government that they were wrong in assuming that Fenianism was dead in Ireland.[4] A fictitious rebellion was one thing, but foreign strangers on the streets implied a real threat to civil obedience.

Commissioner Lake agreed that warrants should be issued if the government advised it and once they were signed, Superintendent Ryan moved into action. On the morning of 15 November, his detectives arrested John Walsh in a Capel Street public house and brought him to Chancery Lane station. Constable Donohoe identified him in the presence of Inspector Doran. Despite such a prominent arrest, the superintendent's brother James was annoyed that the rest of the assassination circle remained at large. He felt that Walsh's arrest ought to be followed up with a large-scale operation. Otherwise, those who were not in custody might 'grow so very apprehensive about their own safety that they will abscond'.[5]

To complicate matters, one of Alfred Aylward's 'pets' believed that G Division harboured IRB sympathisers who were prepared to spoil police raids by sending an advance warning to suspects.[6] The division had been aware of this danger since 1866, when William Kearney communicated with the police for the stated purpose of betraying James Stephens. They soon learned that his real motive was 'to get money and learn the habits of the detectives'.[7]

A markedly more successful attempt at infiltration was achieved by Michael Breslin, who joined Exchange Court as a C Division sergeant in late 1865, probably as one of those men whom Superintendent Ryan drafted in from outlying stations to bolster the detective force.[8] He was a florid-faced, heavily-bearded man from Clontarf, who liked to wear a silk hat and pilot overcoat. He had several brothers. Thomas was a B Division policeman, while John Breslin was a hospital superintendent who worked at the Richmond Bridewell. Niall, known simply as 'Big Breslin', was a Fenian centre. Although Michael failed to warn James Stephens about an 1865 police raid on Fairfield House where he was arrested, he did manage to supply the false keys needed by his brother to plan an escape for Stephens from the Bridewell where he was being held. Such activities were perceived as risky by John O'Leary and James Stephens, who believed that it might lead to exposure of their members. In short, it was 'too much in the nature of playing with edged tools'.[9] In the case of the Breslins, their fears were unfounded. Michael continued to work as a clerk at Dublin Castle for over a year at considerable personal risk until, remarkably, he was promoted to A Division as an inspector. The unsuspecting prison authorities similarly rewarded his brother John with a salary increase.

On Saturday 16 November, Superintendent Ryan received two warrants for the arrests of assassination circle members Patrick McGarry and Michael Feely. They had been named by Alfred Aylward as such and Ryan acted straight away for fear that an informer might spoil the raid. It was rumoured that the gang was once again planning to attempt to shoot Head Constable Talbot. Aylward advised the detectives to track Feely after Sunday Mass as he made his way to his regular IRB council meeting. Feely, whose gold watch chain and black frock coat marked him out as a 'respectable tradesman' had made enemies both inside and outside the shooting circle. The previous Sunday, Patrick Lennon had threatened to hit him with his revolver when he refused to divulge details about the gang's activities.

On the morning of Sunday 17 November, a group of detectives trailed Feely from Mrs Fagan's lodging house in Stoneybatter and arrested him on Mabbot Lane. At the same time, McGarry, a Dublin centre who had been prominent in the National Brotherhood of St Patrick, was arrested at his home in Lisburn Street. The two portly IRB men immediately voiced their suspicions that someone had given them away and the following evening one of Alfred Aylward's informants, a 'clever picker-up of trifles', wrote excitedly:

> I have just heard in two reliable quarters that the President of the Tontine Society [the assassination circle] whom Paddy [Patrick Lennon] disputed so freely with on yesterday week has been arrested at his residence on yesterday day [*sic*] upon information. This of course will cause Paddy the trouble of going to London to

complain of him for of course, Bishop [James Cooke] ... will not now allow him to have office after being arrested on suspicion of being connected with a gang of infidels as Fenians undoubtedly are. The arrest has not yet appeared in print.[10]

Later that night, Inspector Doran's colleagues led a raid on Curran's public house. The Wellington Quay establishment was promising enough given its reputation as an unlicensed, alcohol-selling 'free and easy' and it had been under police observation for almost two weeks. When Sergeant Carey's small raiding party of five entered the upstairs room, they found themselves in the midst of two hundred patrons, most of whom were tradesmen. The piano player and singer suddenly stopped. 'Go on with it,' one of the men urged. 'Put them out!' another cried.

The sergeant interpreted the last comment as a threat, but the room was gloomy and he could not see who had made it. Seeing that he was outnumbered, he sent one of his men back to College Street station for more officers. When they arrived, he supervised a search of the clientele but found nothing suspicious.[11]

On 23 November, the *Penny Dispatch* reported the details of a more successful police raid, this time on O'Rourke's public house in the Coombe. Inspector Doran believed that John Walsh was using it as a halfway house for the storage of incriminating material in case his own room was raided. It was directly across the road from Flanagan's pawn office where he had worked before his arrest.

On the night of the swoop, Doran was assisted by two promising young acting inspectors. John Egenton was a Kingstown detective who had been promoted to third-rate inspector on 1 November, the day after Inspector Rice retired.[12] Up until recently, he had also been involved in the hunt for John Walsh. Joseph Clarke was one of those assigned by Superintendent Ryan to break up the assassination circle. Together they were supported by a group of uniformed A Division officers led by Inspector Ronan.

Descending through the tortuous maze of streets that led to the Coombe, they filed quietly through O'Rourke's back yard, up the communal staircase and onto a landing. Bursting into a bedroom, they startled two young men – practically boys, according to *The Irish Times*. Such a discovery was not unusual, since young lads were often recruited by the IRB as look-outs and messengers. Those who showed most promise were later sworn in and assigned to carry out small-scale larcenies or arson attacks. Such were the two young men now caught – William Hopper, whom the police suspected of masquerading as a constable to steal a revolver, and his colleague Stephen John Henrick. Acting Sergeant Patrick Doyle searched a coat that had been draped across the bed and found £5 9s, a letter addressed to Hopper signed 'John Walsh' and a key. He gave the key to Inspector Clarke who searched the adjoining drawing-room and found three trunks, one of which held two pairs of boots and a military belt which Hopper confirmed belonged to John Walsh.

Downstairs, one of the constables discovered a glazed leather travelling bag behind the bar, but it was too heavy to lift. When Henrick refused to hand over the key, Inspector

Doran instructed one of the constables to force it open. It held eight very highly finished five-chamber revolvers. Although it would take some time to make the tally, there were also two unloaded pistols, 197 rounds of ball cartridge, 376 percussion caps, a filled powder horn and a bullet mould. Although many weapon factories had been dismantled since the rising, some remained in operation and were elaborately fitted up with lathes, furnaces and smelting pots. They required the services of skilled tradesmen and judging by the discovery of the bullet mould, it seemed as though there was such a factory nearby. Doran decided to interrogate Henrick further:

'Who does this bag belong to?'

'A young fella handed it over the counter last night.'

'What time was that at?'

'Between nine and ten.'

'What young fella?'

'I don't know who he is, but I've seen him twice or thrice before.'

Despite William Hopper's insistence that he was the manager, Doran demanded to see the proprietor, Mr O'Rourke. When he appeared, he fawned over the police, but the inspector was unimpressed. 'How did these arms and ammunition come into your hands?'

'I've never seen them before, Mr Doran. I've been sick for a long time and sure I'm very little about the shop these days.'

Doran decided to arrest Hopper and Henrick along with the shop porter John Keogh. Two men who had the misfortune to be drinking at the bar were also arrested. The first was an ironmonger named John Quinn. The second, John Kelly, was a corporation worker who was involved in weights and measures.

The police at Chancery Lane waited until the following day to open the trunks. At first glance, the contents were quite mundane – another pair of boots, some clothes, books and bills with the owner's name on them. On closer inspection, however, one of the books was found to hold a slip of perforated card with Walsh's name written on it in chalk. Between the leaves, there were also some *cartes de visite* photographs of him and his wife. Superintendent Ryan knew that the latter's maiden name was Fraser and that she was a sister of Mrs Thomas Clarke Luby. Her husband had recently inducted Henrick, Hopper and some others into the IRB.

The detectives kept digging. They found a piece of an IRB account book hidden in one of the boots. It was damning evidence as it listed the names of many men involved in the assassination circle. The majority were pawnbrokers' assistants and clerks, a group that Superintendent Ryan believed had been instrumental in keeping the Brotherhood alive in Dublin. Behind it was a note written on a slip of a Cork newspaper, torn along the edge:

Dear B – Yours to hand. I should like to know why the friend who signs himself 'W' has written too late about the bugger as he has left now. Let W write. Would let us know more fully what they are doing in Dublin. It may be a guide to us in Cork to know how to act and let him sign his name as he has. You will of course know mine. We are about getting the other counties to unite with Cork in electing a Councilor [*sic*]. Have you Dublin done the same yet? I don't want to know who you have chosen. Only is one chosen and by who? Is it by the Centres as we want information. Let W give all he can and I will write further next time. I must now close for the post, M.[13]

Evidently, the letter was written by Cork centre John Murphy and concerned the forthcoming elections for the IRB's Supreme Council. It betrayed some confusion on the part of the Cork IRB as to what exactly was required of it. Superintendent Ryan initially assumed that 'Dear B' was a man named Broe – a fellow employee of the pawn office where Walsh had been recently employed. Later, he realised that it was more likely to be one of Roberts' American emissaries, a builder and house repairer named William Brophy who had first come to police attention in 1864 when he frequented Judge's Tavern with James Cooke in Capel Street.[14] On 9 April 1866, he was shot in a Thomas Street bar by a man named William Weber. After piercing his body, the ball had enough force to puncture the half-inch deal board seat behind him. Weber's protest that the shooting was accidental was belied by the words of a Mrs Graham who reportedly said 'that's done'.[15] Though grievously wounded, Brophy was later discharged from Dr Steevens' Hospital and was well enough to take part in the March 1867 rising. A letter from the New York consul to Lord Stanley in the Foreign Office suggested that he had returned to Ireland to liaise with the IRB. He visited Cork at least once and was seen in the company of John Walsh, who elected him to the Directory.

On 24 November, Henrick, Hopper, Keogh, Quinn and Kelly were brought up before Magistrate Edward Spencer Dix at Capel Street and charged with having arms in a proclaimed district. Inspector Doran told the magistrate that he had seen a photograph of William O'Meara Allen, the Manchester convict, during the course of the raid. Undoubtedly, it had been purchased from its sole agent, Mrs William F. Roantree in High Street. Looking at Doran, Henrick stated, '*He* was a man, every inch of him.'[16]

A Thomas Street ironmonger named Elliot Cooke, whom Superintendent Ryan recalled had once given employment to an IRB agent, spoke for John Quinn. He said that Quinn had been his employee for two years, was very constant in his work and had business in the Coombe about the time of his arrest. The magistrate discharged him but remanded Hopper, Henrick and Keogh for a week. Aghast at the prospect of having to run his business without experienced employees, O'Rourke pleaded for their release on bail, but this was refused on the basis that the police had seized 'one of the armories of the shooting circle'.[17]

15

THE FELON'S TRACK

On the morning of 20 November 1867, a retired army sergeant named John Bermingham was passing the corner of Peter Street opposite Morahan's public house when he heard the report of a gun. He wheeled about but was surprised to see that the street was empty. Finding a bullet hole knocked through the soft felt of his hat, he went immediately to the offices of the *Daily Express* and then to the *Freeman's Journal*. Inexplicably, he did not give a statement to Inspector Bennett of A Division until one o'clock that afternoon.[1]

Superintendent Ryan sent two detectives to investigate. First, they went to Chancery Lane station where they invited Bermingham to come before Magistrate Dix who was still hearing the Coombe cases at Capel Street. When he refused, they decided to go directly to the scene. The morning had been a clear, frosty one, but neither Mrs Mordant, the proprietor of a nearby public house, nor her neighbour John Roche had heard anything.

The next morning, the Earl of Mayo read about the strange incident in the *Times*. He dispatched a telegram from the Irish

Office to Thomas Larcom: 'Is the statement … that a man was shot at last night [*sic*] in Bride Street correct?' The incident had caught the attention of the government. Believing that it was nothing more than a fabrication, Superintendent Ryan briefed Commissioner Lake:

> He persists in stating that he was fired at but cannot adjuce [*sic*] a particle of proof in support of his assertion and declines to swear he was fired at. I am not aware of how he or any person could be punished by the criminal law for making a false statement of the kind and would be very glad to be instructed on the point.[2]

The incident also interested Robert Atkinson who, having caught the undercurrent of street opinion, was entirely convinced the attack was real. He wrote immediately to Crown Solicitor Samuel Lee Anderson:

> The cases of the two policemen recently shot on Wellington Quay and the attempted assassination of ex-Sergeant Bermingham yesterday in Bishop Street, proving the reckless daring of the members of the Fenian conspiracy, tend to make me ill at ease in resuming (when fully convalescent) my avocations as commercial traveller in the city or suburbs. In fact, anyone of the size of a policeman and wearing a beard and moustache is looked on with suspicion and in danger of the knife or bullet of an assassination.[3]

The *Freeman's Journal* revealed that the army pensioner was a close neighbour of James Dondrell who had been arrested on South Great George's Street a fortnight earlier. The most likely explanation for the attempted shooting was that he, like Atkinson, had been mistaken for a detective.

Across the city and country, the police continued to pursue all avenues of enquiry in their hunt for the man who had shot Constable Keena and Sergeant Kelly, no matter how desperate they seemed. Suspicious conversations were listened to eagerly, particularly those carried on in public houses. In Mayo, a drunk was arrested after he boasted that he was the murderer. The newspapers reported the astonishing rumour that the 'Fenian assassination committee' extended to London where it aimed to 'take the lives of eminent public men'.[4] By now, however, at least half of the thirty-strong gang was in prison and on the evening of 22 November, Justice O'Donnel, the magistrate who had attended Mercer's Hospital, agreed with Superintendent Ryan that if those named on the Coombe list were also seized, 'it would … secure the tranquillity of this country during the present winter'.[5]

In Manchester, at a quarter to five the following morning, William O'Meara (Philip) Allen, Michael Larkin and Michael O'Brien (William Gould), all of whom had been found guilty of involvement in the rescue of Colonel Kelly and Captain Deasy, began their final hours at Salford's New Bailey Gaol. Shortly before eight o'clock, the executioner, William Calcraft, and his assistant visited the prisoners and pinioned their arms as officiating priests looked on.

The city had come to a standstill; it was closed to all traffic including the railway line that ran along the north side of the prison and the New Bailey Street viaduct. From an early hour, a hostile, anti-Irish crowd, well fortified by the gin palaces of Deansgate and by the nearby beer and coffee stalls, had begun to gather outside. Standing in the drizzle, they gazed up through the dense grey fog in expectation of seeing the black gallows door open. Separated from the mob by barricades, the scaffold topped a high, forbidding wall. The area underneath was manned by several hundred police officers with an additional two thousand swarthy mill and factory hands drafted in on special duty.

At the appointed time, the prisoners filed up a wooden staircase past two flanking platforms occupied by soldiers from the 72nd Highlanders. When the door opened, they were greeted by a cacophony of jeers. Then silence descended. Allen, pale-faced and miserable, was joined by Larkin who glanced towards the railway line as if expecting help to come from that direction. O'Brien was a little stronger and provided solace to his companions. When Larkin mounted the last step, he almost fainted and needed to be supported. Eventually, he took his place beside the others on the wooden drop. Calcraft, nervous on account of death threats he had received, placed the noose and white cap around their heads and necks. Then he stood back. There was a click of bolts. The trapdoor fell.

O'Brien and Larkin struggled for some time. Indeed, the latter's death throes were so violent that the entire scaffold shook – a distressing scene from which the crowd was shielded by heavy black draperies. Calcraft, despite his long career, was notorious for misjudging the correct length of rope required, and dressed in his black suit and skullcap, he descended into the pit to pull on Larkin's legs and finish him off.[6]

That night, the Irish administration was on high alert. Requiem masses were held in several black-draped churches across Dublin and 'funeral' processions were scheduled for 1 December in Cork, Limerick and Kerry. The men became known as the 'Manchester Martyrs'.

That evening, as people waited to buy their newspaper in Westmoreland Street in Dublin, a B Division constable noticed something odd on the building next to the Ballast Office. The premises, owned by Mr Delaney, tailor and woollen importer, had burned down the previous June and its roof gaped open and chimneyless against the night sky. A roughly scrawled placard was posted on one of its boarded-up windows:

> Irishmen – now is the time to prove by deeds that it was no error when we said we would have a tooth for a tooth and an eye for an eye. He that strikes a Saxon down wins a wreath of glory and revives his country.[7]

The policeman removed it before a crowd had time to gather, noticing as he did so that the flour paste used for the adhesive was still wet. The words were remarkably similar to those written by Young Irelander James Fintan Lalor and published in the *Irish Felon* of 22 July 1846: 'Who strikes the first blow for Ireland? Who draws first blood for Ireland? Who wins a wreath that will be green for ever?' These and other sentiments were later popularised by the Fenian Thomas Clarke Luby who had them published for a popular readership.

That night, Superintendent Ryan organised ten simultaneous public house raids across the city. Of those named in John Walsh's account book, some such as Thomas Reilly and John Griffin were of particular interest because of their connection with the fictitious Liverpool 'loan fund' society, set up to purchase arms for the shooting circle. Griffin was a sallow-faced, balding shoemaker who lived in a new stone house on Gardiner's Row. He was said to command two companies of men and was very determined. Alfred Aylward advised that his quarters should be thoroughly searched as he saw him 'send from his room to another, five stone of bullets for safe-keeping'.[8]

Each raid began at half-past nine and was led by an inspector, two G Division officers and a party of uniformed constables. It was an impressive operation involving over one hundred men.[9] Unfortunately, it was also largely ineffective, since the police soon discovered that many of the suspects had already absconded. The Ryan brothers grumbled that here was proof positive it had taken too long to process the warrants.

The only success reported was by Inspector Doran who discovered that Thomas Francis was hiding at a house in New Street.[10] Little was known about him except that he had possibly been involved in the assassination of George Clarke in 1866. He was a shoemaker with an English accent and red Yankee tuft beard who led sixty-five men. He began to change his lodgings frequently after the Temple Bar shootings. Unlike some of the other IRB men who mingled freely in Dublin pubs, he was said to meet none except his deputies, who in their turn met their own men in places apart from the head centre. On the night of the raid, he managed to flit about the city's public houses, disposing of five hundred raffle tickets. They looked innocent enough, but were a front for an IRB fund-raising effort:

> To be raffled – Monday Evening, December 2nd, 1867 at the
> house of Mr Byrne, 14 Nicholas Street, a splendid picture for the
> benefit of a distressed family. Tickets 6d each. Winner & setter-
> up to spend 2s 6d each. Raffle at 8 o'clock.
> George F. Nugent, Printer, 21 Aungier Street, Dublin.[11]

On Sunday 24 November, extra police patrols went out on duty and the outlying stations were instructed to report on the state of their districts twice during the night. These precautions were deemed necessary to ensure that there were no reprisals or petty disturbances in the wake of the Manchester hangings. In the early evening, uncoordinated crowds of people gathered on the streets to sing ballads and some were arrested for drunk and disorderly behaviour. Later, the cold fog that descended over the city seemed to dampen any remnants of revolutionary ardour.

At nine o'clock Inspector Burke returned to the station house at Sackville Place where he completed some paperwork. Two men had just been arrested in Capel Street for cheering Allen and the others who were executed in Manchester, but there was no Fenian activity to report. As he left the station to walk the short distance to his Marlborough Street home, he stopped to talk to a reserve constable.

Suddenly, a shot whistled out of the dark from the direction of Nelson's Lane. Surprisingly, neither man was hurt. It seemed as though the fog and the shadow cast by an awkwardly mounted gas lamp had saved Burke. Pursuing his attacker into the dark, he was unable to make out anything except the sound of running feet, but it appeared as though there were at least two men ahead of him. He was disappointed when the trail came to an abrupt end in North Earl Street and although he stopped a number of night-time strollers, none were willing to tell him the direction in which his attackers had run.[12] The only thing he discovered with certainty was that 'two men had just run fastly up the lane'.[13] The same lack of public co-operation had dogged every effort by the police to disrupt the assassination circle's activities thus far.

In the early hours of the morning, two constables were fired upon from the west side of Stephen's Green. They ran to the top of Grafton Street to investigate but found that the streets were empty. Even if the gas had been lit, most of the lamps on the north side of the Green were broken, as were those along Kildare Street, Merrion Row and Baggot Street. Turning about, they walked to the adjacent shelter where a cabbie called Moran sat with James Alton, an old man who sold coffee at a stand. They had easily picked out the flash of the shot in the darkness but could not identify the perpetrator. It seemed as though it had come from the University Club or one of the adjoining houses.

In many respects, the area around Stephen's Green was no safer than it had been when eighteenth-century bucks and cut-throats prowled the city. Indeed, one of the ugliest tools used by the criminals who walked the locality after dark was the garrotte – a piece of cord used to strangle victims from behind. Gangs roamed the poorer parts of Dublin, particularly around Summerhill where they threw stones at passers-by and quarrelled among themselves. Their arguments sometimes escalated into pitched street battles such as those fought between the 'Boltonites' who hailed from the crowded inner city tenements north of the Liffey and their hated rivals the 'Georgians' who lived around South Great George's Street. The rank and file of Fenianism was recruited from this stratum, the majority of whom worked as casual labourers. They and their large families formed the basis of the city's working poor. In some instances they were drawn by necessity into Fenianism, since a number of Dublin builders allegedly refused employment to labourers unless they joined the Brotherhood.[14] Others were attracted to the IRB because it provided a social outlet beyond the public house. Considering such decidedly apolitical motives, it was unsurprising that the organisation was rife with informers.

The following morning, Sackville Place was in uproar. A group of officers measuring a straight line from the station door along the trajectory of the shot, discovered a bundle of burnt wadding sixty yards away. It proved that a large-barrelled pistol had been used, since wadding papers were normally used to jam the ball into the bore of such weapons.

Inspector Burke called to see James Fitzharris of Marlborough Street whose brother he suspected as the assailant. Fitzharris admitted that his brother kept a gun and when the inspector searched the room, he found a pair of small pistols in a drawer and on the top shelf of a press, a horn with a small quantity of powder.[15] Fitzharris, who had no arms licence, was taken into custody. He was hauled in front of Magistrate O'Donnel that evening at Capel Street police court, where Charles Fitzgerald, the solicitor who defended the Ryan's public house gang appeared in his defence. He argued that the pistols were out of repair and that his client was an upstanding citizen. The magistrate was unmoved. Whether they were broken or not, he reminded Fitzgerald that the weapons still came under the terms of the Arms Act and gave Inspector Burke just one week to gather enough evidence to bring a case against Fitzharris.

16

A MOCK FUNERAL PROCESSION

On Thursday 5 December, the following placards appeared all over Dublin:

GOD SAVE IRELAND!

A PUBLIC FUNERAL PROCESSION
In honour of the Irish Patriots
Executed at Manchester, 23rd November,
Will take place in Dublin
On Sunday next, the 8th inst.

The procession will assemble at Beresford place, near the Custom House, and will start from thence at the house at twelve o'clock noon.

No flags, banner, or party emblems will be allowed.[1]

The event was planned by a committee chaired by James Scanlan. It comprised John Martin, proprietor of the *Irishman*, subeditor John Waters, a vendor of Catholic religious goods called J.J. Lalor and Donal Sullivan, brother of A.M. Sullivan. Only Waters could be said with any certainty to be an IRB member

Junction of Eustace Street and East Essex Street where Sergeant Kelly was shot on the morning of 31 October 1867. *Courtesy of National Library of Ireland (Lawrence Collection).*

Exchange Court (*c.*1892). This photograph was taken by government investigators shortly after an explosion rocked the premises on the night of 24 December 1891. *Courtesy of An Garda Síochána Museum and Archives.*

College Street Station (*c*.1960). During the early part of the twentieth-century, it was used as a convalescent home for soldiers returning from the Great War. It was later demolished. The current police headquarters is in nearby Pearse Street.
Courtesy of Peter Pearson (private collection).

Green Street Courthouse (*c*.1910) – the scene of many Fenian trials.
Courtesy of the National Library of Ireland (W.D. Hogan Collection).

COLONEL W. R. ROBERTS,
PRESIDENT OF THE FENIAN BROTHERHOOD

Above left: Colonel William Randall
Roberts. *Courtesy of Kilmainham Gaol
Museum.*

Above right: Surgeon Richard George
Herbert Butcher. This caricature
depicts the surgeon as he was best
known to Dubliners in the late
nineteenth century. *Courtesy of the
RCSI.*

Left: Dublin Metropolitan Police
sergeant (*c.*1890s). Many officers were
permitted to wear modest beards as
protection against the cold winter
weather. *Courtesy of An Garda Síochána
Museum and Archives.*

PHOTOGRAPH AND DESCRIPTION

OF A PRISONER ~~WHO WAS FORMERLY~~ IN CUSTODY UNDER *Committal*

for Trial Charged with High Treason & Murder

AND DISCHARGED

COUNTY OF DUBLIN GAOL,
KILMAINHAM.

As stated by Prisoner.

Name Given. *Patrick Lennon*

Parish and County where born, } *Dublin*

Trade or Occupation } *None*

Education, *R & W*

Religion, *R.C.*

Age, *24 yrs*

Complexion, *Fresh*

Eyes, *Brown*

Hair, *Dark Brown*

Height, *5 ft 9 ins*

Make, *Ordinary*

Marks on Person.

OBSERVATIONS.

D. on left side, altered into a "Flag"
the red marks denote the alteration

Henry Price Governor.
5 Feby 1868

Patrick J. Lennon pictured in Kilmainham
Gaol shortly after his arrest in 1868.
The governor took particular note of his
deserter's brand, which Lennon had altered
to look like a flag.
*Fenian Photographs Fp.272, courtesy of the
National Archives of Ireland.*

Left to right: 'Ryan's gang' – Thomas Rooney, Peter McDonnell and John Dowling.
All photos from the Fenian Photograph Collection, courtesy of the National Archives of Ireland.

Patrick Hayburne, the first man to be arrested in connection with the Temple Bar shootings.

James McGrath helped to raise funds for Patrick Lennon's trial and was later arrested.

Informer, Jack Cade O'Loughlin.

18-year-old Arthur Forrester, arrested on 25 March 1867.

Shooting circle members Michael Feeley and Patrick McGarry, arrested on Sunday 17 November, 1867.

Fig. I.—Showing where the Bullet entered.

Fig. II.—Showing position of Wound made for extraction of Ball.

Sergeant Stephen Kelly pictured shortly after his operation in Mercer's Hospital. The route taken by the bullet is clearly shown in the anterior and postero-lateral views. From Richard G.H. Butcher, *On Gunshot Wounds and their Treatment* (Dublin, 1868). *Picture courtesy of the RCSI.*

Far left: Woodcut of bullet removed from Constable Patrick Keena. Its shape matches that of the eponymously titled 'Minié' ball. *Left*: Woodcut of bullet removed from Sergeant Stephen Kelly. The first two letters of the word 'police' are visible where it glanced off the officer's tunic button. *Picture courtesy of the RCSI.*

Sketch taken from *Shaw's Dublin Pictorial Guide and Directory* (1850). It shows the extent of the crown witness depot in Chancery Lane. A DMP lamp standard can be made out over the entrance gates. *Courtesy of the National Archives of Ireland.*

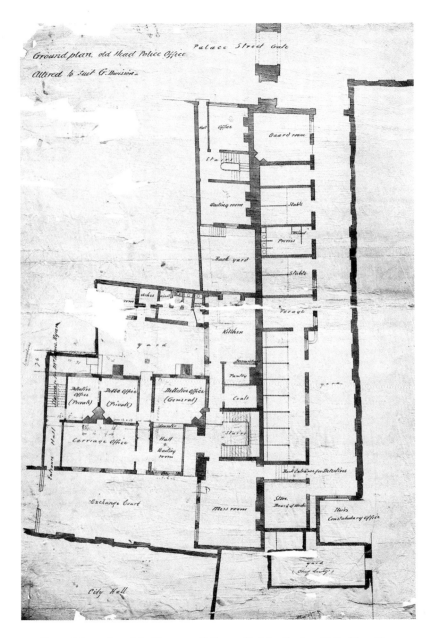

Ground floor plan of the Detective Offices in Dublin Castle, *c*.1860. The offices extended from Exchange Court as far as the Palace Street Gate. *OPW U16 7 misc. 2.*

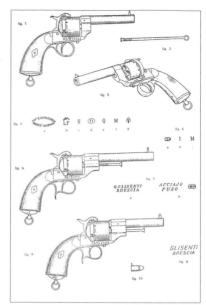

Blueprint of a Lefraucheux 12mm pin-fire revolver. These six-chamber, single-shot Belgian weapons were typical of those used by the Fenian assassination circle. *Courtesy of www.littlegun.be.*

Above: Copy of a threatening letter sent to Inspector Burke. *NAI CSORP 1867/19983, courtesy of the National Archives of Ireland.*

Right: G Division Police Report. *Courtesy of the National Archives of Ireland.*

and the committee was determined not to allow the procession to be dominated by any single political agenda.

Four days earlier there had been a series of countrywide marches and the latest preparations generated a great deal of interest. The windows of drapery establishments were stocked with funeral knots, badges, scarves and hat-bands made from crêpe and green ribbon.

Lord Strathnairn returned to the city from London on 3 December and his arrangements for maintaining civil order, outlined in a subsequent letter to Captain Wesley, demonstrated a marked subtlety:

> All the military arrangements were in place for placing the troops out of sight, *not like Hyde Park*, in different places from whence they could have given assistance to the Civil Authorities if they had not dispersed on their order.[2]

The mention of Hyde Park was a reference to an English working-class riot in favour of universal male suffrage. Although Strathnairn did not want to make the same self-avowed mistakes as Commissioner Richard Mayne, the acerbic Dublin-born commissioner of the London Metropolitan Police, in the handling of a public demonstration, he saw no essential difference between the procession organisers (almost none of whom were IRB members) and the working-class English Reform League.[3] Overriding this, however, was a dogged insistence on the part of the administration to interpret the entire proceedings as a 'Fenian' event.

Police preparations formed a useful counterpoint to those

made by the military. Rank and file RIC constables stationed at the Phoenix Park depot were armed and prepared for trouble as were the officers on duty at various DMP stations throughout the city. The detective branch made its own arrangements. From Dublin Castle, Superintendent Ryan ordered lookouts to prepare a list of any known Fenians spotted in the crowd and when a drunk called John Bryan proclaimed that 'he would shoot the police like rats', he was hauled off to the cells.[4] No chances were being taken.

On Sunday morning, soldiers from the various city barracks were kept in readiness. Among these was a squadron of 12th Lancers. They had been sent to Dublin Castle from the Royal Barracks and they kept their horses saddled and ready in the riding school of the Lower Castle Yard from six o'clock. Across the city mounted military and police orderlies were stationed, ready to convey urgent intelligence.

The day dawned on streets muddied with half-melted sleet. From ten o'clock, crowds congregated in Beresford Place. Some newspapers estimated that almost 10,000 people had gathered in the space of an hour and A.M. Sullivan later wrote:

> The space from the quays, including the great sweep in front of the Custom House, was swarming with men and women and small children, and the big ungainly crowd bulged out in Gardiner Street and the broad space leading up Talbot Street. The ranks began to be formed at eleven o'clock amid a downpour of cold rain. The mud was deep and aqueous, and great pools ran through the streets almost level with the paths. Some of the more prominent of the men and several of the committee rode about directing and organising the crowd. A couple of thousand

young children stood quietly packed in the rain and slush for over an hour; while behind them were over two thousand young women.[5]

Among the two and a half thousand or so tradesmen, the appearance of five hundred men from the Guild of Incorporated Brick & Stonelayers served as a barometer of nationalist sentiment. A large number were Fenians who had suffered imprisonment for the part they played in the 1867 rising. Waiting in front for the signal to start were two four-horse teams. The foremost was draped in black cloth with white plumes and the hearse, covered with black palls, bore the legend 'William P. Allen' on its side. The second displayed the name 'Michael Larkin'. Four mourning coaches waited patiently behind them. Somewhere further back was a hearse for Michael O'Brien.

When the head of the procession moved off at half-past twelve, there was already a slight edginess in the air. As one of the bands prepared to strike up a march near the Abbey Street Wesleyan House, a policeman bluntly told them that it was a place of worship.

Moving up and down the footpaths unseen, various plain-clothes detectives continued to watch for known republicans. Among them was Acting Inspector Mathew Carey from Kingstown. He recognised nine IRB members in total, including a monkey-jacketed sailor with a black crêpe armband named Henry Law, who was on leave from the *Royal George*. Law had obviously ignored the general prohibition on sailors taking part in the procession.[6] Carey continued to keep pace as the cortège moved slowly down Abbey Street and onto Capel Street. Plodding slowly past the closed doors of the various public houses, it moved along the quays, up Stevens' Lane and onto James' Street. After passing James' Gate, the band stopped playing and on passing 151 Thomas Street, every head was uncovered in honour of the United Irishman Lord Edward Fitzgerald, who was executed by the British in 1798. At St Catherine's church, the police took careful note of a group of 86th (Royal County Down) Regiment soldiers who were conspicuous in their uniforms. It was a reminder of the strength of nationalist feeling within the army – something that the leaders of the abortive rising had often recognised but failed to harness. Afterwards, Lord Strathnairn took the matter seriously enough:

> I am much obliged if you have the goodness to find the man who saw the so-called soldiers take their caps off opposite the place of Emmet's execution.[7]

As the crowd passed Patrick Hayburne's barber shop, the gesture was repeated. Hayburne was the first man to be arrested in connection with the police shootings and had been transferred to Mountjoy on 27 November. The home of treason-felony convict William Roantree provided a similar focal point in High Street and an emblematic harp displayed in his wife's drawing-room window drew loud cheers. Eventually, the throng doubled back along Dame Street and headed over Carlisle

Bridge, towards North Frederick Street, Blessington Street and thence by Upper Berkeley Street to the North Circular Road.

At Glasnevin, a shorthand reporter named Hill had been paid over £6 by Acting Inspector John Mallon to transcribe John Martin's oration, given as he stood in the window of a house overlooking the open space in front of the cemetery gates. Although he occasionally struggled to distinguish the *Irishman* proprietor's words from those of the crowd, he was able to obtain a fairly accurate transcription:

> Fellow countrymen – this is a strange kind of funeral procession in which we are engaged today. We are here, a vast multitude of men, women, and children in a very inclement season of the year, under rain and through mud. We are here escorting three empty hearses to the consecrated last resting place of those who die in the Lord (cheers).[8]

The last words of these opening remarks were an obvious nod to the inscription written over the cemetery gates nearby (*Beati mortui qui in Domino moriuntur*). Martin continued to speak for half an hour before passing through the gates and visiting the grave of United Irelander Terence Bellew McManus. Remarkably, there was no violence and despite an insistence by *The Irish Times* that the day was marred by broken headstones and drunken hooligans, the demonstration passed off peacefully. Mr Coyle, secretary to the cemetery board was reported by the *Freeman's Journal* of 9 December 1867 to have said that 'not one sixpence of damage had been done'.

The administration did not view events so favourably, however. After the march Strathnairn wrote to the lord lieutenant, alluding to the shooting of Sergeant Kelly and Constable Keena as well as to the attack on Sergeant Brett in Manchester and describing them as 'an insult to every principle of good government and to the morality which teaches that treason and assassination are crimes'. As far as he was concerned, this mock funeral made a grim mockery of Constable Keena's funeral procession just a few weeks earlier. He intended to mount a blistering attack against the chief secretary but later reconsidered and crossed it out:

> I am astonished at Mayo's extraordinary reasoning that the meeting must be put down by barricades drawn across the street to stop the procession with soldiers or police at each barricade. If any non-commissioned officer under me had proposed so utterly irrational and most unmilitary a plan, I should have said he was a Fenian who wished to give success to the illegal procession. I myself think that I might have been consulted, considering that I am selected to command the troops in Ireland.[9]

The new *de facto* leader of the assassination circle, Patrick Lennon, watched the day's events from a footpath on Winetavern Street. He had not yet been officially announced as its leader, but Superintendent Ryan had a fair idea through an informant of who the successor might be in the event of an election.[10] No doubt he took an interest in the marshals with their hastily crafted wands, courtesy of the carpenters' guild. Lennon had participated as a steward during the Terence Bellew MacManus funeral in 1861 – an event that was something of a coup for the ordinary rank and file members of the National Brotherhood of St Patrick. It enabled them to show their 'trusted' republican leaders that they could agitate for themselves and IRB dictator James Stephens had no choice but to go along with the arrangements. The Martyrs' procession was similar in some respects. As Lennon watched it pass, he was joined by a friend named Luke Gibney. He complimented him on his new coat and on how well he looked.[11] Standing among the umbrella-bedecked crowd, it was relatively easy for them to slip away afterwards.

17

DESPERADO

Evidence produced at the November 1867 treason-felony trial of William G. Halpin, a military officer who had been appointed to command the Dublin district during the Fenian rising, showed how Patrick Lennon might have become involved with President Roberts' faction and through it, members of the shooting circle such as John Walsh. In court, Constable Worship Lee read a letter that had been found with the prisoner on board *The City of Paris* on 4 July 1867. Addressed to Halpin and written by 'W. Dunlop', it showed that, not long after the rising, Colonel Kelly had begun to fall out of favour among the Manchester and Liverpool IRB:

> I will tell you a tail [sic] about K. And I am sure it will startle you and all honest men; their [sic] is a man here whom he sent to the detectives to give information about an honest man that stood in his way. The man of course had his little game exposed and for doing so he got this tool of his to go and give information about him and for such he got £10 and gave it to K. Now what do you think of a man that would be guilty of such an act and what does he deserve? *Death* worse than Massey; for God's sake, get shut of him as easy as possible for

I am very much mistaken if he is not doing the same thing in Dublin.[1]

Among the first recipients of this letter were Patrick Lennon and his friend Michael Monks. They, along with other prominent republicans, had been encouraged to give an ear to President Roberts' envoy. During the March 1867 rising, Lennon led attacks on police barracks in Milltown, Dundrum, Stepaside and Glencullen and later went into hiding, presumably in the north Wicklow, south Dublin area. He escaped to England shortly afterwards. Joseph Clarke, who met him in London, described him as 'a kindly faced, priestly looking man of hesitating speech with a record of fierce exploits behind him – a modern soldier of fortune and altogether the most fearless creature'.[2] He was well known for being a teetotaller and did not smoke, but he made up for such reserved habits in other ways.

Some years before, he had served in the British army in India under the alias 'James Clarke'. While he was there he had witnessed the sepoy mutiny. It began with Hindu and Muslim Indian army infantry privates or 'sepoys', who protested that their rifle casings had been greased with animal fat, and quickly escalated into a bloody uprising. Although traditional set battles certainly formed part of the ensuing campaign, the accompanying civilian rebellion, multifarious and hard to pin down due to the use of guerrilla tactics, probably gave the young soldier an introduction to other forms of warfare. He deserted the 12th Lancers in 1860 and was later reported as having stolen an officer's horse. When the army caught up with him two years later, he was branded with the mark of a deserter – an excruciatingly painful letter 'D'. He escaped again, went to America and joined the Union Army for the last two years of the Civil War. There he fought a guerrilla campaign in West Virginia as a lieutenant of the 11th New York cavalry.

Having escaped an effort by the informer Corydon to have him arrested in Liverpool in June 1867, he joined President Roberts' faction and returned to Ireland. During the summer, his role as John Walsh's 'best friend' was to take the letters of other Directory members to him. The shooting circle had become bolder and more daring, possibly due to Walsh's executive position on the Directory.[3] This culminated in the attempt on the life of Head Constable Talbot on 12 September 1867. According to Thomas Larcom, the policeman was known to make his habitual homeward journey along the quays from the Phoenix Park and with their plan formed, the men lay in wait:

> A man was seen approaching. Walsh at once pointed him out as Talbot. Lennon then put the others back, went up and fired two or three shots at this man who turned out to be a Mr Robert Atkinson, a tobacconist. The assailants seemed to perceive their mistake and decamped … Mr Atkinson was badly wounded in the neck but he failed to identify any of the parties and accordingly all escaped punishment.[4]

Atkinson's business was located at 22 Ellis Quay. He was shot near the entrance to a narrow passage adjoining Ormond Market called Water Row. It led to what *The Irish Times* of 14 September 1867 described as a maze of 'dark and filthy laneways communicating with Pill Lane and Charles Street'.

Atkinson had been carrying a sword cane, but was shot twice before he could brandish it. His life was probably saved by the failure of the assassin's weapon – presumably a pistol – to fire on the third attempt. Clutching his wounded neck and shoulder, he ran along the quay towards the Four Courts where he met two soldiers running in his direction. Evidently the assassin waited for a moment since the soldiers were just in time to see a stout, low-sized individual running away. Afterwards, Private Charles Hallam reported that two 'grown-up boys' ran off with the assassin, but he was unwilling to pursue them.[5]

A few days after this shooting, the informer George Black (who was prompted by the chance of obtaining a £50 reward) told Dublin Castle that Captain Lennon was in charge of the 'Fenian Police'. One of their duties was to threaten 'backsliders' within IRB ranks.[6] Listing his address as the 'General Post Office Dublin', he made two anxious postscripts. First, he asked Superintendent Ryan to delay Lennon's arrest until he had a chance to provide a more detailed description. Then, changing his mind, he decided that it would be best to have the Fenian captain captured along with some others to make the arrest seem accidental. He gave details of Lennon's whereabouts and the names of some of his associates, but the police were unable to track him down.

As the current leader of the shooting circle, Michael Feely did not trust Lennon fully and, according to an unnamed informant of Alfred Aylward's, refused to tell him 'all of the important little things … he wished to know'. To remedy this, Maurice Donohoe, one of Roberts' men who had sailed with

James Cooke from New York in May 1867, planned to back Lennon by complaining about Feely to Cooke in London. Aylward crowed in a letter to the police that this was a prime example of how little unanimity existed within the Dublin assassination circle.

In mid November, Inspector Patrick Travers was sent to Enniscorthy barracks with a colleague to see whether they could identify a prisoner as the man who shot at George Reilly. On their return journey, they were amazed to encounter a fellow traveller on the Dublin-bound train whom they believed to be Patrick Lennon. He 'had a narrow escape'.[7] A few weeks later, he turned up in London with a large sum of cash for which he had agreed to act as guarantor and there met President Roberts' arms agent, James Cooke.[8] In all probability, the trip was financed by Lennon's Dublin associates with additional money from William Brophy.[9]

Around the same time, Roberts' financial agent Daniel O'Sullivan was almost betrayed to the London police by some of Colonel Kelly's followers who resented his success in converting men to the senate faction.[10] Having shaved off his characteristic foxy whiskers and moustache, O'Sullivan quit the city and by 22 November was living at 23 rue de Turin in Paris. Considering the bitter dissension within the London IRB, all of Lennon's movements while he was there were planned cautiously.

On 25 November, Superintendent Ryan paid Acting Inspectors Doyle and Entwhistle £15 to shadow Lennon in the British capital. On the same day, Gathorne Hardy's private secretary informed him that a 'strange fellow' had been seen trying to get into his house on Eaton Square. Despite his best efforts, he could discover nothing about the intruder, but the Earl of Mayo informed him darkly about the 'coming of some desperado from Dublin'.[11] Whether or not this was Patrick Lennon, the police were soon able to learn that he was lodging with Cooke and his wife, and on 1 December, Robert Anderson arranged to have a photograph of the arms agent sent to Dublin through the Irish Office.[12] By now, even the private secretaries at Westminster carried revolvers and ordinary citizens braved the London fog to go on duty as special constables.

Dan Ryan believed that Lennon and Cooke were planning something – perhaps the assassination of Colonel Kelly, who was believed to be in London on business. This was certainly possible, since Cooke had already been implicated in a similar attack. On 28 September, while he and another IRB man named John Groves were drinking at the Turk's Head, they singled out a man whom they believed to be John Joseph Corydon among a group of after-hours revellers.[13] All were bandsmen from the 2nd Life Guards. The two IRB men probably would not have noticed the musicians, had one of them not made a scene by asking the barmaid for a glass of Cooper ale. Afterwards, Cooke and Groves followed them into the street, making grunting, pig-like noises. Incensed by their taunts, the bandsmen turned to challenge them at nearby Vernon Place, Bloomsbury Square. In reply, Groves levelled a revolver at 'Corydon', wounding him fatally. It was a case of mistaken identity. The victim turned out to be a soldier called Edward McDonald. He survived just long enough to put the blame on Groves, who was hauled before his hospital bed by Inspector Thompson. Cooke managed to evade arrest.

It was likely that Lennon had been in London when this incident occurred. While in England, he pressed ahead with a plan to overthrow Michael Feely. In a conversation with Maurice O'Donoghue, he indicated the extent to which Feely had 'lost the favour of the members of the society' and even suggested that he was an informer.[14]

At the same time, the authorities mounted a concerted campaign to trace the source of William Hill's weapons, some of which had already found their way into the hands of IRB assassins in Dublin. At the start of the month, Inspector Manners was sent to Belgium and by mid November he had discovered the route of their importation through Harwich. The customs officers were briefed about what to look out for on the quayside. Guns were liable to arrive packed in crates without a manifest or marked up as 'hardware'. One ill-destined supply of revolvers seized at the Dublin docks bore the label 'swords'. Despite such measures, the home secretary still lacked the legal wherewithal to stop the arms trade and his attempts to create a firearms registry was hamstrung by the realisation among his cabinet colleagues that to do so would also require a full public disclosure of the source of government weapons – inadvisable at a time when Fenian raids against gun shops and armories were commonplace.

As an example of such government impotency in the face of Fenian gun-running, a man calling himself 'Phearson Thompson' was arrested on 28 November in Manchester with forty revolvers in his possession. Convinced that this was Patrick Lennon, the Manchester police wrote to Crown Solicitor Samuel Anderson for a photograph and description of the infamous Fenian leader.[15] The police also felt that Alfred Aylward might be of some assistance. He had been living in Manchester for some months under the pseudonym 'Charles Rivers' having elected to go to England instead of America out of fear of assassination.[16]

Aylward was suspected by many Fenians of playing a 'double game'. In March 1867, he helped to plan the rescue of General Godfrey Massey, an American who was to have led the rising at Limerick Junction, but who was arrested as he stepped off the train from Cork. Suspicions were further raised by Aylward's presence in court during the trials of General Thomas F. Burke and Patrick Doran when, rather naïvely, he allowed the prisoners in the dock to see him speak to prosecution lawyer Isaac Butt. Inevitably, he became a target for assassination.

On the night of 16 May 1867, he went to meet an acquaintance in Dublin, but two strangers turned up instead. He reluctantly followed them but took fright when five men appeared out of the shadows near Harcourt Terrace. Mr Moir, a merchant tailor, later reported that he saw the gang follow Aylward into a nearby field where six or seven shots were fired in quick succession. He was set upon in the grass, but managed to escape and stumbled into the arms of a soldier, urging him, 'for God's sake … conduct me to a cab'. When he was asked if he knew who had attacked him, he replied, 'Oh yes I do, they are persons whom I thought my best friends.'[17] At nearby Mercer's Hospital, suspicion was cast over his injuries when no trace of gunpowder could be found on his skin and although there was some evidence of a knife wound, the police suspected that Aylward had inflicted it on himself to increase his value as an informer.

At the beginning of September, he claimed that he was tracked for two full days by a man whom he identified as Captain Patrick Lennon and that he escaped a hail of bullets by barring the door of a barber's shop with a table, much to the proprietor's horror. On another occasion, Lennon attempted to assassinate him in the Camden Street workshop of an IRB man named James McGrath.

Since moving to England, Aylward's dispatches through George Bolton were cobbled together from snatches of conversation he overheard in Fenian beer houses. This caused the home secretary (who sanctioned occasional payments to Aylward) to regard his information with ambivalence and he instructed the post office to open his mail. Trawling through copies of these intercepted letters, whose contents were now 'free of charge', Gathorne Hardy was able to learn that most of the 'Kellyites' had gone to ground after the Manchester escape and that they lacked accurate intelligence. Aylward suspected home office subterfuge of this kind, however. When he wrote again to Bolton around the beginning of December, he tried to prevent the letter being picked up by the home office by listing his address as the Manchester GPO:

Sir, surmising that this will find you at home, I write private. I presume you received in due course mine of Wednesday ... I went to look at the man called McPhearson [*sic*] who was taken for the revolvers. He was like Lennon but is not him. He was in Roberts' employment, bringing the arms to Arthur Forrester who is head of that party here. Forrester has promised four hundred to his men here but the other party, Kelly's, say they are glad of the arrest.

Aylward had little to fear from the Kellyite faction. Its adherents knew that he was a probable informer, but in the absence of strong leadership they were disorganised and unable to confirm these suspicions. Of far greater concern was the Roberts' faction, which had begun to grow in importance, and by mid December many of Patrick Lennon's associates had begun to arrive in Manchester. It would seem that President Roberts had discovered that in order both to retain and appease his new adherents, it was necessary to arm them. According to Aylward, the assassination circle was also known in Liverpool where it called itself the 'Tontine Burial Society' – a tongue-in-cheek reference to a fictitious loan-fund organisation allegedly established to purchase weapons. 'Burial' alluded to its more sinister aims.[18] This created a dangerous tension, for while Roberts' decision was probably made in an attempt to forestall another rising before it could be properly organised, he was also putting guns in the hands of IRB radicals – men who had few qualms about their premature use.

Superintendent Ryan put little faith in Aylward's negative identification of 'Thompson' since he believed that the law clerk had never actually seen Lennon at close quarters. Instead, he sent Acting Inspector Clarke, Sergeant Sheridan, Sub-Constable

McIlwaine and Constable Dolan to Manchester. Of the four RIC men, Sheridan was the most crucial, since Lennon, who had force-marched him across the foothills of the Dublin Mountains on the night of the rising, knew that he could positively identify him. Commissioner Mayne later sent John J. Corydon and John Devaney by train to Manchester, but was at pains to ensure that their visit remained secret.

At the same time, Thomas Larcom wrote that 'Thompson' might be made an accessory 'upon his part in the Manchester business' and recommended that he be sent to Ireland to see whether he could be identified as the man who shot Constable Keena and Sergeant Kelly.[19] Crown Solicitor Samuel Lee Anderson agreed wholeheartedly and even proposed the services of Robert Atkinson as a witness. If he was willing to take the stand and identify Lennon as the man who shot him near Water Row Market, it might help to bolster the government's case against the Fenian leader. To secure his compliance, the chief secretary temporarily withheld payment of medical expenses and deferred compensation for his loss of business earnings. Their hopes were soon dashed by Under-Secretary Adolphus Liddell, however. The Manchester police had been unable to obtain a positive identification of the prisoner from any of the RIC officers or crown witnesses:

> I am to transmit to his Lordship … a police report in which it appears that the man now in custody at Manchester for having Revolvers is not Patrick John Lennon.[20]

Part of the problem in trying to locate Lennon was due to the

fragmentation of British police boroughs. It rendered communication difficult, exposed investigative efforts to infiltration
and left Irish detectives stationed in English cities under-
utilised. The Earl of Derby's government settled on a scheme
to better organise its intelligence-gathering activities and when,
in November 1867, the chief secretary proposed a special
Fenian department of police, separate from Scotland Yard, with
Inspector Adolphus Frederick Williamson at its head, a new
bureau was born.

The previous year, responsibility for tackling the activities
of the IRB had been vested in the Irish Office. That gave
both Samuel Lee Anderson and his younger brother Robert,
a barrister, an unprecedented opportunity to organise Dublin
Castle's secret service, but they soon found they had their
work cut out. All kinds of secret documents regarding diverse
Irish political groups lay 'in an undigested mass in an office
cupboard'.[21] By late 1867, however, the papers had been sorted
and Robert had written a *History of Fenianism*. It proved to be
of immense value to the government since it had been almost
entirely unaware of the existence of the IRB prior to 1864.[22]

In September 1867, a man named John Francis was arrested
in Manchester. His premature release raised suspicions that
he was an informer, and arms agent Ricard O'Sullivan Burke
targeted him for assassination. Francis sought protection
from the English police who obliged by arresting Burke in
late November with the help of John Devaney. Once Burke
was in custody, the government refused to prosecute him
merely on grounds of his supposed Fenianism, however. The

chief secretary was dismayed. He instructed the Dublin police magistrates to issue a warrant for his repatriation on a charge of attempted assassination, but there was a considerable delay in carrying it out. Amid fears that the case might collapse, he telegraphed for the Andersons to bring all the information respecting the accused from Dublin.[23]

Some days before they arrived, Burke managed to write a note in invisible ink and had it smuggled out of his prison cell in Clerkenwell. Destined for a group of Fenian radicals in London's West End (among them James Cooke), it detailed a dazzlingly audacious escape plan. The signal was to be a white rubber ball, thrown over the wall while Burke was at exercise. He and a fellow prisoner named Casey were to retreat to a safe distance while a hole was blown in the perimeter. Outside, a cab would be waiting with suitable disguises. The police received advance notice about the plot through Superintendent Ryan, who sent all the details from Dublin. However Richard Mayne refused to believe that the Fenians would be so brazen.

The prison wall was weakest at a point where recent sewage works had been carried out. It adjoined a row of close-packed tenement houses, but the West End gang reasoned that given his army career, Burke was bound to be familiar with the effects of explosives and (perhaps by extension) that his instructions on setting the charge would have a mitigating effect on the number of civilian casualties.

On Thursday 12 December, they wheeled a barrel containing five hundred pounds of gunpowder to the site and threw the ball over the wall as planned. Burke began to move to the other side of the yard, explaining to the warders that he had a pebble in his shoe. Meanwhile, Joseph Clarke, head centre for Marylebone (who was against Burke's scheme) dispatched his deputy to organise the removal of the barrel. For the government, this was a moment of unknown assistance from the mainstream IRB. When they arrived, the Marylebone men found that the barrel had failed to ignite and were able to wheel it away without being challenged by either prison warders or police. Afterwards, Clarke was relieved to hear that it had been safely stowed away.

The radicals had not abandoned their scheme, however. The following morning, they managed to retrieve the barrel for a second attempt. Under the eyes of the authorities, they wheeled a tarpaulin-covered object up to the prison wall. A nearby police officer assumed that it was a beer keg and failed to act. Once the penny firecracker fuses had been lit, it was too late. Constable Moriarty tried to flee, but his clothing was ripped to shreds by the explosion. Huge chunks of brick and masonry were flung across the exercise yard – empty because of the prudence of the prison authorities who suspected an attack was imminent – and debris rained down on the buildings beyond. The charge was at least twenty times too great for its purpose. Had Burke and Casey been at exercise, they would undoubtedly have been killed. Fortunately for them, the authorities had seen to it that their daily exercise was switched to the female prisoners' yard.

The breach was huge. Within minutes a crowd began to gather. The panicked warders – unable to discern through the dust and smoke whether or not the onlookers were Fenian raiders – opened fire over their heads. Two houses in Corporation Lane had been completely destroyed and many more were badly damaged. A rescue team descended on the area. It comprised firemen, policemen and medical staff from the nearby Royal Free and St Bartholomew's Hospitals. Three bodies were recovered and dozens more injured were taken away for treatment. As night fell, they continued to pick through the ghastly scene by the light of pipes attached to the gas mains.[24]

At St Bartholomew's, the stream of arrivals was slow at first but the casualties quickly filled the corridors of the old hospital. Most were blackened and many looked as though they had been showered with glass. Brandy was given liberally to the injured and, amid the constant shrieks of women and children, the more serious cases were carried to the wards, either on stretchers or in the arms of the house surgeons and their young interns. Afterwards, the *British Medical Journal* recalled poignantly that:

> Two of them, Mary Ann Hodgkinson and William Clutton, were found to be dead when brought in. One poor child, Minnie Julia Abbott, suffering great agony, apparently from the severity of the wounds on her face and neck, which were bleeding copiously, after swallowing a little brandy, expired while being carried to the ward.[25]

One of the less immediate problems concerned the pregnant women who lived in the vicinity of the explosion. Forty were hospitalised prematurely and at least half the babies died.

This was the fraught situation into which the Earl of Mayo and Robert Anderson arrived on the night of 14 December.

The next morning, they joined Crown Solicitor Matthew Anderson for a meeting at the Irish Office – a series of old law rooms in the heart of London. The group, chaired by Permanent Home Office Under-Secretary Sir Adolphus Liddell, discussed the formation of the new service and resolved to appoint Lieutenant Colonel Percy Feilding as its head, assisted by Captain William Whelan. Feilding had recently arrived in London from Ireland, but he made it clear that he had a moral distaste for secret service work. He had built his reputation on finding and court-martialling military Fenians – those men who had been encouraged to join the IRB by John Devoy. Regardless, he soon launched intelligence operations in Paris and Italy 'to uncover the great international assassination conspiracy', reporting to the home secretary with Robert Anderson as legal advisor and secretary. Small mechanical incendiary devices called 'infernal machines' were said to be under construction in Naples and Milan, and investigations into this and other matters were paid for by a 'secret service' fund, thus opening the way for an extension of Dublin Castle's anti-Fenian intelligence network into England.

The prime minister was unsure as to whether Feilding's international mission would produce anything of value, however, and he was more interested in tackling Fenianism at home. In Britain, efforts were already being made in that direction by Commissioner Mayne. He took personal responsibility for the Clerkenwell bombing, but the home secretary refused to accept his resignation.

On the night of 16 December, Mayne dispatched a ciphered

telegram to Dublin to inform the authorities that Patrick Lennon was on his way back from Holyhead. Commissioner Lake ordered a watch to be placed on the incoming Kingstown and North Wall steam packets as well as on ships entering Queenstown and Galway harbours. Railway routes were kept under surveillance and passengers were searched. The suspect was said to be wearing a deerstalker hat and American square-toed shoes. He spoke quickly and had rather long features. Despite these efforts, he managed to evade his would-be captors.

Some unexpected assistance came from informer Jack O'Loughlin, who had been expelled *in absentia* from the Brotherhood.[26] He and Francis Murray had pleaded guilty to having arms at the November special commission, a crime for which they received twelve months' imprisonment.[27] On 7 December, Acting Inspector Rotheray escorted the truculent Irish-American from the Richmond Bridewell (where he had spent almost a month) to Kilmainham. He had agreed to allow Superintendent Ryan to interview him there.[28]

Unlike many other Irish-American prisoners, he had not sought either the protection or advocacy of the American Consul, William West.[29] Before the March insurrection, he had become involved with the Athboy Fenians led by Skibbereen schoolteacher James Pallas. Pallas had been imprisoned with O'Donovan Rossa after the Phoenix Society round-up of 1858 and many of the new Athboy members received the oath from the former in the back room of a grocery and public house owned by a young Fenian named William McLoughlin. On the night of the rising, the men, armed with a handful of revolvers and pikes, were hopelessly out-manoeuvred by a well-prepared constabulary who filled their barracks windows with sandbags, took possession of two nearby residences and drafted in help from the outlying police stations. McLoughlin would later recount in a letter to John Devoy that Jack O'Loughlin had been a frequent visitor:

> He was an unbeliever and spoke his mind about the clergy, particularly about a certain 'Red Headed' gentleman in Dublin [Cardinal Cullen], but Pallas objected to him coming again to Athboy. He thought they were too religious but your humble didn't care a damn.[30]

Having been curtly dismissed by Pallas, O'Loughlin returned to Dublin where he became involved with the shooting circle. He was able to furnish Superintendent Ryan with a description of Patrick Lennon and the names of his associates, which Ryan accepted as being 'thoroughly reliable'.[31] He was assured that Lennon could easily be implicated in the shootings of Sergeant Kelly and Constable Keena. In return, the superintendent promised a reduced prison term and some assistance in leaving the country.

O'Loughlin's testimony served to intensify the pace of the investigation. In the weeks before Christmas, Inspector Doran stepped down as its head and two G Division detectives were nominated in his place. The first was thirty-three-year-old Acting Inspector John Egenton, who had worked on the Blackrock shooting case and the Coombe raid. The second was thirty-one-year-old Acting Inspector Mathew Carey, fresh from his undercover duties at the recent Manchester Martyrs' procession. He was one of the few Dublin-born detectives in the division. Both worked in the Kingstown area where Lennon was known to have associates and Egenton had actually seen him on one occasion.

According to a Castle report of 19 December, recent arrests had the effect of reducing the number of active IRB circles in the city. Since the capture of John Walsh, Michael Feely and Patrick McGarry, the Dublin Directory had ceased to exist. From Mountjoy, the hapless Patrick Hayburne promised to leave for America in the space of two months and there were now perhaps no more than ten 'assassins' still at large.[32] Despite these successes, the police commissioners were not prepared to rest on their laurels. They authorised an extraordinary amount of expenditure in their search for Patrick Lennon and in gathering intelligence about the Martyrs' processions – about £120 per week until 22 January 1868. It would finally amount to a grand total of £572 11s 3d.[33] The Irish administration was determined that the investigation, in the hands of G Division, would run the city's remaining IRB radicals to ground.

18

HOME FOR CHRISTMAS

On Monday 9 December, *Saunders' Newsletter* reported that Sergeant Kelly was 'going on favourably' and he was soon able to sit up and dress himself. On Wednesday, a police comrade helped him to walk about the ward. The same afternoon, James Robinson, photographer and optician, arrived to take his picture.

Surgeon Butcher explained that the photograph was for a treatise he was thinking of writing. For many years, he had drawn his patients in lateral and anterior aspects, demonstrating a desire to represent their ailments visually as well as descriptively. For all his efforts, however, he could not match the precision of a photographer's lens. The sergeant posed shirtless on the edge of the bed while a Mr Oldham from Suffolk Street made woodcuts of the bullets. When the *Saunders'* reporter called again two days later, he was informed that the sergeant was likely to leave the hospital in a matter of weeks.

There was a rather festive air in the hospital as the staff began to prepare in earnest for their Christmas Eve amateur concert, the centrepiece of which would be a rendition of

George Frideric Handel's *Deeper and Deeper Still*. It was a significant choice, since the composer had performed his *Messiah* in aid of Mercer's (among other Dublin charities) in Fishamble Street in 1742.

The day before Christmas Eve, Doctors Butcher and Tisdall decided that Sergeant Kelly was well enough to be discharged. Once he had dressed, he asked for some jotting paper and a pen. Writing from his bedside, he copied a letter several times and had it dispatched by hand to the *Freeman's Journal*, the *Dublin Evening Post* and *Saunders' Newsletter*. Addressed to the editors of each, it read as follows:

> Sir; the attempt to take away my life in the discharge of my duty at Eustace Street on the morning of 1st November last is still fresh in the recollection of the readers of your influential journal. Although, at that time, no hope was entertained of my recovery, I am now by the will of providence, so far recovered as to be able, with safety, to leave Mercer's Hospital on this day. I am convinced that my recovery is mainly due to the skill and unremitting attention of Surgeon Butcher. Therefore, I desire, through the medium of your journal, publicly to tender him and his colleague, Dr Tisdall, my most sincere thanks.

Afterwards, he left the ward with his wife Anne and emerged into the brilliant sunshine of Mercer Street. It was the first time he had stood outside the hospital in almost two months. Almost immediately he was accosted by well-wishers, but there were no newspaper reporters to pester him for an interview. The city had moved on.

The following day, Police Secretary James Hanlon wrote to the lord mayor. He thanked him on behalf of the commissioners for the £100 cheque he had enclosed for the Keena and Kelly families, adding his relief that 'so deserving an officer as Sergeant Kelly has been spared ... very many manifestations of sympathy with the police in the dangerous and responsible duties which for the last two years have devolved upon them, have been shown by citizens of worth and position.'[1]

The Kellys had married eighteen months previously in St Andrew's Church, Westland Row. It was Stephen's second marriage but Anne's first. She had come from a South Prince's Street tenement. They had no issue, but the sergeant had one adult child from his first marriage and after their wedding they lived above John Byrne's grocery, tea and tobacco shop at 20 Mark Street. The basement and ground floor were liable to flood at high tide and it was probably because of this that they took rooms upstairs with the grocer and his daughter Elizabeth. She owned a dressmaker's and millinery establishment at 3 Church Lane. Such *petit bourgeois* surroundings could not put Sergeant Kelly at more than a discreet remove from the people he policed, however. Had he been a higher-ranking inspector or superintendent, he might have afforded a house in the suburbs. Instead, he was obliged to return to a rabbit-warren neighbourhood of lanes and red-raddle painted hallways – one that continued to harbour an unquantifiable menace.

On 27 December, the Fenian assassination circle decided to attack again, this time with letter bombs. The first two were destined for Superintendent Ryan and Commissioner Lake. The remainder were addressed to the lord lieutenant and his private secretary at the vice regal lodge.

At a quarter past four, a man walking up Church Lane past Mr Madden's shop noticed a bright light in the postbox and immediately alerted the staff. The street was dark apart from some lamps in the higher-end tailoring and dressmaking establishments. Besides being a manufacturer of account books, Madden, who occupied No. 2, was also a stationer and printer. He operated the postbox on a franchise basis and it could only be opened from behind the counter. Fumbling for the key, the shop assistant unlocked the box and found to his dismay that something was burning inside. Cautiously, he managed to remove all the letters and parcels and emptied them onto the wooden counter. Among the envelopes were four matchbox-sized tin cases, each covered with cartridge paper and tied neatly with red twine. One of them had caught fire. He dispatched a messenger to the nearby College Street police station. When Sergeant Gannon and Constable Hilles arrived, they tried to remove the packages but one of them exploded in the constable's hand. Evidently, whoever had planted them had not intended them to flare up until they were handled by the recipients. Since the four o'clock collection had just been taken away, the packages must have been deposited quite recently.

The two intact cases were conveyed to College Street where precautions were taken to prevent their ignition. In the centre of each the police discovered a holder into which a cork had been inserted and tightly screwed. Commissioner Lake and Superintendent Ryan were briefed. Of the many threatening letters Superintendent Ryan had received, this was perhaps the most sinister. However, despite the letter bomber's careful arrangements, his *modus operandi* was severely flawed.[2] The four parcels when bundled together had allowed their address tags to be appraised collectively, thereby arousing suspicion about their full intent. Posting them individually might have produced better results.

Constable Hilles was left with severe burns and in an effort to avoid further casualties, Acting Superintendent James Ryan sent an officer to the GPO in Sackville Street with instructions to speak to the comptroller. Similar packages had been put into postboxes throughout the city and arrangements were made to seize them before they could be delivered. Soon after Ryan's messenger left, a boy threw an explosive parcel at the sentry on duty in Foster Place. It failed to ignite in the muddy street but when the sentry took it to College Street it flared up violently and filled the station with sulphurous smoke.

Later that day, another anonymous package was delivered – this time to the postmaster of Middlesborough GPO. A device consisting of three five-inch long paper tubes rammed hard with powder and tied together was sent, but the plot was foiled when the bomb ignited before reaching him. The *Manchester Courier* added to the growing panic by reporting on a similar post office plot in Liverpool and in the afternoon, packets of explosive material were removed from the London sorting office. News of this latter event was not made public.

The Irish Times of 28 December attempted to define this new method of Fenian warfare. No longer able to 'delude by the assemblance of any force in the open field', the Brotherhood was now attempting to 'avenge its ignominious discomfiture by cowardly personal outrages'. News of the Dublin post office explosion was received negatively by the American press, whose nationalist sentiments seemed decidedly moderate.

It is debatable of course whether the IRB had ever attempted direct confrontation with the forces of the crown 'in the open field' as *The Irish Times* suggested. When Colonel Kelly and others organised the March rising, they planned to proceed on the basis that direct confrontation was to be avoided, except where the rebels had the superiority of numbers and a likelihood of victory. Guerrilla tactics such as the cutting of communications and disruption of railway lines had been encouraged.

Towards the end of December, Thomas Larcom received a letter from Toronto in which the writer, who described himself as an orderly room clerk to President Roberts, warned that thirty-two men armed with needle-action revolvers had left New York on board a Danish brig bound for England. Their intent, he said, was to assassinate the queen, the Earl of Derby, the Irish lord lieutenant and many others. In short, they aimed to 'accomplish their object or perish in the attempt'.[3] When the Governor General of Canada, Lord Monck, dispatched a similar telegram to the British authorities around the same time, it made no mention of the senate faction connection. Despite his belief that the invaders were not Fenians at all but anti-monarchists and anarchists, the home secretary, whose Essex home had been guarded all Christmas, saw fit to alarm the queen with stories of projected attacks on gasometers, telegraphs and railways with the use of 'some deadly explosive or chemical'.[4]

In Ireland, Strathnairn's approach was reactionary. He sent orders to Dublin Castle to ensure that:

> All Grenadier Guards and soldiers are furnished with proper orders … sentries with their arms loaded will be most careful not to fire on any person except those who give reason to fire.[5]

The chief secretary agreed and the lord lieutenant was briefed. With numerous small-scale attacks having occurred on police barracks across Ireland, proposals for fortifications flooded in. Well-drawn, detailed plans from reputable contractors were sent to Dublin Castle. On 28 December, the *Nation* reported that each barracks was to be fitted with bulletproof shutters and the front and back doors were to be made of bulletproof iron. The upstairs windows would be protected by projecting angular loop-hole shutters of the same material. On a more domestic level, householders were given handy tips on how to extinguish Greek fire. An *Irish Times* article of 26 December advised its readers to 'keep on hand a small supply of sand or dry ash dust'. Police stations, commercial offices and other institutions kept buckets of damp sand in readiness, with porters assigned to water them regularly.

In the midst of all of this, President Roberts' tenure came to an abrupt end, occasioned in part by his failure to unite the Brotherhood, but more particularly by his alleged mishandling of the Fenian desperadoes in Ireland and England. Despite his confident assertions in Cleveland, the Fenian Brotherhood was sorely in need of capital and it seemed that several of those who had pledged money at that convention had reneged on their offer. Moreover, many of his followers believed that recent events in London had caused the organisation more harm than good. Joseph Clarke's sister Harriet caught the mood of the London Irish:

> A terrible calamity came upon us – the Clerkenwell Explosion, of which I suppose you have read and which has brought disaster on many and ruin on almost all ... of course a cry was raised of 'down with the Irish assassins and child murderers'.[6]

It was rumoured that Roberts' own arms agent in London, James Cooke, had been involved.[7] From Paris, Daniel O'Sullivan quickly recognised the damage that this would do to the Brotherhood and did his best to minimise it by writing to the English newspapers. In his article, he disowned the bombing as something that was instigated by a small splinter group of the IRB. At the same time, an anonymous letter was sent to the home secretary by the so-called 'Fenian Brotherhood of London'. They called for the release of Burke and warned him that 'we will have our scouts by day and night in town or country and when you little think, your life will be swept out of your worthless body'. With more than a hint of agrarian Ribbonism, they informed him that he was dealing with 'men from the bloodstained county of Tipperary who have always wiped out a wrong by a life'.[8]

Inspector Williamson of the Metropolitan police had meanwhile begun to make enquiries about another of Roberts' affiliates, Philip Kennedy, who kept a tobacconist shop at 5 Keppel Street, Chelsea. Although the informer Patrick Mullany later stated that to the best of his knowledge Kennedy had not been involve in the Clerkenwell plot, his subsequent discovery in hiding at rue Lafayette in Paris was most suspicious.[9] The response from the IRB hardliners was equivocal:

> Occasionally they are heard to disclaim all connection with the Clerkenwell outrage and again they are heard to say it was a grand plot, and proves what they can do. It really has given the timid conspirators confidence in their capacity to do mischief.[10]

Regardless of who had been involved, the international standing of the organisation was at stake. The incident had destroyed the influence of the London Directory to manage IRB affairs there and even the *New York Tribune*, a radical Republican newspaper that had favoured subjection of the Confederacy instead of a negotiated post-bellum settlement during the Civil War, had begun to comment. 'The Fenians,' it deplored on 18 December, 'are losing the countenance of their best friends. The spectacle of an oppressed people struggling manfully … cannot but awaken enthusiasm in honourable breasts. But the incendiary and the assassin is every man's foe.' Whether or not Roberts was directly involved in the Clerkenwell plot, his position made him accountable for its disastrous outcome.

John O'Neill made an address to the senate wing of the Fenian Brotherhood on New Year's Eve. That morning, James Gibbons had resigned his vice-presidency and O'Neill was elected in his stead. The atmosphere at the Fenian Brotherhood headquarters at 10 West Fourth Street, New York, was electric. O'Neill spoke about the damage which incidents such as the blowing up of the prison wall or the attempt to bomb Warrington gas works on 23 December was doing to the movement. With regard to the recent post office incidents, his stance was uncompromising: 'The sending of explosive or deadly missiles to individuals through the mail – are neither authorised, approved or encouraged.' In the past, Irishmen had 'met the minions of English tyranny on every battlefield of Europe, but they met them as soldiers, not as assassins'. Appealing again to the ideal of a struggle against despotism, he called for solidarity between the English working class and their Irish counterparts:

> The Fenian Brotherhood [wage] war not against the lives, liberties, or properties of their English brethren, but against the brutal tyranny which degrades human nature in England and Ireland alike ... they neither employ in their struggle the secret weapon of the assassin nor the torch of the incendiary.[11]

It was a strongly worded attack. William Roberts, known for his powerful voice, parried as best he could, but he had failed to raise enough funds or to unite the organisation according to his grand vision. Not only had he embarked on a determined slander campaign against James Stephens, he had also acted as a kind of puppet for the kind of men that General Millen, himself a British *agent provocateur*, described as 'American political speculators'. Millen, who delighted in his own divisive strategy, claimed to John O'Mahony that it was these interests, rather than those of Roberts, which had influenced his disastrous raid on Canada. In addition, he pointed out that the two wings of the Fenian Brotherhood had their own 'distinct and different policies' which rendered Roberts' unification scheme wholly unnecessary.[12]

A letter from an unnamed Fenian Brotherhood correspondent in late 1867 further accused Roberts of 'narrow, petty, intriguing means, beneath the dignity of men' and, perhaps more tellingly that this was 'injurious to [our] reputation as an honourable, suffering, struggling people'. The writer further suggested that he had been involved in subversive terrorist incidents, something he called 'schismatic crime'.[13] Whether or not Roberts had taken an active part or had simply failed to rein in the activities of Fenian gunmen, the point was now moot. He could do nothing more than try to assert the honourable nature of his motives:

> Neither the interests of the Fenian Brotherhood, nor the honour of the Irish people, have suffered at my hands ... at no period since my election to the office of President has the organisation been so strong in numbers, or its resources so great as at present.[14]

The change in leadership left Roberts' European agents in an uncertain position – none more so than Daniel O'Sullivan, his secretary for civil affairs. The Irish police continued to search for him in Cork, but he stayed in Paris, having moved from rue de Turin to 44 rue de la Rochefoucauld in Montmartre.[15] Undoubtedly, such detailed intelligence about his whereabouts had come from Lieutenant Colonel Feilding's team which was now stationed in the French capital and working in tandem with the Parisian secret police. Their reports were forwarded through the British ambassador on the direct orders of a jittery Emperor

Napoleon III. In England, the Lancashire police had instigated a separate search for O'Sullivan at the behest of Commissioner Mayne who distrusted Feilding's discovery.

James Stephens lived around the corner from O'Sullivan in penury. Writing to his wife on 30 December, he expressed the hope that 1868 would be happier than the previous year, but his landlady had already called twice for her rent money and like a Parisian Raskolnikov he was wont to rise late for purely 'economical reasons'.[16] Up until that point, he had attempted to undermine O'Sullivan's efforts through a double-crossing Fenian named John Power – a nominal member of Roberts' faction who later played politics with the Manchester IRB, advising its members to hold aloof from the senate president and Colonel Kelly to see what they could gain from either. Power kept O'Sullivan purposely in fear of the police, even after they had escaped to France. O'Sullivan had been preparing to quit the city, but after Roberts' resignation he stayed put and awaited further instructions. For such men living in the Parisian shadows, it remained to be seen what the New Year would bring. For a short time at least, there would be a power vacuum in the Irish IRB due to Roberts' departure – one that Dublin Castle might exploit to its advantage.

19

A DISCREET ARREST

On 30 December, the *Freeman's Journal* reported jubilantly that Sergeant Kelly had spent Christmas Day at home. There was further good news on 3 January when the lord mayor announced that he had forwarded £300 for the use of his family, as well as that of Constable Keena.[1]

Meanwhile, all haste was made at the Castle to take whatever measures were necessary to capture Patrick Lennon. Police duties were rapidly re-arranged so that the entire force could be brought into action on very short notice and efforts were made to improve communications between stations. Reserves were reinforced and constables armed with revolvers and cutlasses continued to go on the beat in pairs. In London, officers working near Chatham dockyard were trained in swordplay, a policy that continued despite a stream of letters to the newspapers highlighting the inadequacy of such weapons against firearms.

Having learned from bitter experience, the DMP superintendents received instructions to keep a close eye on the gunmakers' shops within their respective districts as they would be held accountable for any thefts. In the wake of the

Manchester executions, a garrisoned Martello tower near Cork had been successfully raided for weapons by Fenians who arrived armed with pistols and large canvas bags. Other robberies followed. On 31 December 1867, Mr Allport, whose Cork city-centre shop had been burgled, received an anonymous letter:

> Dear Sir – Agreeable to my promise I send you an account of the number of revolvers which we took from your shop yesterday – the number was 63. I hope we do not put you to any inconvenience, and strongly recommend the sub-constable on duty at the other side of Patrick Street when we were taking them, to promotion.[2]

The need to ensure the safety of businesses took up valuable police time. In the case of Albert French, who kept a ramshackle shop in Lincoln Place, Dublin, Inspector Harrington noted that despite his installation of iron window bars, he continued to display his guns openly and often left the premises in the charge of an elderly woman. The chief superintendent warned him in no uncertain terms that 'he should exhibit only a small portion of his stock in his window, merely to show he was in the trade', but in the meantime officers from College Street were diverted from other duties to keep watch. After almost a month of such activity, French's arms licence was revoked.[3]

In the first few days of the New Year, Superintendent Ryan's strategy of increasing payments to informers began to bear fruit, but before he could act, his men needed to eliminate a plethora of false leads. Insubstantial rumours notwithstanding (it was said that Lennon's brother lived at 159

Capel Street and that 'Paddy' donned disguises out of an old clothes shop near Mary Street), it took several days to locate suspects with similar-sounding names. The first of these, an army pensioner named John Lennon, was already in gaol. The others were more elusive. Among them were Joseph Lennon, who had been elected to an IRB committee during a Rotunda meeting; Edward Lennon, who was already a suspect for his supposed Fenianism; and finally John Lennon, an ex-member of the St Patrick's Brotherhood, who also had an Abbey Street background.

On the morning of Tuesday 7 January, Dublin Castle's pedestrian gates at Cork Hill, Thomas Street and Ship Street were ominously closed – a prudent security measure in case Lennon or his men attempted to attack the chief secretary – and in addition to the usual military sentry, a police constable was placed on duty. Later that afternoon, Superintendent Ryan met Commissioner Lake who agreed to take further measures. At a quarter past four, orders were given to the officer of the main Castle guard to close all the entrances and to admit no person without authorisation or a satisfactory explanation of his business. There had been strange portents: some officials believed they had seen Patrick Lennon skulking near the Castle gates that evening and there were rumours that the Earl of Mayo would be assassinated.

A.F. Foster, a well-educated bookkeeper, believed he had overheard just such a plan as he sat alone in Jude's coffee rooms on Grafton Street. The premises had a seditious past, the son of its proprietor having been arrested there on 20 September

1865.[4] Three well-dressed men with sallow complexions, one of whom sounded decidedly 'Mexican', sat at a table near him. He spoke about how 'the Prime Minister, the Secretary Hardy and the Lord Mi-o [Mayo] would be got into the cellar [i.e. the grave]'.[5] Whether or not the projected attack was to be made on 7 January, the chief secretary trumped them all by planning a day's hunting fourteen miles away at his estate in Naas.[6] If the rumours were true, then this would be the second attempt on his life, both taking place during his third term in office. According to an *Irish Times* correspondent, whose letter was printed in the newspaper on 15 February 1872, the plans for the first effort were betrayed by Alfred Aylward around 1866 when he warned Mayo not to pass through the Lower Castle Yard. Some years later, Mayo ventured his own philosophy that 'these things, when done at all, are done in a moment, and no number of guards would stop one resolute man's blow'.[7]

On the strength of information he had received from Jack O'Loughlin, Superintendent Dan Ryan briefed Detectives John Egenton and Mathew Carey. He told them that Lennon was due to meet William Roberts' envoy on the evening of 8 January at Denis Downey's tailor shop in Dawson Street. He did not doubt his men's enthusiasm, but they were young and in need of guidance. As a result, Ryan felt a need to:

> … apply a certain amount of training … in order to make them efficient … as any mistake on my part in the public interest would be placed to my credit. No arrest of any importance whatsoever was made, save by my directions and under my immediate guidance.[8]

Lennon's case was no exception. Considering the likelihood that he would be armed, Ryan reasoned that it would be better 'to come at him from behind and seize him firmly by both hands and arms'.[9] His fears were not unfounded considering the number of attacks that had been made against the police since November 1865. During the hunt for the murderer of Constable O'Neill in 1866, Inspector Clarke was almost shot when he stopped Patrick Kearney for questioning in the damp quarters of a tenement hallway. He had attempted to draw a revolver from his pocket, but the inspector seized it and told him that 'he would send the contents thro' him if he attempted to resist'.[10] There was no reason to assume that Lennon would be any less dangerous.

On the afternoon of 8 January, Detectives Egenton and Carey set out for Dawson Street. There had been no rain during the previous twenty-four hours and the streets were quite dry. A light, damp fog hung persistently in the dusky air – ideal conditions for an ambush. At half-past five, they watched as a smartly dressed man in a thick winter coat and bowler hat approached Denis Downey's shop. He had a long, angular face and a high-bridged nose. Only his destination marked him out among the evening strollers.

Waiting inside for him were the tailor, his brother Christopher, their cousin James Turner, an acquaintance called Matthew O'Neill and William Roberts' emissary William Brophy. Turner, who was erstwhile carpenter to the Royal Barracks, had most likely concealed arms in the window and door sills of the Downeys' former Trinity Street premises and O'Neill was no less active. He had assisted James Stephens' prison break-out before being seconded as centre by James Cody in 1866. Afterwards, he escaped briefly to England. It seemed likely that the men were meeting to discuss what should be done in the wake of Roberts' resignation.

When the Dawson Street meeting ended, the suspect chatted casually on the footpath for a few moments with Denis Downey. Then he walked down Duke Street in the direction of Grafton Street. The detectives followed. There was a watchmaker and jewellers on the corner and a hotchpotch of businesses further down – the Bailey tavern, some provision dealers and the premises of Brown Thomas & Co. The suspect paused to look in a shop window but took little interest in the display. He appeared to be marking Acting Inspector Egenton's position in the reflection of the glass. Taking advantage of his own anonymity, Acting Inspector Carey strolled by as if he were an ordinary shopper.

Suddenly, the suspect bolted in the direction of Duke Lane. The detectives were taken by surprise. Egenton realised that he had been recognised and that the fugitive, whose free hand rested on an outside coat pocket, was trying to lure him down the lane. Then Carey pounced on him before he reached the corner but was almost knocked off balance by his 'desperate plunge' off the footpath.

A gruff conversation ensued: 'Who are you?'

'A police constable.'

'Where's your uniform then?'

With Carey pinioning the prisoner's arms, Egenton relieved him of a six-chamber revolver, twelve patent cartridges, a small unloaded single-barrelled pistol and a dagger. The ammunition was made for a Belgian pin-fire weapon similar to those allegedly imported through James Cooke and Denis Downey. However, the most inflammatory discovery by far was a copy of a Fenian oath:

> I solemnly swear before Almighty God that I will preserve unavoidably [*sic*] the secrets of the Fenian plans in Ireland, England and Scotland save as I shall communicate them to the members of the Association when they take the oath, similar to that which I now take.[11]

There was also a list of residences around Bray, Enniskerry, Ballybrack and elsewhere. Lord Powerscourt, Lord Monck, the attorney-general, Mr Lawson, the Honourable John Plunkett, the late Chief Justice Lefroy and others were named. Of rather uncertain importance was a small piece of paper which outlined the titles of officers and men and their composition in an army company.

The policemen called a cab from the nearby stand. The whole arrest had taken just minutes and had few witnesses. On the way to Chancery Lane, the prisoner spoke jovially, his attitude possibly calculated to annoy rather than win over his captors: 'Ah, you have disarmed me.'

The detectives were not amused.

'What were you doing carrying those weapons?'

'I carry them for my own amusement. By night, every man should have them.'

Superintendent Ryan waited anxiously for their return.

Of late, he had been working feverishly at his office, sleeping only in short bursts and having his food brought to him. The following June he wrote, 'I feel that the past five years have had a worse effect on my constitution than the twenty-three that preceded them.'[12]

When the detectives eventually arrived, they informed Ryan that their prisoner was uncooperative. At Chancery Lane, he gave his surname as 'Ferguson' (a stock Fenian alias) and said that since he did not recollect when he was baptised, he could not tell his name. As a result, they were unable to trace his lodgings. When asked again, he repeated that they might call him any name they pleased, but Ryan instructed them to strip him to the waist and to examine his left side. There, impressed into the soft skin under his elbow was a letter 'D', altered into the shape of a flag. His identity as Patrick Lennon was indisputably confirmed. He sat down and did not speak for a few minutes.

'How's old Sheridan?' he eventually asked with a kind of weary humour.

The reference was to Francis Sheridan, the DMP sergeant who had been sent to patrol the Milltown viaduct on the night of the March rising. He, together with a group of other captured officers, had been force-marched to the RIC barracks at Dundrum and Stepaside which Lennon and his men then attacked. Later, he named the Fenian leader at the November special commission.

'He has a very bad cold. You kept him out too long that night. Besides, ye gave him nothing to eat,' Ryan said.

'Lies,' Lennon retorted. 'We gave him lots of dry bread.'

'Aye, but you gave him nothing to wash it down.'

'That's true, but begob, we hadn't that ourselves.'

After a moment, he spoke again, afraid perhaps that Superintendent Ryan would try to play up his standing in the Brotherhood to further justify his arrest.

'Well, I suppose when you have me now, you'll make a brigadier general of me.'

'I have no power to make one of you, either in the British army or the Fenian army,' Ryan answered, 'but I'll treat you decently.'

While they talked, the police made further enquiries. Another slip of paper found on Lennon mentioned a man named Joe Taylor, and James Ryan waited for him at his Upper Wellington Street home until after midnight. When Taylor arrived, Ryan discovered nothing apart from the fact that he had been recently employed as a waiter at the Angel Hotel, Inns Quay. Later he learned that he had hosted an IRB meeting attended by a number of men including Patrick Lennon and John Waters. Waters was sub-editor of the *Irishman* and alleged head IRB executive for Leinster. He was already due to stand trial at the next commission for his part in organising the Manchester Martyrs' procession.

That night, Lennon was held in a rather noisome cell underneath Exchange Court. Used for accommodating police court prisoners, it was originally built as a wine cellar and extended under the Lower and Upper Castle Yards as far as the City Hall foundations. Upstairs, Commissioner Lake was informed about the prominent arrest. Superintendent Dan

Ryan believed that Lennon's trial should be arranged without delay.[13] He admitted that he had failed to caution his prize prisoner and consequently, it would be not be politic to linger on the circumstances of the arrest in court. Until a case could be prepared for the police shooting, he suggested that he should be incarcerated on the basis of his participation in the March rebellion.

The next day, John Mallon escorted Lennon to Kilmainham Gaol. Continuing to insist that his name was Ferguson, he was ushered into the photographic department. In his first picture he adopted a Napoleonic pose – right hand stuffed into his breast pocket, left hand gripping a chair. For the second, Deputy Governor Mr Flewitt asked him to remove his hat and measured his height at five feet, nine inches. He noted the alteration to his 'D' brand. He then returned him to the Lower Castle Yard to await his preliminary inquiry.

Superintendent Ryan obtained a warrant for Denis Downey's arrest but did not act on it straight away. The tailor's subsequent movements might yet reveal something of value to the case. The offer of a reward for the capture of the man who had shot the policemen continued to appear in *Hue & Cry* until 14 February 1868, but as far as the administration was concerned, the case was already closed. The Earl of Mayo wrote immediately to Prime Minister Lord Derby, asserting his belief that Lennon had been out to assassinate him:

> We did not catch him a bit too soon as he was waiting for several hours at the Castle Gate the night before last for me, but luckily

it was the only night for more than a week that I had not been here as I had gone out hunting. Ryan's information as usual is wonderful. His men showed great courage in his capture for they knew quite well who he was and knew if he had slipped out of their hands he would have shot them.[14]

Derby was well aware of who the Fenian was, since the chief secretary had written about him on a number of occasions. Earlier that year, Mayo had given Derby a brace of pheasants. Now it would seem as though his penchant for hunting had saved his life. Commissioner Lake wrote to the Earl of Mayo, his tone that of a well-wisher commiserating with someone who had been ill. He was sorry for the fear Lennon had caused him, writing that he would soon be 'safely housed in Kilmainham Jail'.[15]

There was a stir among the IRB in the city that evening. Earlier that day, James Ryan had raided two premises and it was now impossible to hold any further meetings at Joe Taylor's house since the police had him under surveillance. A hurried gathering was arranged elsewhere. William Brophy felt nervous about remaining in the country so Dr Waters paid for his return fare to America. Another centre named Charles McNamara, who presided over 'one of the largest and most respectable circles in Dublin', considered making for Canada where it was still possible to get gas-fitting work during the summer.[16]

The home secretary gave a full account of the capture to the queen who agreed that it was most satisfactory. 'The police deserve great credit for the coolness and skill shown by them,' he told Mayo. 'Ryan must have a reliable informer.'[17] No one understood the desperate need for security more than Gathorne Hardy, since a warning had recently reached him from America that he would be assassinated along with the Prince of Wales and the prime minister to balance the account for the Manchester executions. The special precautions established to protect the monarch's life would need to continue.

In Ireland, the administration continued to buzz with the news of the arrest. On 12 January, Lord Strathnairn took some time out from a busy inspection schedule of Munster's military installations and principal ports to profess his delight that Lennon was taken. 'It is a great capture,' he wrote. 'I have been carrying it all over the country – Duncannon Fort, Cahir, Clogher, Lismore, Kinsale, Skibbereen, Bandon, Kilmallock, Charleville ...' However, these lines were no more than a footnote in a deluge of correspondence dominated by the issue of the Ballincollig Powder Mills and their 400,000 lbs of powder and magazine which were 'neither bomb nor splinter-proof'.[18] Strathnairn, who could not understand why the IRB had not yet attacked the installation, sent an urgent telegram to the lord lieutenant outlining his concerns. The malaise he encountered in Munster had encouraged him to consider bolstering the army and he listened with growing alarm to rumours of a supposed Fenian plot to destroy the military barracks in Cork. As a result, the RIC was instructed to conduct nightly inspections of the underground Great Southern and Western Railway tunnel that ran underneath it for evidence of explosives.

When the newspapers began to report on Lennon's arrest, some, such as the *Irishman*, indulged in wild speculation. One article detailed the time he had supposedly spent in Dublin with Colonel Kelly. In short, he was said to have:

> ... returned from America to England in company with several of the leaders of the Brotherhood and to have travelled from London to Holyhead several times by railway without being captured. This is in a great measure owing to the fact that he possessed great facilities for disguising himself.

Other publications were openly hostile. To unbiased observers, the speculation seemed like a crude attempt to ensure Lennon's conviction before the case even came to trial. Similar tactics had often been employed in the English press by what the *Irishman* (guilty itself of fanning the flames) called 'England's literary detectives', but one reader appealed to the editor of the *Evening Post* for a greater sense of fair play:

> In two of your morning contemporaries of this day, there is a short article ... in which Lennon is described as 'the notorious member of the Fenian conspiracy' and it is stated that 'the police are in possession of evidence against him of a most conclusive character', that facts connected with his career prove that he is a 'daring and desperate character'. If this be considered fair play in the year 1868, what is to be thought of public opinion now as contrasted with times long since passed?[19]

Despite such opinions, the unsympathetic articles continued. Reporting on a piece in that Saturday's *Weekly News*, the *Evening Mail* of 12 January gave a rather sensational account of Lennon's arrest, revealing that a plan had been found on his person for 'a simultaneous rising ... by armed bands in London, Dublin and Cork, the particulars of which were given with much minuteness of detail and the names of leaders specified'. Such manifest nonsense served no purpose except to fuel public fears.

On the morning of 11 January, parties of police scoured the streets and public houses along the route to Kilmainham Gaol where Lennon's preliminary inquiry was due to be held. Such hearings were often detrimental to the accused despite legal safeguards such as a right to hear and cross-examine witnesses and an entitlement to a formal caution as a guard against self-incrimination. The usual venue was Dublin Castle, but the inquiry was moved to Kilmainham due to significant security concerns raised by the vacancy of the former La Touche & Company bank. Its rear wall abutted one of the Castle buildings and the administration considered it to be at risk of attack. In fact, the threat was considered so serious that the Earl of Mayo wrote to the secretary of the treasury to inform him that:

> The extreme danger of such close proximity in the event of any attack on the Castle or any attempt to injure it by fire or explosion is so evident that His Excellency desires it quite necessary to seize the opportunity now afforded of precluding the hostile occupation at any time of the premises by purchasing these for the use of the Government accommodations.[20]

At one o'clock, the prisoner was brought into the schoolroom at Kilmainham flanked by two warders armed with wire-covered leaden truncheons known as 'life-preservers'. Besides its use for legal inquiries, the room was sometimes used by prisoners for writing letters at exercise time.[21] Although Lennon still wore his winter coat, his dark brown hair was uncovered for the want of his customary bowler hat and, grimacing with evident discomfort, he appeared to have suffered on account of his confinement. The deputy governor allowed him to sit down. Facing him were Acting Superintendent James Ryan, Magistrate Dix and Crown Solicitors Anderson and Murphy. The clerk informed him that the magistrate would hear his 'county charge' for treasonable activities during the rising. A second 'city inquiry' would be held when the crown had gathered enough evidence about the police shootings.

Up until the Dublin-based trial of *New York Herald* correspondent, Stephen J. Meany, the crown had been hindered by common law which afforded a prisoner the right to stand trial in the county where his alleged crime occurred. To the chagrin of the Dublin legal profession, that meant that prisoners had the right to have their trials split between 'city' and 'county'. On the one hand, it necessitated the use of the poorly resourced provincial assizes. On the other, it gave rise to a ludicrous practice adopted by some barristers who, in dealing with the same prisoner, saw no ambiguity in working for the prosecution in one court setting and for the defence in another.[22] Almost all of the special commissions of 1865 and 1866 were conducted in this disjointed way.

Meany's case, which came to court in 1867, marked a turning point. Although he had maintained a rather blameless existence after his arrival in England, he was arrested in

London and sent to Dublin where he was put on trial for acts of Fenianism he had allegedly committed in America. When no evidence could be produced to prove that he had ever been active as a Fenian in the British Isles, the crown prosecution argued that the acts of his co-conspirators 'were legally his acts and that because he was a British subject, he was responsible for them although in America'.[23] The trial judges reserved the point for consideration by the Court of Criminal Appeal who gave a majority judgement in favour of the crown. From then on, it was possible to try any Fenian in any county where acts of other Fenians could be proved to have occurred. Dublin quickly became the chosen venue on account of its experienced judiciary, court officers and grand jury. For Patrick Lennon, this meant that his county case would not need to be heard elsewhere. As was now becoming customary, it could be handled in its entirety at Green Street.

Dix began proceedings: 'Is your name Patrick Lennon?'

'It is, sir.'

'Have you any person engaged for you?'

'No sir.'

The witnesses waited in another part of the prison and were produced one by one. Detectives Egenton and Carey were the first to give evidence and their statements were brief. They informed the magistrate that the man they had arrested as 'Ferguson' was in fact Patrick Lennon and that he had been involved in a raid on four police barracks on 5 March 1867. RIC policeman Thomas Doran was interviewed about one such attack at Stepaside. 'At about twelve o'clock that night, a number of persons came up to us on the road. The persons numbered about 400 or 500. A great deal of them were armed with pikes, rifles, swords and revolvers. We were surrounded by them and ordered to give up our arms. Our revolvers and cutlasses were taken from us and we were made prisoners. A party of men took charge of us and told us to "fall in", and we went to the police barrack at Stepaside. I heard one man call on the police in the barrack to "Surrender to the Irish Republic". The police did not surrender for a considerable time … I now see and identify Patrick Lennon, who was one of that party, in company with another man. Lennon and the other man took command of all the party by giving them orders to "take charge of the police", and to "surrender the barrack". I also heard Lennon say he would make an example of some of his own men for not obeying orders.'

The prisoner refused to cross-examine him. Dix conferred with Crown Solicitor Patrick John Murphy: 'Does that close the case?'

'Yes.'

'Upon that evidence, Mr Murphy, what do you require me to do?'

'I ask you to commit the prisoner on a charge of high treason.'

'Very well. Of course, Mr Murphy, when I commit the man on a charge of high treason, it will be to the next commission.'

Waiving his right to speak, Lennon was removed from the schoolroom and shown to a cell. Samuel Lee Anderson wrote to his brother Robert in London, informing him that the trial was scheduled to take place on 10 February.[24]

20

SERGEANT KELLY
HAS A VISITOR

On Saturday 18 January, Acting Inspector Egenton had taken informer John Devaney to Kilmainham to identify deposed assassination centre John Walsh. The visit was unsuccessful and Devaney returned to England on the evening mail boat accompanied by a police sergeant.[1] Robert Atkinson had also been invited to visit the prison by Samuel Lee Anderson to see whether he could identify Patrick Lennon, but he could not. If the police hoped that Denis Downey would be of any more help, they were similarly disappointed. Before he was handed over to the prison authorities, he denied he knew Lennon, said that he could not recall who he had spoken to at the door of his shop and repeated that he was determined to mind himself.

On Sunday, Sergeant Kelly was sitting at home reading about the Duke Street arrest when a solitary cab rattled along the broken cobbles of Mark Street. Passing the Widows' Almshouse, it jingled to a stop outside No. 20. He recognised its passenger as Acting Inspector Egenton of G Division. After exchanging pleasantries, Egenton proposed that the sergeant accompany him to Kilmainham the next day to see whether he might be more successful at identifying the prisoner. Constable Hickey and Mary Donnelly had been similarly notified.[2]

On Monday morning the two men set out for the prison. Along the route, many of their colleagues now patrolled the beat in groups of four or six and carried swords and pistols. Searches were planned for different parts of the city. According to the *Belfast Newsletter* of 17 January, every last vestige of Fenianism was being ferreted out from its hiding place.

On arrival, the two officers were greeted by Governor Price, a short, powerfully built man whose long yellow moustache, side whiskers and shaggy eyebrows lent him a forbidding appearance. This belied his true feelings. His nervousness about holding Lennon in custody had caused him to increase security measures at the prison and he was on constant guard. He conducted the men to the hall where a parade of thirteen or fourteen similarly dressed inmates had assembled. Sergeant Kelly walked quietly along the line, but stopped when he came to a man with a long scar over his right temple. He looked him up and down carefully. The prisoner had recently shaved and had a cut on the left side of his chin. 'Would you say "Stand" please?' he asked. Lennon just muttered something inaudible under his breath.

Next, Mary Donnelly was brought into the hall. Prisoner John Francis Nugent recognised her immediately. He had met her after a visit to the city to meet an IRB arms dealer. On 16 May 1866, he had escaped from police custody by jumping through the back window of his father's house into a yard, but was rearrested in Manchester after the prison van breakout. He noticed that although Donnelly also stopped at Patrick Lennon, she would not swear positively to him being the gunman.

Having left Kilmainham, Egenton and Kelly made their way directly to Exchange Court where they told Superintendent Ryan about the morning's events. Sergeant Kelly concluded by saying that he had no doubt about Lennon's identity as his attacker. The sergeant's only regret was not asking him to walk, since he had been impressed with the gunman's peculiar gait. Ryan pressed him as to whether he would prefer swearing on oath that he had doubts but his mind was made up. To make doubly sure, the superintendent embellished his subsequent report:

> He [Kelly] immediately riveted his eyes on Lennon and walked up and down two or three times … Lennon did say 'Stand' when Kelly requested him to do so but he spoke in rather an undertone and he betrayed very great emotion and absolutely shrank from the gaze of Kelly.[3]

A letter from Strathnairn to Lieutenant Colonel Feilding was similarly overblown. While he echoed the chief secretary's fears that Lennon had harboured designs on his life, he added that he was:

> A very gentlemanly man and he has apologised in the handsomest terms for shooting the two policemen, 'conveying as I did, papers of extreme importance to my Government. I had nothing left for it but I was really compelled, much as I regretted, to shoot the men who stopped me.'

Lennon had admitted nothing of the sort. Leader of a rebel band he may have been, but he absolutely refused to admit to murder and the wording may have been supplied by Superintendent Ryan. Strathnairn thanked Feilding for sending some Fenian plans of operations and concluded that:

18 of the 21 number of the United Irish American Assassination Company have been taken but not least Lennon, who as chief member, assassin-in-chief was holed off for Mayo.[4]

By now, A.F. Foster's letter had found its way to the chief secretary by a circuitous route via the Home Office. The conversation he had overheard in Jude's coffee rooms also included a threat against Gathorne Hardy and he professed his anxiety to 'preserve the life of the best Home Secretary of my time'. Mayo's response was animated: 'enquire about the author of this … as soon as possible'. His concerns were possibly heightened by the receipt of a ciphered Home Office telegram in December 1867 warning him about three men who were 'sworn' to shoot him and advising him to retain a detective. Superintendent Ryan was suspicious, however, and he informed him that Foster was a drunkard who was not to be relied upon.[5] It was an example of the voluminous, low-grade information with which the administration was inundated on a daily basis, but could not be ignored for fear of future liability. Foster, who claimed to have a long list of acquaintances in the 'most respectable society', awaited an audience with his lordship but Mayo did not meet with him.

Meanwhile, Ryan pressed for Patrick Lennon's committal on a charge of shooting Sergeant Kelly and hoped that a murder trial would follow. Crown Solicitor Matthew Anderson urged caution. While he agreed that a second preliminary inquiry was expedient, he also recognised that the two cases against Lennon would need to be handled differently. The second was, he said, 'of far more importance and will require extreme care'.

Almost a week previously, Superintendent Ryan had requested warrants for John Waters, Charles McNamara and William Brophy on the basis that they might try to abscond. Unknown to him, Brophy was already steaming his way back to New York, but the others were not so lucky. When Waters was picked up on his way to the *Irishman* offices, its proprietor John Martin immediately denied his connection with the newspaper.

Charles McNamara went to Cork, from whence he dispatched a false letter claiming that he had quit Ireland from Queenstown. At the same time, he wrote to a companion in Dublin, asking for news of Patrick Lennon whom he supposed to have already appeared in front of a magistrate. The reply (which he did not receive until it was too late) was discouraging:

> Dear McN – I rec'd yours this mng. I am happy to hear of your getting down safe. I cannot send you the paper you require, for the very reason that Lennon has not been brought up for examination at all. Enclosed, I send your wife's letter. I transmitted the letter you sent to her by the boy. I'll say no more until I hear from you again; well I hope you will be in New York. With best wishes, Dear McN – yours sincerely Thomas Ward.

Curiously, Lennon's preliminary examination of 11 January had already been widely reported and Ward must have had access to at least some of these newspapers. That meant he was guilty of misconstruing the facts, but McNamara was still at liberty and perhaps Ward hoped that this letter would be enough to put the police off his trail. From Cork, McNamara travelled north to take the Canadian packet boat, but his wife Sarah had some worrying news:

> Dear Charles, I received a note this morning which eased my mind very much. We are all well. The report is out that you are an informer. Please send me word where you are. Yours, Sarah McNamara.[6]

Shortly before ten o'clock on the morning of Tuesday, 17 January, Head Constable Bailey of Londonderry observed a middle-aged, well-dressed man in a top hat walking towards the Canadian tender with a lady. Sub-Inspector Stafford managed to get a closer look, noting that he walked fairly erect as though he had seen military service. He was dressed in a blue pilot jacket and carried a light-coloured tweed overcoat over his arm. Following him on board, the two officers arrested him and seized a letter with some travel papers. The passenger protested that his name was Charles Ryan and that his Drogheda-bought passage ticket would prove it. Undeterred, they searched his trunk and discovered a copy of the *Irishman*. His travelling companion, who turned out to be his sister, said that it did not belong to them. She informed them that she had left Drogheda to join her husband in New York and that they were respectable travellers. Despite her protests, McNamara was bundled into a cab on the quayside a few minutes later. 'It's all up with me,' he whispered.

That evening, he was brought before the lord mayor in Londonderry. The only person who knew about his travel plans had been Patrick Lennon, whom he immediately suspected.[7] Echoing the concern outlined in his wife's letter, others believed that the opposite was the case – that in fact it was McNamara who had given Lennon away. In court, he stoutly denied owning a copy of the *Irishman* but before he was remanded, Head Constable Bailey told the court that he had reason to believe that McNamara belonged to a secret society.[8]

Shortly after five o'clock, an envelope was delivered to McNamara's lodgings at 2 Foyle Street, Londonderry. Mr Andrews, the proprietor, who had heard about his arrest decided to open it. There were three letters inside. Having read Sarah McNamara's line about her husband being a suspected informer, Andrews sent his son to the police station.

Unaware of these events, Patrick Lennon returned to the schoolroom at Kilmainham for his second inquiry. This time, he was to be examined on the 'city charge' of shooting with intent. The 20 January edition of *Saunders' Newsletter* carried a bold headline: 'The late murder at Wellington Quay – Investigation at Kilmainham – Committal of the Alleged Murderer'. Magistrate Allen was appointed to hear the evidence and four witnesses waited in a nearby room – Sergeant Kelly, Constable Hickey and the two prostitutes, who were chaperoned by Inspector Cunningham.

The sergeant was the first to be examined. Despite Mr Butcher's assurance that he was 'strong and lusty and in excellent spirits', it was obvious that he was still quite weak.[9] He asked for a chair, and Lennon, in keeping with his gentlemanly conduct during the rising, immediately offered up his. The governor curtly refused. Another was brought and Kelly read his statement, beginning with his dash along the quay with Constable Morton. Lennon interrupted when he reached the part about his confrontation with the gunman: 'Look at me and say that I was the man.'

'I am sure,' Kelly answered.

'But did you ever give a description of the person who fired at you?' Lennon persisted.

'I did, and the description was taken down in writing.'

Unsatisfied, Lennon demanded to hear the description.

'A better course for you to take is to let the description be identified by Sergeant Kelly,' Crown Solicitor Murphy said. 'At the trial, if you think it for your advantage, you might use it.'

Lennon considered this for a moment. The newspapers were already printing prejudicial articles: 'I don't want to shirk the scaffold,' he cried. 'I have been charged with another offence which might bring me to it, but I don't want to go to the scaffold on a charge of murder. I can produce evidence to prove that I didn't shoot the policemen.'

Next, Mary Donnelly was sworn in and Anderson read her statement. The magistrate asked her whether she was sure that the assassin was Patrick Lennon. 'I would swear to his eyes,' she answered hesitantly, 'but his features are very much altered. To the best of my opinion, he is the man.'

Recalling the details outlined in Sergeant Kelly's statement, Lennon attempted to wrest an admission from her: 'Did the man have a beard?'

'Oh, he seemed to have a dark shade down his cheek.'

Ann Clarke was the next witness to enter the room. She looked the prisoner up and down: 'He's the same kind of man.'

In response to a question from Lennon, she said that she could not tell whether he looked the same from behind without seeing him walk so he obliged her by walking a few paces.

'Can you say now?' he asked.

'Yes,' she replied. 'You're the kind of man I saw and you have the same coat on now that you had on about eleven o'clock that night, for I saw you about eleven o'clock passing Merchant's Hall.'

Lennon declined to cross-examine the last witness, John Hickey, possibly on the grounds that he had not even seen the gunman, but he panicked when the magistrate committed him to trial on a charge of murder: 'I have never had a beard in my life and will bring a thousand people to prove that!'

A reporter from the *Daily Express* noticed that although Lennon had begun to grow a beard, he was incapable of ever growing hair around his chin or upper lip. As a result, he could never have been as hirsute as the assassin was purported to be.[10]

'Do you have anything to say?' the magistrate asked.

'Only that I deny the charge teetotally [*sic*],' Lennon said bluntly. 'Can I have some newspapers? It has been reported that I have admitted the charge by which the jury might be prejudiced against me.'

'We cannot interfere with or go into that matter now,' Samuel Lee Anderson said.

Newspapers were prohibited in the gaol, but Murphy tried to persuade the prisoner that they could not affect the outcome of his trial. It was a naïve under-estimation of the power of the press and Lennon was no fool: 'They may prejudice the jury.'

'They cannot possibly do so ... I hope they will not,' Murphy answered.

Eventually they settled on a compromise. It was decided that although the warders would fetch the newspapers, Lennon could not keep them and they would have to be taken away when the warders left the cell. He would also need to apply for counsel when the trial began at Green Street. If he could not choose a professional advisor, the crown would assign one as well as an attorney. In the meantime, Murphy promised to provide him with a copy of Sergeant Kelly's contentious statement.

The trial by newspaper recommenced the next day and several key points were tweaked to make Lennon's description match that of the gunman. Although the London *Times* of 21 January commented on his evident distress, it added some glaring embellishments, saying that Mary Donnelly had testified that his eyes and height were the same as the assassin's. An *Irish Times* article was terser, but gave great play to the notion that the prisoner had been extremely pale and agitated during the Kilmainham line-up.

However, if the newspapers were out to make him a scapegoat for the perpetrator of the October shootings, the police were still a little doubtful or at the very least anxious that the evidence of their key witnesses would not be enough in court.

21

A BELATED CONFESSION

On the morning of Patrick Lennon's second inquiry, Constable James Donnelly made a surprise appearance at Exchange Court. He asked Superintendent Ryan whether he might be allowed to see the prisoner. He explained that on the night of the police shooting, he had seen a man in a round jerry hat and blue pilot coat standing near Kilroy's public house at the corner of Anglesea Street. His back had been towards the road and his hands and arms were out of view, as if in his pockets. The sergeant had noticed him as he ran past.

This statement annoyed the superintendent because notwithstanding its importance, it could also have been taken along with all of the others over at Kilmainham earlier that day. There was still a considerable burden of proof on the part of the crown so Ryan wrote immediately to Commissioner Lake. He reminded him that it would be very important to establish Patrick Lennon's presence in Temple Bar at the time of the shootings and he hoped that Constable Donnelly might be allowed to see the prisoner at Kilmainham.[1]

The reply took some days due to the misplacement of an

annexed letter, but Donnelly was eventually allowed to visit Kilmainham with Acting Inspector Egenton on 28 January. On arrival, they went to the yard where there were a number of prisoners walking around at exercise, one behind the other. Donnelly's attention was drawn to one man who fell out of the ranks to take a drink. His first impression was that the prisoner was the one who had shot the two policemen. After he left the yard, one of the warders informed him that this was Patrick Lennon, who had been committed for murder.

Superintendent Ryan was happy with the sergeant's state-ment and explained to Commissioner Lake that 'if he was on his oath and under examination, especially if he was pressed to the definite, he would have no hesitation in swearing to the identity'.[2] This was most unusual. Some of the other witnesses had encoun-tered the gunman at closer quarters. If Mary Donnelly could not verify that Patrick Lennon was the same man, how could the policeman claim to do so when he only had a fleeting glimpse? The superintendent's theory was that the gunman, whom he now concluded to be Lennon, must have heard Donnelly's approach and stood still, hoping to escape notice.

Later that day, Ryan sent Constable Donnelly on an errand, this time to Temple Bar with Sergeant Kelly and some others to meet city surveyor John Guilfoyle. He recorded the distance from Kilroy's at the corner of Anglesea Street to Sergeant Kelly's original position and found it to be about thirty Irish perches. The sergeant then stepped the distance from there to the gunman's position and concluded it to be twenty-seven paces or yards.

Commissioner Lake discussed the matter of Constable Donnelly's delayed testimony with the attorney-general, Robert Warren. He was one of two MPs elected to Westminster from Dublin University and was described by the *Irishman* of 15 February as a 'keen-looking little man with spectacles and a regard for the outward trappings of his office ... dressed with a scrupulous exactitude'. He was a full member of the Irish administration, but, unlike his English counterpart, acted as a public prosecutor. Warren felt that Donnelly's testimony had some merit and in turn, Baron Deasy, whose services had been secured four days earlier to oversee the county charge, instructed Lake to show Donnelly's statement to Samuel Lee Anderson whose job it was to advise Warren and his deputy, Solicitor-General Michael Harrison, during the murder trial.

As a result, Samuel Lee Anderson decided to convene a meeting at his Inn's Quay office with Sergeant Kelly and Constable Donnelly. He had a history of taking this kind of hands-on approach, having secretly questioned some Kilmainham prisoners about their involvement in the ill-fated *Erin's Hope* expedition in May 1867. At the meeting Sergeant Kelly recollected the whitish bundle that the gunman had carried. He had made no mention of it to Inspector Doran, but the crown solicitor was sympathetic and thought that an explanation could be found for this later recollection. As Kelly's initial statement had surely been made under fear of death, Anderson believed that the jury would undoubtedly accept a lapse of memory under the circumstances. Next, he took a belated statement from Constable Donnelly. Three months before the shooting incident, he had been moved to E Division in Ringsend – a type of exile normally reserved for men found drunk on duty. Just before that, he was demoted from the rank of station sergeant. This certainly left the reliability of his evidence open to question.

Meanwhile, Acting Inspector Mathew Carey travelled to the north of Ireland with a colleague to collect Charles McNamara. The Castle authorities felt that it would be more prudent to try McNamara in Dublin where a positive identification could be made. When the detectives arrived in Londonderry on 23 January, the area around the courthouse was thronged with people. With some help from the local constabulary, they took a back road to the station and bustled the prisoner onto the one o'clock train.[3]

With the exception of Thomas Rooney, who had been discharged from Mountjoy after just three weeks, most of the assassination circle was now in prison.[4] Francis Murray had been found guilty at the 23 December commission and there was little point in him making an appeal. John Dowling felt that he stood a better chance since his wife and two children relied on his meagre income for subsistence. Now they were 'in great want owing to his being in prison'. However, Superintendent Ryan felt that while he was of no further use as a prospective informer, his previous experience as a dog trainer at Dublin Castle might give him access to government information. In short, he wrote:

As an individual, he would not be capable of doing much mischief in a political line but as a spy for a gang of miscreants who would resort to assassination, he would be very dangerous.[5]

A barrage of letters followed, including one from the proprietor of the public house in which Dowling had been arrested. Prisoners who could not afford to hire their own brief often called upon friends or acquaintances to act as witnesses to character and in Dowling's case, the most representative was Thomas Reynolds:

> I consider he was in the company he was arrested with because he was getting drunk from them. I frequently knew him to neglect his work and his family and go off with parties on drinking excursions. I also know him [sic] to lose employment as a sportsman with gentlemen in consequence of his pawning his clothes for drink which they bought for him. Under all the circumstances, I believe it was this evil propensity that has brought him to this present position.[6]

A few weeks later, the crown finally recognised Dowling's repeated requests and he was allowed to sail for America. On 23 January, the Mountjoy medical officer also reported that constant confinement had begun to damage Peter McDonnell's health and Patrick Hayburne decided to argue likewise.[7] His request was accompanied by a memorial signed by several Catholic clergymen. A disgruntled writer to the *Bristol Daily Post* argued that if the Irish church 'set about suppressing Fenianism with the same heartiness which they show in opposing proselytism, pauperism &c, the Habeas Corpus might be restored in Ireland before midsummer'.[8]

Many of the shooting circle prisoners argued that continued incarceration was causing hardship to their families. Chief among these was Thomas Francis, whose wife had already sold the few articles of furniture she owned and was ready to enter the poor house with their five children. It caused an exasperated Superintendent Ryan to remark: 'It is very difficult to deal with those cases in a manner which will insure [*sic*] the public safety and relieve the distress of the families of the prisoners at the same time.'[9]

Meanwhile, the crown continued to gather evidence against Patrick Lennon for his county charge. Thomas Larcom sent a letter to the military secretary on 5 February, enclosing a photograph with a description based on the one taken in Kilmainham. 'There are some grounds for supposing that the prisoner is a deserter from Her Majesty's army,' he wrote. 'It is believed one of the regiments of Lancers is requesting enquiry may be made into the matter.'[10] The task fell to a Liverpool detective named Maher. He visited Lieutenant Colonel Bidwell and adjutant Captain Graves, who told him that the man in the photograph seemed like Lennon. He got a second opinion from the recruiting office in Birkenhead where Lennon was believed to have engaged the services of Sergeant Hutchinson to train him in swordplay. The officer recalled his proficiency at it and said that he was more experienced than the other men.[11]

Maher sent his report to Samuel Lee Anderson, who scarcely had a chance to review it. On 6 and 7 February, he was engaged at a court martial at the Royal Barracks with James Murphy and the recently appointed law advisor, Charles Shaw.

On Saturday 8 February, he spent all day at Dublin Castle with Murphy, Peake and Barton, preparing a return of the previous year's arrests for the chief secretary. The work continued into Sunday with precious little time to devote to Monday morning's trial.[12]

On Sunday morning, Thomas Larcom sent a telegram to Commissioner Mayne in London. In an ironic re-enactment of General Halpin's court case, he asked him to send over John J. Corydon to appear as a crown witness on the following Wednesday.[13] The informer had escaped his brush with James Dondrell unscathed. Now, he was ready to take the stand against the leader of the shooting circle.

22

COMMISSION OF 'OYER AND TERMINER'

Aside from convening for specific business outside the normal dates, the commission court of 'Oyer and Terminer', its purpose literally to 'Hear and Determine', was a similar, albeit more expensive version of the bi-annual county assizes. In the aftermath of the Cork and Limerick commissions of April, May and June 1867 – courts which were set up to try a large number of Fenians – there was a substantial adjournment, occasioned by the manner in which the attorney-general had arranged the trials. Judges Deasy and Fitzgerald impatiently lobbied the secretary of the treasury for an increase in their salaries and the Earl of Mayo approved on the basis that there was a marked difference between the Fenian insurrection of 1867 and the Young Irelander rebellion of 1848. Then, the movement was quelled with little or no violent aftermath. Now, the prisoners were not merely defeated and captured insurgents, but members of a seditious conspiracy:

Not only are the informers who have given evidence and policemen who have been in the discharge of their duty marked for murder when an opportunity shall appear, but there is good ground to believe that the assassination of at least one of the judges has been contemplated.[1]

The police magistrates were similarly concerned. As early as 15 November 1865, just four days after he had committed James Stephens to the Richmond Bridewell, Sir John Calvert Stronge received an anonymous letter:

I will put six shots, ten pikes thro' four detectives out of the G Division and let Mr Stronge and Lord Wodehouse [the lord lieutenant] mind themselves. There is only opportunity wanted.[2]

Despite such threats, Stronge had gone on to preside over the preliminary inquiry into the murder of George Clarke in February 1866. By 1867, however, the situation seemed increasingly portentous and many of the magistrates were afraid to conclude their examinations after dark. Before John Walsh's inquiry, Magistrate Dix (whose attitude was representative) complained that the case was 'too heavy' for him to handle on his own.[3] The government agreed and appointed Samuel Lee Anderson as crown solicitor. As an incentive, the judges assigned to hear Patrick Lennon's case were each awarded a salary of £1,500 (around €65,280).

On Sunday 9 February, 1868, there was another attack on the police, this time in Cork city. It was most probably the work of the men of William Francis Lomasney, alias 'John Mackey', a local IRB leader.[4] The *Cork Constitution* reported that none of the three constables involved in the incident on Sunday were injured. In the meantime, Lomasney was due to appear at the next assizes for shooting a policeman who tried to arrest him on suspicion of robbing a gun shop. With little evidence that the streets were any less dangerous than they had been when the shootings occurred in October, the magistrates had every reason to be cautious.

Spurning such fears, Justice John David Fitzgerald, a man who, according to A.M. Sullivan, had 'his own peculiarly calm, precise and perspicuous style' decided to take a walk through Temple Bar on Monday morning.[5] The Liberal judge had ample experience dealing with Fenianism, having handled a number of such trials in 1863 and 1866. The morning was cloudy and the footpath almost dry after the previous night's rain. A light mist was falling, but not so much as to interfere with his observations.

Before turning onto Wellington Quay, he took a note of the position of the gas lamps and looked along the length of Eustace Street where Sergeant Kelly had been shot. Then, turning his back on a strong south-westerly wind, he walked to the quayside corner and noted that the distance between it and Duffy's shop, where the fatal shot had hit Constable Keena, was about fifty paces. The stroll from the shop to Parliament Street was no more than a hundred paces. Having made a mental note of these calculations, he continued over the river towards Green Street.

Rather dramatically, the *Nation* of 15 February described

Green Street as 'guarded on all sides like a beleaguered fortress'. Security had been tightened since the October shootings and the court policemen were now armed with revolvers.[6] It was necessary to defend the judiciary from the perennial threat that the dispensation of law in a community of ramshackle tenement houses and markets presented. During the March rising, a cart loaded with pikes and rifles had been discovered in nearby Halston Street and the area harboured a number of Fenian drill halls. As a result, a reporter for the *Irishman* wrote with frustration that 'every passage was blocked up by athletic police constables who appeared determined to allow no person to pass unchallenged'. As he and a colleague elbowed their way towards the gate, they were stopped firmly but gently by 'the goliath' who guarded the entrance: 'Where are you going?'

'To the courthouse.'

'Are you a juror?'

'No.'

'Well then, friend, you have no business here.'

Resolutely, the constable closed the gate, but after the journalists explained that they were armed with nothing more than 'a few cedar pencils and a few slips', he reluctantly let them in. Inside, the reporters' gallery was packed. The courtroom hosted two or three barristers as well as the prisoners' counsel, a strong force of policemen, some detectives and a large body of grand jurors whose purpose was to consider whether the case could proceed to trial. Consensus would be required from no fewer than twelve jurors.

Proceedings began shortly after eleven o'clock when the

crier called, 'Order, hats off!' Solicitor-General Michael Harrison and Charles Shaw, law advisor, made their appearance, followed by the full crown counsel team. They were followed by Justice Fitzgerald, Baron Rickard Deasy and the lord mayor. A ruddy-faced gentleman informed the *Irishman* reporter with a sigh that it would be 'a very heavy commission'. In turn, the journalist remarked wryly to himself that 'if the amount of wisdom according to the proverb be at all commensurate with the number of counsellors, the crown should be well shielded from all mishaps'.

The prisoners were conveyed from Kilmainham under a strong guard of carabineers and mounted police. Among the cases before the bench were those against nine men for marching in the 8 December mock funeral procession and against Richard Pigott and A.M. Sullivan for printing 'seditious' articles about the Martyrs' trials in the *Irishman* and *Nation*. There were also a number of Fenian cases to consider besides Lennon's city case. Stephen John Henrick and William Hopper were due to appear for having arms in a proclaimed district, and their head centre John Walsh for shooting at crown witness George Reilly.

Handling the newspaper case first, Justice Fitzgerald read the portion referring to the prosecutions from a printed brief. He praised the literary ability of one of A.M. Sullivan's articles and agreed that it was the 'emanation of a man accustomed to write', but reminded the court that its object was no less mischievous.[7] Patrick Lennon's case came after those of Peter Reilly for murder, Richard Fitzgerald for manslaughter and

Bartholomew and Margaret Lowry for neglect of a child. Not yet having had an opportunity to hire his own counsel, the prisoner listened as his membership of an unlawful association was cited and the events of 5 March 1867 described.

Outlining Lennon's city case, Justice Fitzgerald informed the jury that bills would be laid against him for the wilful murder of Constable Patrick Keena. 'Gentlemen,' he said, 'that this unfortunate man Patrick Keena was murdered, there can be no doubt.'

When a barrister named Joseph Barnes objected to this statement, the judge was incensed and threatened to have him expelled. Barnes displayed a particular penchant for obstructing Fenian trials and the prosecution was well aware of a previous outburst during which he cried that the Manchester executions constituted nothing less than 'legal murder'.[8] He delighted reporters with similar statements whenever he could manage them.

Once order had been restored, Justice Fitzgerald reminded the jury that the only direct evidence they had in Constable Keena's case was his dying declaration. Recalling his brief detour that morning, he said: 'It is plain that he [the gunman] did not return the way he came, because it was obvious if he did, he would have been intercepted by Police Constable Morton who said he did not meet anyone save a carman when he came up to the murdered man. He may have proceeded in the opposite direction.'

In considering the second shooting, he attached great significance to Sergeant Kelly's evidence, but warned that the case would hinge on the amount of credit the jury attached to the accuracy of his statement. He was prepared to accept Inspector Doran's preliminary notes since these were taken when the sergeant thought he would die and his initial assertion that he would not know the gunman again was also extremely significant. Mary Donnelly and Ann Clarke were legally obliged to take the stand, but the jury needed to agree on the solidity of their evidence. Fitzgerald instructed them to allow for the time of night and sense of confusion and reminded them that, having decided whether or not Lennon was the gunman, they would need to agree on whether he injured the sergeant with intent to murder.

The county and city grand juries retired to consider their verdict. They scrutinised printed copies of the two indictments, replete with witness statements and returned after just ten minutes. True bills would be brought against Patrick Lennon to certify that there was sufficient evidence to commit him to trial for murder, treason-felony and shooting with intent to kill.

23

TRIAL

As Patrick Lennon's trial got under way, news of his indictment was already on its way to America via the new transatlantic cable. On the morning of Tuesday 11 February, he was escorted to Green Street by a troop of mounted police and 12th Lancers in a van that resembled a long, black, wheeled box. Inside, it was lit solely by a grating in the door and by two ventilators in the roof. The Kilmainham prisoners were locked into six small cells with a constable assigned to guard them. In the aftermath of the Manchester escape, the military secretary had grumbled about the condition of the vehicle, as well as the inconvenience of trials taking place at Green Street rather than at Kilmainham. In response, the police commissioners bought two new horses, but did little else to address the problem.[1]

It had become almost routine for the judiciary to assign counsel to the accused in murder trials and those cases in which no defence lawyer was provided were now relatively rare (nine were listed in *The Times* trial reports for 1860–9).[2] Barristers were chosen in a variety of ways. If there were no volunteers, the presiding judge could call upon the most senior counsel.

Otherwise, the prisoner could pick his team from among the unengaged barristers in court.

At that time, there were about four hundred lawyers in Dublin, but only enough work to occupy forty. John Martin of the *Irishman* saw it as a profession in decline and believed that the Act of Union had been designed to carry away the superior courts and the remains of the bar to Westminster 'and to turn that beautiful building upon the quay [the Four Courts] into a barrack like the Linen Hall, or an English tax-gatherer's office like the Custom House'.[3] As a result, Lennon had no difficulty securing the services of two able men, the first of whom was Theobald Andrew Purcell, a barrister of many years standing who had published a number of books including a *Summary of the Criminal Law of Ireland*. He was supported by John Ayde Curran, a thirty-year-old Dublin barrister who had considerable experience handling Fenian trials. His first address to a jury in the same courthouse some years before had caused a colleague to remark, 'Mr Curran, do you intend continuing at the bar, because if so, my advice to you is to give it up. You will never be any good at it.' Fortunately, he had cultivated a great facility for speaking and had a marked influence on jurors.[4]

As was typical in murder cases, the two men had little or no brief to work from, apart from a copy of the indictments which they only received when the trial opened. Despite this disadvantage, they were fortunate enough to secure the services of an attorney named Rodgers. Although they were not legally entitled to sue for fees, one of Rodgers' responsibilities was to handle the money that had been collected in Lennon's defence by a man called James McGrath.

By contrast, the crown was represented by an experienced team of professionals, most of whom had had weeks to prepare their brief. Among these was attorney-general and MP, Robert Warren. He was unlikely to take a lenient view of the case since he was one of those named as a target on the list found with Patrick Lennon. He was joined by William Owen, QC, and Dr John Thomas Ball, an MP and barrister from the Liberal benches who was tipped to shortly succeed Michael Harrison (also present) as solicitor-general. Ball's inclusion in the trial was widely remarked upon as unusual, not least by the *Irishman*, which felt that the crown was going outside Tory lines in a measure to ensure the security of the state. The law advisor was Charles Shaw. Shortly after his controversial appointment in December 1867, an unnamed member of the bar had written to the editor of the *Dublin Evening Mail* to accuse the administration of nepotism, as Shaw was alleged to be the cousin of the Earl of Mayo. Springing to his defence, the *Daily Express*, the self-proclaimed organ of the Earl of Mayo, refuted the accusation.[5] Instructing this cross-section of Irish judicial life was Crown Solicitor Samuel Lee Anderson. Like John Ayde Curran, he had a fair degree of experience with Fenian state cases, having acted in his father's stead at the 1865 treason-felony trials.

When the proceedings commenced, the prisoner confirmed that he was fit to stand and pleaded not guilty. Curran and Purcell pushed for the murder trial to be postponed until

Wednesday so that a proper defence could be mounted. In the meantime, they were fully prepared to tackle the challenge of defending his treason-felony charge. 'I believe this is the proper time to make an application in this case,' Purcell said. 'I am instructed that the prisoner at the bar is a naturalised citizen of America and therefore he claims to be tried on the present indictment by a *jury de medietate linguae*.'

In times past, the 'jury of the half tongue' had been established to protect the rights of Jews on trial in Britain and in Patrick Lennon's case it presupposed his right to a mixed American panel. Clearly his defence team hoped to raise some difficulty between the two countries as had happened in the trial of Colonel John Warren, a naturalised American citizen who was put on trial in Green Street for treason-felony in October 1867. In practice, however, the American approach was cautious and diplomatic. On 1 November 1867, Charles Francis Adams wrote to the US Secretary of State, William H. Seward, to clarify the issue. America, he said, could not claim indignation if a mixed jury was not used, particularly since the system was practised almost nowhere else.[6] Similarly, Baron Deasy was not prepared to allow the *medietate* system to be used where there were other more ordinary recourses open to the prisoner. Purcell was allowed to challenge the nineteen jurors peremptorily and, after a brief deliberation, chose to remove three of them. Once he had finished, the attorney-general took the floor: 'It is sufficient to say that the prisoner will prove to be a member of the Fenian conspiracy or party to an act of violence connected with that conspiracy, the object of which is to overthrow the queen's government in this country and to establish in its stead an Irish Republic.'

In short, the crown aimed to demonstrate that Patrick Lennon had led a band of Fenians in open insurrection. Essential to its portrayal of him as a dangerous rebel, his relationship with General Halpin and a previous leader of the assassination circle, James Cody, would also be examined. Realising that this information might influence the testimony of the crown witnesses, Purcell requested that they be ordered out of courtroom. Halpin's counsel had taken similar steps three months earlier.

When the attorney-general resumed, he began by outlining the prisoner's alleged command of an insurrectionary party, revealing that his plans to field a cavalry unit had gone unrealised. Raids had nevertheless taken place on a number of barracks across South County Dublin and Wicklow. 'Manifestly,' he said, referring to the list of gentlemen's residences, 'I presume that amongst the plans of the Fenian Conspiracy was one to divide the property of the country amongst the insurgents.' Lennon's list could have come from an IRB sympathiser on the staff of *Thom's Directory*, but such subterfuge was hardly necessary since the addresses were publicly known.

The informer John J. Corydon was the first crown witness to take the stand. His presence signalled the prosecution's intention to link Lennon's case with those of Cody and Halpin. The nationalist playwright and novelist John Denvir described him colourfully as:

... a third-rate actor or circus performer. He wore a frock coat, buttoned tightly, to set off a by no means contemptible figure, and carried himself with a jaunty, swaggering air, after the conventional style of a theatrical 'professional'. He was about the middle height, of wiry, active build, with features clearly cut, thin face, large round forehead, a high aquiline nose, thick and curly hair, decidedly 'sandy' in colour, and heavy moustache of the same tinge. His cheeks and chin were denuded of beard.[7]

Corydon, avoiding Lennon's gaze, informed the court of their first encounter: 'I saw him on George's Street, Dublin, a day before the rising of March 1867. He met me and asked me if it was true that Massey was arrested. That was General Massey. I saw him give money to this man for Fenian purposes. He did so on some small street near Beggar's Bush barracks. I received money at the same time myself.'

Introducing the court to a world of intrigue and rebellion, he confirmed that Patrick Lennon was to have had command of the Fenian cavalry in Dublin under General Halpin. The two men exchanged money and on the evening of the rising, Corydon helped Lennon to load and clean revolvers. When he finished speaking, he was examined by Purcell, whose distaste for the witness was evident: 'Did you give this information because of your loyalty?'

'No, not exactly,' Corydon faltered. 'It was to break up the swindle. I was swindled myself and I was determined that I would not allow others to be swindled.'

'Did you ever suggest any Fenian movements?'

'Sometimes.'

'You were at Chester?'

'No, I frustrated their designs, sir.'

Purcell persisted with a barrage of questions: 'What for? For the public good? When did you leave Ireland?'

'About fourteen years ago.'

'Are you an Irishman?'

'I believe I am.'

The barrister shook his head. 'I am sorry for it.'

'I am not,' Corydon replied.

The court then heard reports from various RIC sergeants as well as from Detectives Egenton and Carey who had handled Patrick Lennon's arrest. Egenton had some business in Kingstown that morning (the arraignment of two youths for robbing money and brandy from a locked shop) so his report was concise. Afterwards, Mr Purcell addressed the jury. They would need to satisfy themselves that the witnesses who had attested to Lennon's role on the night of the rising were trustworthy and reliable. He underscored this by reference to one man in particular: 'The evidence of Corydon is not such as would be relied on by twelve men of intelligence to convict a dog,' he said.

Baron Deasy agreed, but reminded the jury that the informer's testimony had been corroborated by trustworthy witnesses. They retired to deliberate and returned after just ten minutes. Head juror Edward Cottinge pronounced the verdict: 'Guilty.'

Lennon was composed. He had expected nothing less. He listened impassively as the attorney-general informed the court that the second indictment – shooting a police officer with intent – would be examined the following morning.

He emerged from the courtroom to find that the day had grown warmer and sunnier, but within moments he had been plunged back into the semi-darkness of the prison van, with its musty aroma of horses, leather and wood. A mounted party of 6th Carabineers led by Captain Hall was assigned to ensure his safe delivery to Kilmainham. The escort comprised one major, a sergeant and twenty-eight regimental soldiers, all of whom had seen service in the Crimea, India and Meerut. Shortly after their arrival in Ireland, they had helped to quell the rising in Tipperary.

Capel Street and the quays were thronged with people, all eager for a glimpse of the infamous Fenian rebel, so Captain Hall made a last-minute decision, writing afterwards that 'we thought it advisable to adopt a different route back as a great crowd had assembled along the route we took this morning'.[8] Out of sight of the waiting reporters and onlookers, they set off over the cobblestones of North King Street. Half an hour later, the prisoner was back in his cell.

That evening, Samuel Lee Anderson met Dr Ball for a consultation which went on until half-past nine.[9] Despite his laudable legal career, Anderson had something of a reputation for indolence as John Ayde Curran had already discovered during their time together on the provincial assizes. Fatigued by heavy summer weather and an onerous schedule, he was not much inclined to work, but often invited the young barrister up to his room after dinner where he usually found him:

Lying on his back in bed, a most striking figure with his black hair on a white pillow. I then read for him slowly each brief – there were always a number – and left him at last to go to sleep.[10]

According to the *Rules for Crown Solicitors and Sessional Crown Solicitors*, it was more proper for the entire counsel to meet to discuss important cases and although a more informal strategy was sufficient for the home circuit, it remained to be seen whether it would do for Green Street. By now, however, Superintendent Ryan knew that Patrick Lennon would be tried for Sergeant Kelly's shooting, but not that of Constable Keena. This puzzled London's new satirical magazine, *Tomahawk*:

> Great deference is we know, paid to success now-a-days, but a curious mode of showing it has been adopted by the prosecution … the same person who fired at Kelly undoubtedly killed Kenna [*sic*], but for some mysterious reason, the accused Lennon has been put on his trial only for the shot which was unsuccessful.[11]

The Irish Times provided the likely reason for this. The attorney-general had clearly found it difficult to amass enough evidence to prove that Lennon was involved in Keena's shooting – a situation that was complicated by his death and a lack of witnesses.

The next morning, the city petty jury panel needed to be called over three times. Over sixty men had been summoned by the sheriff and they waited in the courtroom for a small handful of their number to be selected. It was not unheard of for jurors to be threatened during Fenian trials or to find their names vilified by the nationalist press. Justice Fitzgerald was concerned about the insufficient number of respondents, particularly since the prosecution and defence had the right to dismiss some of them on the basis of a pre-emptory challenge. Others could be removed by the prisoner due to their supposed personal, racial or class-related bias (a challenge for cause). He decided to postpone the case until midday by which time the city jurors had been empanelled on penalty of a £50 fine.

When the murder trial began, Patrick Lennon seemed to be very weak. He was pale and found it difficult to stand. After scrutinising the faces in the gallery for several minutes, his attention was eventually drawn back to the jury by Mr Smartt, deputy clerk of the crown, who reminded him of his right to challenge. 'I do not wish to challenge any,' he said indifferently. 'I will take the first twelve.'

'You must leave that to me,' Purcell advised. Under his guiding hand, almost twenty men were removed. One was a justice of the peace for Galway. Others were challenged on the basis of their non-residence in Dublin. As a matter of course, any vintner, publican or retailer of 'spirituous or malt liquors' could also be removed.[12]

With the preliminaries out of the way, the trial began in earnest. Attorney-General Robert Warren stated the case for the prosecution. He had stood to greet Constable Keena's cortège at Broadstone and his speech was sprinkled with phrases designed to contrast the supposed actions of Lennon with those of decent, law-abiding citizens. Once again, Mr Barnes found a reason to protest, much to the delight of the courtroom reporters. 'Mr Barnes,' Justice Fitzgerald thundered,

'If there is another interruption, I must pursue the same course I pursued before of having you removed from the court.'

Once order had been restored, Warren reminded the jury of the seriousness of the crime: 'The main part of the evidence, on which you will be called upon to arrive at the conclusion, will be of a very simple character. It is a case in which your verdict will be founded not upon circumstantial but upon direct evidence – [that of] Kelly himself. If you believe what he says, you will have no doubt whatever of the prisoner's guilt.'

But how could the crown explain away the sergeant's assertion that 'he would not know the man again'?

'We can all call to our minds circumstances under which events have passed by and about which, if we were asked would we know a certain man again, we might say no and yet if he were produced, a remembrance of his features would come to mind as certainly as possible.'

Next, he began to relate the details of Patrick Lennon's arrest. To Purcell, this was little more than an attempt to link the two events in the minds of the jury and, by extension, imply that his client was the one who shot the two policemen.

'I really do not see in what way the attorney-general intends to use the circumstances connected with his arrest,' he said.

'They are clearly admissible,' Justice Fitzgerald answered. 'Their effect may be very light.'

When Sergeant Kelly took the stand, he was questioned by Solicitor-General Michael Harrison. He was obviously still weak from his ordeal. Inexplicably, he now decided that his assailant had first fired a warning shot and his recollection of the man's appearance had suddenly become curiously specific: 'He was dressed in a short black lounge coat with a whitish trousers and a hat with a very low crown and a small leaf. He had some whitish thing hanging on his left arm when he fired the shot.'

Although the description of the hat had not appeared in any police correspondence, it seemed remarkably similar to the one given by Sergeant Sheridan at General Halpin's trial.

'Do you see the prisoner at the bar?' Harrison asked.

'Yes. That's the man that fired the shot,' the sergeant replied.

He was cross-examined by Purcell, who began by asking him about his clandestine visit to Kilmainham with Acting Inspector Egenton. He freely admitted that he had read about Lennon's arrest in the newspaper. This implied identification by association: 'You stated that you always had an idea that you could recognise this man? That you always recollected that he had something whitish on his arm and that he never wore a cap?'

The sergeant nodded.

Purcell fetched a printed copy of the policeman's statement from the bench: 'In your dying declaration in hospital made under the belief that you were about to meet your God, you say, "I would not know the man again who fired the shot at me".'

'Yes.'

It was obvious where this line of questioning was leading. Besides testifying to Police Magistrate O'Donnel that his attacker was 'low-sized', Sergeant Kelly had been otherwise unable to describe him. Now he was able to produce vivid details.

'Did not Mr O'Donnel, the magistrate, read the declaration for you?' the barrister asked.

'He did.'

'Did you state in that, that your dying declaration was what you believed to be true?'

'Yes. But at the same time, I was in great pain. Two men had to lift me up and turn me around.'

'Had you then the slightest idea of who it was fired at you?'

'Not the slightest. The man who fired at me had a slight beard on his chin – a "meg" it is called.'

Sergeant Kelly admitted that he had read the opening charge in Monday's newspaper, but then added, 'I mentioned about the whitish thing being with the prisoner on Saturday week to the crown solicitor.'

The slip was exactly what the barrister had been waiting for.

'Ah. You were asked about the declaration and information made by you and it was said that in neither of them you made reference to the white parcel you say the prisoner had on the morning of 31 October. When did you first make any statement about the parcel to anyone representing the crown?'

'On Saturday last week.'

Mr Harrison objected on the grounds that Purcell's line of questioning did not arise out of the cross-examination. Justice Fitzgerald disagreed. He recognised the insinuation that the witness had based his trial statement on a reading of the opening charge.

Next, the crown called surgeon Richard Butcher. He took

the stand dressed in a velvet waistcoat with a white silk stock at the neck fastened by two chain-linked diamond pins. His sleeves were replete with ruffles and his ringletted hair was well-oiled. He recognised most of those present. On 5 February, he had seen both Baron Deasy and Justice Fitzgerald at the lord lieutenant's first drawing-room of the season. Lord Strathnairn, Thomas Larcom, Dr Nedley, Commissioner Lake, Samuel Lee Anderson and many others connected either directly or indirectly with the case had also attended.

To begin with, Butcher recounted Sergeant Kelly's arrival at the hospital. Then he produced the distorted bullet and showed it to the court. There was already a plethora of textbooks on medical jurisprudence to guide his conduct, many of which had been published in America and were widely subscribed to in Britain and Ireland. Francis Wharton, Moreton Stillé and Alfred Stillé's *A Treatise on Medical Jurisprudence*, published in Philadelphia in 1860, contained a substantial section on gunshot wounds and provided prospective medical witnesses with solid legal grounding. On the subject of shooting injuries, it advised them to limit their testimony to the treatment of the patient and to abstain from venturing an opinion about the trajectory of the bullet or the distance over which it had been fired. Butcher took a similar approach and his cross-examination was brief. J.A. Curran merely enquired as to how the sergeant had been that morning: 'Was he quite capable of asserting that which he really believed?'

'Yes, but he was very weak, and if he could speak more he might recollect many other things.'

'But did he understand was he was saying?'

'Oh, perfectly. I may mention that this bullet is now a remarkable one. It penetrated the uniform coat of the sergeant, striking one of the buttons – a circumstance that saved his life since the bullet was directed towards his heart. The bullet cannot be counterfeited. It has "PO" stamped upon the lead.'

Constables Morton and Jordan were questioned separately by Law Advisor Charles Shaw. The ensuing cross-examination revealed that they only heard two shots – not the three testified to by Sergeant Kelly. On face value, the evidence supplied by Constable Hickey seemed similarly insubstantial, but there was also a glaring inconsistency with regard to the timing of events. When he put Constable Keena on the car, he said he heard a second shot and screams of 'murder', but this made no sense. Such timing would have placed him on the street-corner with Constable Morton who said he had seen no one. Either Morton had hesitated before running down the quay or Hickey was mistaken. The latter did not seem likely. The obvious answer – one that the *Daily Express* had picked up on shortly after the shooting – was that Morton and Kelly had dallied for up to five minutes that night before coming to Constable Keena's aid.

Moreover, if Constable Hickey heard a second report, this meant that there was a strong possibility that the Essex Street cabbie, whose stand was directly behind the assassin's position, had seen him at some point. Three or four local jarveys had been questioned on Wellington Quay but the Essex Street driver did not appear as a witness.

Mary Donnelly was a picture of sobriety when she took the stand. She was dressed in a cloak and green-ribboned bonnet. Some months before, Acting Inspector John Mallon had even spent eight shillings on two new chemises for her.[13] Before commenting on such crude attempts at respectability, Curran quizzed her about Patrick Lennon: 'Did you ever say you did not know him?'

'I said I believed he was the man and pointed him out. I saw his face that night. I observed his nose. It is a remarkable nose.'

He read her original statement in which she had said that the gunman was low-sized and that she would recognise him by the fierce glance he gave her. She spoke sharply, her voice ringing shrilly in the courtroom: 'I swear he is the man.'

'Of course you do,' Curran soothed. 'Did you not also swear this: "His features are very much altered. I can only swear to his eyes." Are you not ashamed of yourself?'

'No.'

'What do you expect to get for this?'

'It is not for gain I do it. I would do the same thing if I saw my father shooting a man.'

'But you are well fed by the police?'

'Yes.'

'And supplied with the clothes to make you look respectable?'

'Yes.'

'What it is to get your spoon into the porridge at the Castle.'

He dismissed her with theatrical aplomb: 'You may go down for I am tired of you.'

Ann Clarke fared no better. During her examination, she told Mr Harrison that she had seen the gunman passing Merchant's Hall a couple of hours before the shootings that evening: 'I was after seeing Morton, the policeman, passing before that. The prisoner was then going towards Essex Bridge. That leads me to the opinion ...'

'Don't state that,' Curran cautioned.

Emboldened by her favourable treatment, Clarke had forgotten herself a little, but Curran started by asking her to recount her visit to Kilmainham on the orders of Inspector Cunningham: 'You obeyed orders?'

'Yes.'

'You generally do, except sometimes when you are told to "move on".'

That produced a peal of laughter in the courtroom and he forced her to admit that she had been drinking on the night of 31 October. Then she ruined her own testimony by telling one of the jurors that 'it was a very fine night'.

Constable Donnelly discredited his evidence in the same way. Before allowing him to leave the stand, Curran wanted to know two things. How could he claim that Patrick Lennon was the gunman? Secondly, how could he purport to describe the coat he wore?

Once the two detectives who arrested Lennon had spoken, City Surveyor John Guilfoyle spread his map of Temple Bar on the table. It showed where the principal parties had stood and their approximate distances from the gunman. Standing in front of it, Purcell summarised the day's proceedings: 'My client does not deny that he was rightfully convicted of being a member of the Fenian organisation, but he does deny emphatically, indignantly, that he is the assassin of Constable Keena and the attempted assassin of Sergeant Kelly. He has a right to claim that he acted as a member of the Fenian conspiracy conscientiously, though he might be mistaken, but he can claim no consideration for the commission of such a crime as is now imputed to him.'

Lennon's counsel felt that the prosecution's handling of the case had been nothing short of devious. By first obtaining a successful conviction for treason-felony, the shooting trial was open to bias. Secondly, it seemed no accident that Acting Inspector Egenton had acted as chaperone to Sergeant Kelly during his visit to Kilmainham. Could the jury convict on such 'evidence'? For Purcell, the most striking circumstance was that Keena's assassin carried a white bundle which Sergeant Kelly said nothing about in his initial declaration. This simply highlighted how fleeting his glimpse of the gunman had been.

Superintendent Ryan had already admitted that Kelly could not identify his attacker. To make up for this, it appeared (at least to the counsel for the defence) that he had received significant coaching. Moreover, Ryan later claimed to Lord Strathnairn that Lennon had 'apologised in the handsomest terms for shooting the two policemen'. With reference to the bundle the gunman carried, Ryan also alleged that Lennon had written the following to an unnamed member of the Brotherhood: 'Send the box as it is and make a bundle of me frise [*sic*] coat and any of the books, put them in an old bag and send them to me.'[14]

The tone and character of the confession was noticeably similar to the 'assassin's' letter that had appeared in November's *Irish Times* and it supported the notion that the gunman had been interrupted on some clandestine mission. Whether or not the evidence had been fabricated, it meant that either the newspaper letter or confession was contrived.

By now, it was late afternoon and the lengthening shadows set the court attendants to work, silently stepping around the edges of the room with lighted tapers. Under the glimmering chandelier-light, witnesses for the defence were produced. The appearance of John Francis Nugent was a surprise to many. The Drogheda escapee had been present in the line-up on the day that Patrick Lennon was paraded. Speaking in his characteristic monotone, he distinctly recalled seeing Mary Donnelly.

'Did she leave without identifying Lennon?' Mr Curran asked.

'She did.'

Next, Mr Flewitt, Deputy Governor of Kilmainham Gaol, took the stand and proved, with the aid of photographic records, that the prisoner measured five feet nine inches in his boots.

Justice Fitzgerald was surprised: 'Without a hat?'

'Yes,' Curran confirmed.

This was precisely what Lennon's defence counsel needed – an admission that their client was a tall man. By way of explanation, Curran reminded the jury that each prosecution witness had recalled the gunman as low-sized.

'That is a matter of opinion,' Solicitor-General Harrison said.

But Curran was not to be dissuaded: 'I would ask your lordship's permission to let the prisoner come onto the table.'

What followed was a remarkable piece of courtroom theatre. The plan of Temple Bar was moved aside to allow Patrick Lennon to stand over the court. It was now obvious to all that he was not the short man described in the witness statements.

The trial adjourned shortly after six o'clock. Although the defence counsel intended to call more witnesses, they were deferred until the following day. Once again, Capel Street and the quays near the courthouse were densely crowded with people and large crowds lingered about Essex Bridge until eight o'clock in the vain expectation of seeing the prison van pass. For their part, the jurors were accommodated or 'locked up', as Samuel Lee Anderson put it, in the newly renovated Gresham Hotel. A guarded escort, sworn to prevent communication between them, marshalled them up the steps and through the front doors. Inside, they were met with:

> ... a grand staircase which is worthy of a palace ... the banisters are of rich gilt bronze, and support finely carved and highly polished oak balustrades, flanked by four 'twelve light' bronze gothic standards of exquisite pattern and workmanship.[15]

The bookings cost the government £1 4s, with a 3s 6d dinner of soup, joint, vegetables and cheese from eight o'clock. As each man settled into his bedroom overlooking a garden behind Sackville Street, he no doubt reflected on the unfolding case.

Michael Scanlon joined the crowd streaming out of the courthouse. Until recently, he had been a commission agent for Mr Manning, a druggist. He talked earnestly with some other young men who had watched all afternoon from the public gallery and after parting with them, went to his dinner. Later, as he took a stroll, he stopped at the corner of Sandwith Street and noted one house in particular. The following day he would play a very important role indeed.

24

ALIBI

The trial resumed on Thursday morning with further witnesses for the defence. The first to take the stand was Patrick McDonnell, the upholsterer who had been walking in Sackville Street on the night of the shootings. To the delight of Messrs Purcell and Curran, he had come forward voluntarily after reading a report of Wednesday's trial in the *Evening Freeman*. He was surprised by the testimonies of Ann Clarke and Constable Donnelly, who both said that the early hours of 31 October had been fine, as well as by Sergeant Kelly's assertion that he had recognised the accused at twenty-seven paces. Immediately prior to the shooting, he had been escorting a young lady home and as he passed under the portico of the GPO, he was unable to recognise a person beyond ten yards. During his cross-examination, he repeated that he had been most taken by Sergeant Kelly's remark. If the assassin could not be seen clearly past ten paces, then how had the crown witness managed to provide a detailed description at twenty-seven?

Next, a succession of witnesses were produced, all of whom were able to provide an alibi for Patrick Lennon's whereabouts.

At least some were Fenians known to the police. Most were unemployed, but with a little money from James McGrath they were all willing to provide sworn testimony. Arthur Forrester later hailed their action as an act of self-sacrifice, since his own experience reminded him that 'a severe punishment was meted out to those who harboured or assisted fugitive Fenians'.[1] On the other hand, British legal reformers bemoaned the practice of giving alibis and called for the inadmissibility of such evidence unless it was produced by a prisoner at his preliminary hearing.

The first to take the stand was Luke Gibney, an unemployed packer who had recently returned from Liverpool to live with his father in Cook Street. Examined by Andrew Purcell, he deposed to having known Patrick Lennon for about eighteen months. He was introduced to Lennon by a man named Howe, but had not seen him for two months prior to the shooting. He recalled the night of 30 October very vividly: 'We [Gibney and Lennon] remained in the Public House [McGovern's, South Cumberland Street] until twenty minutes past eleven o'clock when they shut up. There were three other young men with us named Scanlon, Monks and Garvey. When we left the public house, Monks and Scanlon came with Lennon and me and we all went to Lennon's lodgings at the corner of Sandwith Street.'

Knowing that his father usually locked the door at a certain hour, Gibney told the court that he had accepted Lennon's invitation to stay with him: 'We reached the lodgings at about a quarter to twelve o'clock. Lennon let himself in by a latch key. Monks and Scanlon left us. I slept with Lennon that night in the same bed and remained there until half-past five in the morning. By no possible means could Lennon leave the house during the night. I saw him the day after.'

A cross-examination by Dr Ball elicited few further details apart from an assertion that this was the only time that Gibney had ever slept at the accused man's lodgings and that they met twice afterwards – the first time in Westmoreland Street the day after the shootings (which they spoke of briefly) and the second on the morning of the Martyrs' procession on Winetavern Street. In response to a juror's question about his sobriety, he replied: 'I never was drunk in my life.'

The next witness was a tall, florid-faced man named Michael Monks. He was an unemployed porter who lived with his parents in Townsend Street. Although not mentioned in court, he was already known to the police. He had gone to meet President Roberts' envoy with Patrick Lennon the previous summer and his return from Liverpool was heralded by Alfred Aylward, who informed Dublin Castle that he was a centre who went armed into the streets. He was mentioned twice by Joseph Denieffe in his *Personal Narrative of the Irish Revolutionary Brotherhood* in connection with Lennon, as well as in an intercepted letter from James Cooke to an American Fenian named Daniel O'Connell:

> Send me a long letter and say how is [*sic*] the boys getting on. Is [*sic*] there much men idle over there? Is Mick Monks working? If you see him tell him I was asking for him.[2]

Monks informed the court that he had only known the accused

for nine months. On the morning after the shooting he was sitting in McGovern's reading about it when Lennon came in. He only stopped for ten minutes. In his cross-examination, Charles Shaw asked him about Walsh, the barman who had supposedly taken their orders. He might have helped to corroborate their statements but had mysteriously left for America two weeks before the trial.

Michael Scanlon substantiated the two accounts, confirming to Purcell that the men left the 'shop' together when it shut and that he and Monks walked home at about midnight. In response to a question from the solicitor-general, he recalled meeting Lennon in the street a day or two afterwards and that they spoke of the policemen being shot. He had no distinct recollection of where.

'And were you shocked?'

'I would not like any man's life to be taken.'

'Not even a policeman's?'

'I wouldn't like to see any man's.'

'Even a policeman's sir?'

'No, not even a policeman's. I told the prisoner it was a fearful thing to have these policemen shot.'

John Garvey was the last of the group to be examined. He had met the other men in McGovern's that night but did not leave with them. He had seen both Scanlon and Monks before then, but not the prisoner.

Finally, Christopher Holbrook, the patient from Mercer's Hospital, was called to the stand. When asked about Sergeant Kelly, he said: 'I was in the same ward. I heard him say that night he could not identify anyone. It was while the magistrate was there but I also heard him say it four days afterwards.'

This revelation ought to have entailed the sergeant's recall to the stand, but Purcell was anxious not to confuse matters: 'We only heard of this evidence this morning,' he explained. 'I don't think it necessary to go into it. The matter is so plain on the dying declaration of Sergeant Kelly. We now close our case by reading the dying declaration of Constable Keena ...'

Michael Harrison protested. Aware that the barrister was about to read the young constable's sparse and unofficial statement, he knew that it would contrast with the detailed one just given by Sergeant Kelly. He conferred with the prosecution team and conceded reluctantly on their behalf: 'The crown will not object to the declaration being in evidence.'

Justice Fitzgerald was incredulous: 'If the crown did object, it would not be admissible!'

The task fell to the young Mr Curran to summarise the case for the defence. While Patrick Lennon did not ask for liberty, he did ask for acquittal as an assassin. Reading from a slip of paper on the bench, Curran denied that Lennon's face was of 'pale and ghostly hue' and that his features were 'dull and blunted'. His features did not bear a 'look of malevolence rarely to be met with' or his eyes 'a cold steel grey'.

'What is all this?' Harrison asked.

'Mr Curran is only describing what his client is not,' Justice Fitzgerald replied mildly.

'And the solicitor-general does not like to hear it,' Curran added.

Had he read Wednesday's *Irish Times*, he would have seen how the paper made a savage brute of Lennon:

> The nose forms a strikingly prominent feature, and seems to be the most regularly formed of the whole countenance. About the mouth there is a peculiarly sinister expression.

The article attempted to make him conform to a phrenological type which associated skull shape and facial features with a person's propensity to commit acts of criminality or violence.[3]

Justice Fitzgerald offered his opinion, not merely on the malicious article but on the crown case in general. The evidence of Donnelly, Kelly and Clarke (who all said the assassin was low-sized) was contradicted when the prisoner stood on the table. How could the prosecution get over that? He denounced the way in which the two women had been dressed up to impress the jury. Moreover, to what avail was Sergeant Kelly's later recognition of Patrick Lennon when he had said in his dying declaration that he could not identify his assailant?

In his summation for the crown, the solicitor-general continued to insist that the evidence was sufficient to bring a conviction and that the jury should act upon it. It was true that Sergeant Kelly said that he would not know the man again, but he had been in extreme agony and his recollection strengthened as his health returned. No doubt there was a contradiction but it was explicable, and several of the witnesses reported seeing the gunman's face by gaslight. Finally, there was the alibi to consider. It was highly suspicious and actually served to prove that Lennon was in Dublin on the night of the outrage.

'It was never denied he was in Dublin, both before and after it,' Curran said mildly.

The solicitor-general was undaunted. If Luke Gibney was mistaken or had misrepresented the truth, then the whole alibi failed because none of the others pretended to have been with Lennon all night. It was also curious that neither the defendant's landlady nor the servant had been produced to corroborate his statement.

Justice Fitzgerald charged the jury, whose verdict would turn on evidence given by three or four witnesses. He cautioned them that Patrick Lennon's role as a Fenian captain should not affect their judgement. His weapons were presumably to be used to resist capture but this was quite distinct from their being used to commit murder. Moreover, although there could be no doubt that a respectable officer like Sergeant Kelly would not wilfully misrepresent the facts, they needed to agree on the accuracy of his evidence.

The twelve men retired to consider their verdict. A majority decision was required. At their request, Patrick Lennon's revolver – ear-marked for the attorney-general's trophy cabinet – was brought to their chamber, along with the bullet removed from Sergeant Kelly. An hour of anxious waiting followed and when they returned, the words of the head juror rang out: 'Not guilty.'

The crowd in the public gallery burst into applause just as they had earlier that week when John Walsh was acquitted of shooting George Reilly. The wooden gavel came down repeatedly. The prosecution case had failed. A conditional pardon would now be drafted, addressing Patrick Lennon in collegiate terms as, 'Right trusty and well-beloved Cousin and Councillor'. The crown had 'thought fit … to extend our Royal Mercy'.[4]

Curran and Purcell were informed that the third indictment for Constable Keena's murder would proceed at some indefinite date; presumably once enough evidence had been gathered. Although they were unsatisfied to leave such a serious charge hanging over their client, their request for a *nolle prosequi* or 'striking out' of the offence was unsuccessful. *The Irish Times* of 14 February conceded that there was 'no reason to be dissatisfied' with the final verdict, however, concluding rather triumphantly that:

> Whether or not he [Patrick Lennon] shot the policeman, we must congratulate the public on his having been convicted of an offence which will ensure his being kept out of mischief henceforth. If not a murderer, he has proved to be a traitor and richly deserves any sentence the court may award him.

The following day, the *Nation* found a reason to be jubilant:

> On the trial of shooting Sergeant Kelly, we refer with deep and sincere pleasure to the verdict in this case, showing as it does the disposition on the part of Dublin jurors to interfere at last with the regular current in which these state prosecutions have flowed and to regard the words of the Attorney-General in some other light than those of an infallible authority.

When Lennon returned to the court on Friday, it was simply to receive a sentence for his treason-felony conviction. He took the opportunity to condemn the Clerkenwell explosion as an incident that had nothing to do with the Fenian Brotherhood. When he had finished speaking, Baron Deasy's summation was rather even-handed: 'No one after this acquittal has a right to reproach you for participation in that outrage [Kelly's shooting], but the verdict of the jury against you for treason-felony was equally proper and I think equally right. The charge was proved by overwhelming evidence and I don't think the verdict is questioned even by yourself.'

'And if another insurrection broke out, I would lead another party,' Lennon said defiantly.

In fixing his sentence, the judge made some allowances for the humanity he had shown towards the captured policemen, before condemning him to fifteen years' penal servitude. Lennon was stunned: 'I expect to see the end of the government before that!' he cried.

The parallel with James Cody's trial was obvious. Although the crown did not require any other pretext for fixing Lennon's sentence (his involvement in the rising was enough), what seemed clear was that in both trials, the preparation of the prosecution's murder case was guided, not by a desire to punish the perpetrator, but by a sense of political expediency. Simply put, the government needed to be seen to bring the assassination circle to book.

Before returning to the waiting prison van, Lennon was ushered into a back room where three non-commissioned officers from the 12th Lancers stood in their all-too-familiar red-fringed black tunics. He must surely have guessed why they were there. They identified him as a former comrade and confirmed that his alias at Aldershot was 'Clarke'. Later that day, the military secretary, Colonel Leicester Curzon Smyth, wrote to the lord lieutenant to inform him that the prisoner was now 'fully identified as a deserter'.[5] There was hardly any reason for a separate court martial.

That afternoon, an urgent telegram was handed to the Earl of Mayo in Westminster. It was most opportune. The previous April, he had been forced to explain to an incredulous House of Commons why John Kirwan, Patrick Lennon's erstwhile commander, had escaped police custody at the Meath Hospital.[6] The latest news from Green Street would help to portray the administration in a more competent light.

At Westminster, the Habeas Corpus Suspension (Ireland) Act Continuance Bill was about to have its first reading. On three separate occasions, it had allowed for the detention of suspects on immaterial grounds, but in recent months fears of its imminent expiration had caused hastily arranged Fenian cases to be pushed through the Irish courts. Inevitably, some trials collapsed due to a lack of evidence. In arguing for an extension to the Act, the chief secretary could now outline its usefulness by reference to the shooting circle.

Although he was a personal advocate of reform, Mayo was obliged to take the Tory party line. He informed the house that the progress of the Fenian conspiracy in Ireland was now greatly paralysed, as well as the activities of its members who had resolved to commit 'isolated outrages to keep up a state of alarm and excitement'. With an expedient disregard for the truth, he said that Lennon 'had not been many days in Ireland before [being] arrested by the police in Dublin in the most gallant manner'. In reality, he had acted with impunity for many months, leaving Ireland several times. The chief secretary, whose sights were set on the viceroyship of India, was unlikely to put his career on the line by suggesting that the lives of British citizens had been endangered in any way. Now that its leader was behind bars, he could rewrite the history of the assassination circle howsoever he wanted. Skimming over the details, he emphasised the heroic service rendered by the RIC and DMP:

> Repeated attempts at assassination have been made upon them who are merely doing their duty and I am sorry to say that in some three or four cases, those attempts were successful ... the list of outrages inflicted on them since the commencement of the Fenian conspiracy ... is still a very painful one ... Constable Patrick Keenan [sic] on 31st October 1867 was shot by a pistol bullet and died after seven days; Sergeant Stephen Kelly on 31st October 1867 was shot in the stomach and for three weeks he was at the point of death but happily he recovered though he is still an invalid ... three or four other men have been permanently disabled by wounds received ... and have been obliged to retire from the force with marks of severe personal injury which I am afraid they will bear to the day of their death.[7]

Taken in their entirety, the actions of the shooting circle made a persuasive argument in favour of extending the Act. Several heated questions were fired from the Liberal benches whose occupants hoped to settle the Irish problem by granting concessions. Would nothing be done for the amelioration of the country? What would be done to satisfy the tenant farmers? It was a portent of things to come.

25

A PLOT UNMASKED

After Patrick Lennon's trial ended, the authorities could at last begin to address some of the structural problems that had been caused by the explosion at Green Street. T. Ruckley, builder, was hired to make the necessary repairs to the gas fittings. Further afield in New York, Lennon was already gaining a semi-mythological status, the *Brooklyn Eagle* of 20 February reporting somewhat inaccurately that 'he went out in a blaze of glory, making a speech in which he predicted that the British Monarchy would be overthrown before the expiration of his term'. On 20 October 1894, Arthur Forrester, himself a suspect in the early part of the investigation, added to the Fenian leader's mystique by writing in the *Irish Weekly Independent* that:

> As soon as this verdict of 'Not Guilty' was pronounced and Lennon sent from the dock, he was surrounded by eight or nine tall fellows, who concealed his movements from the alert detectives while he affected some rapid and complete transformation of his dress and appearance which disguised him so effectually that he passed unchallenged out of the courthouse.

The reality was far more banal. Lennon was first removed to Mountjoy, which in response to Australia's refusal to take any more prisoners had become a terrestrial penal facility. The *Hougoumont*, which transported Denis Cashman as well as the infamous assassination circle leader James Cody, was one of the last such ships to leave. English and Irish prisons were fitted out accordingly, but the transfer of convicts to Mountjoy was already quite controversial. During the week of Lennon's trial, Matthew Lynch died from pulmonary consumption there and it was widely felt that he had suffered from neglect. The Earl of Mayo was questioned as to whether the government would retain the prison's medical officer, Dr Young, and it would appear that the controversy which ensued in Westminster after the death encouraged the remaining 'shooting circle' prisoners to apply for release on health grounds.[1]

On 19 February, the home secretary signed a warrant for Patrick Lennon's removal to Millbank prison in London.[2] Six days later, his train left Westland Row for Kingstown. Since many of his friends lived in the locality, Superintendent Ryan ordered a close watch to be kept. The dogged insistence by a shadowy group of Fenians that a breakout plan 'was feasible and effective' was worrying, as was their assertion that 'they could hear all about the removal and be prepared'.[3] Ryan took no chances and kept news of the transfer out of the newspapers.

At Kingstown, a contingent of marines from the coastguard ship HMS *Royal George* waited silently at the Carlisle Pier, led by Captain Thomas Miller. Depending on the security risk, convicts sometimes boarded directly at the Pigeon House Fort, but Lennon was transferred to a waiting mail boat.[4] After the bags were landed at Holyhead, the marines disembarked and formed a line to guard his route to a waiting mail train. A large number of warders – perhaps a dozen or more – came from London to meet them. The following day, a telegram was delivered to Captain Barlow who worked at the militia office in Henrietta Street, Dublin. It simply read 'arrived all right'.[5] The under-secretary was duly informed and Superintendent Ryan wrote a letter of thanks.

There were some further arrests in the weeks that followed. On 18 March, a party of police raided James McGrath's workshop in Clarendon Street. It was probably carried out on the basis that Lennon had attempted to assassinate Alfred Aylward there the previous summer.[6] The police found an account of money expended in Lennon's defence as well as an IRB subscription list. Significantly, they also discovered a letter written in secret ink from President Roberts' envoy Daniel O'Sullivan. When they went to McGrath's Camden Street home, they found a loaded five-chamber revolver and a rare seven-chamber one taken to pieces, together with the barrel and stick of a large Colt and some more Fenian papers.[7] Until his re-arrest some months later, Superintendent Ryan believed that John Walsh was the only IRB centre now carrying on the aims of the assassination circle.

For his part in helping the investigation, Jack Cade O'Loughlin served only half of a twelve-month sentence. He gave some additional information to Superintendent Ryan who honoured his promise and got him away to America.

On 11 June 1868, he was escorted to the North Wall under armed guard by Sergeant John Giles of G Division. The under-secretary noted that 'this course was the most judicious ... for if he had been left to serve the entire of his sentence, he would have remained in Dublin after his discharge'.[8] Despite his penury, Thomas Rooney also managed to raise the price of his steamship fare and left for America with Patrick Hayburne on 23 April 1868. Before his discharge, he was forced to sign an undertaking that he would never again resort to Fenianism.

The arms agent James Cooke continued to operate for some months in London, making efforts to win IRB members over to John O'Neill's faction along with Dr James Keenan, the man supposed by the police to have taken over from Daniel O'Sullivan as Paris pay agent. When Cooke was arrested in London on 11 July 1868, Samuel Lee Anderson was duly informed, and Pat Mullany, the informer from the Clerkenwell trial, was brought to Scotland Yard to identify him.[9] Cooke wrote that he would have killed him if he had 'got a hold of him but he took to his heels like a man'. Later, he boasted that it had taken ten detectives to hold him down. There was not enough evidence to detain him in custody, however, and he was released pending the gathering of evidence for his trial on 23 July. Afterwards he crowed: 'I am a little god with the boys since I was marked', and the police continued to monitor his activities.

At the suggestion of Robert Anderson, a cheque sent from William Roberts' erstwhile secretary Daniel O'Sullivan to Cooke at the beginning of August 1868 was seized by the police, but the Home Office berated Anderson, believing that it would only drive Cooke further underground. Then in early September 1868, two letters from his Euston Road address were successfully intercepted. The first, addressed to Daniel O'Connell in New York, enquired as to how Michael Monks was getting on. The second was more vitriolic. The addressee, Daniel O'Sullivan, had not responded in five weeks, and Keenan, who was supposed to be his new pay agent, had also failed him. 'Why,' Cooke asked, 'should I be left at the mercy of informers without a penny to defend me?'[10] Insolvent and without means, he was faced with a £32 solicitor's bill. A warrant was issued for his arrest.

Such polemics belonged to the legal sphere, however. In Mullingar and Dublin, the lives of two families had been irrevocably altered. Was Patrick Lennon to blame? Undoubtedly he had taken a leading role in the activities of the assassination circle but his direct involvement now seemed unlikely. Despite small but well-intentioned donations from *Irish Times* readers, Sergeant Kelly found it difficult to come to terms with what had happened. His injuries persisted and he left the force on 15 June 1868 on a temporary annual pension of £65, never to return.[11] Although he never found gainful employment again, his life was blessed with two sons, both of whom lived into adulthood. The first, delivered in 1871 was named after his father Paul. When the second was born two years later, his parents named him Thomas, adding the name Patrick.

In part, the commissioners' Victorian approach to policing was to blame for Constable Keena's death. Only officers with three years' service or more were permitted to guard Dublin's main thoroughfares and as a result the inexperienced 'Johnny Raw' was sent to patrol dangerous back streets and alleyways away from the eyes of the 'respectable classes'. In spite of the city coroner's recommendations, the permanent armament of such men proved to be difficult to achieve on ideological and practical grounds and in August 1868, Conservative MP for Armagh John Vance cautioned that:

> However well-justified a policeman may consider himself in firing, the act with all its accompanying circumstances, whether the result be attended by loss of life or otherwise, must become the subject of legal investigation. It therefore behoves those who may be placed in such a situation to be well prepared to prove that they acted with becoming humanity, caution and prudence and that they were compelled by necessity alone to have recourse to their arms.[12]

As a result, the outmoded Fenian arms on loan to the various DMP stations were returned to storage. Ten rifles were presented as souvenirs to those officers whom DMP Commissioner O'Ferrall deemed to be the most deserving, but in the main, the metropolitan divisions regained a more civic aspect.

In the meantime, those who wrote about the incident in its aftermath seemed blithely unaware of the circumstances, apart from the fact that there had been a police shooting and that Patrick Lennon was put on trial. This was probably because Castle files remained confidential. In the absence of more detailed information, Richard Pigott proposed his own theory:

The assassin is said to have been a Fenian carrying documents. If that were so, and as the encounter with the policemen was accidental, the murder could not have been designed by any combination or conspiracy, since it was clearly not premeditated.[13]

The *Irishman* editor, whose account was published in 1883, did not believe in the existence of the shooting circle. Instead, he gave credence to the third, least credible option – the one suggested by *The Irish Times* of 4 November 1867. A letter printed in its columns purported to have been written by the assassin and was remarkably similar to Lennon's 'confession' in which the gunman claimed to be little more than a courier for important Fenian documents. Similarly, Superintendent John Mallon, in a report written just two weeks after the 1882 Phoenix Park murders claimed that 'Constables O'Neill and Keena were murdered because they sought to interfere with Fenians who were in the execution of their duty.'[14]

Such accounts may have originated with Samuel Lee Anderson, who it was rumoured often tried to plant suggestive articles in order to convict known Fenians, and were it not for Thomas Larcom or Patrick Tynan, it might have remained the only version of events. Under-Secretary Larcom wrote that:

During the October commissions, the informers Corydon and Devany [*sic*] were at the Chancery Lane crown witness depot. They were naturally looked upon by the conspirators as legitimate victims. A plan to set fire to the depot was conceived. Eight men were told off for the duty. The principle of these, J.C. O'Loughlin, the murderer of Clarke in the canal … was proceeding with a parcel of Greek Fire from Arthur Forrester's in the neighbourhood of Temple Bar when he was accosted by Constable Kenna [*sic*] who told him to stop.

It was obvious that Larcom had drawn heavily on Superintendent Ryan's reports, particularly when he also described the men as 'desperadoes' and Jack O'Loughlin as a man who 'set no value on human life'.[15] For the most part his account was plausible, however, and there was even evidence to suggest that the informer John Devaney was aware of the threat.

When, almost thirty years later, IRB man Patrick Tynan revisited the 1867 shootings in a book about the Phoenix Park murders, he further asserted that Kelly and Keena had been part of a police cordon formed to protect the Chancery Lane crown witness depot and that the military was not deployed because the government wanted to maintain public calm.[16] Towards the close of 1866, Baron Strathnairn, commander of the Irish forces, had been at loggerheads with the Earl of Mayo (then Lord Naas) over the use of small military street patrols for what he felt were police duties. Keen to insist on the presence of troops as a simultaneous deterrent to lawlessness and an encouragement to the country's loyal citizenry, the chief secretary pursued the matter until the rising effectively nullified the issue. By the autumn of 1867, the country had probably become sufficiently peaceful for Strathnairn once again to push for the removal of his soldiers from civil duty, thus leaving the DMP in a vulnerable position.

If the Irish administration had indeed assigned unarmed

constables to operate a military cordon on the night of 30–31 October, it had effectively signed their death warrants. After the shootings it seemed far more palatable for nationalist newspapers to claim that the injured policemen had carried revolvers since it would not do to suggest that IRB men had gone out to shoot defenceless officers.

On 20 October 1894, Arthur Forrester echoed the same sentiments in one of a series of 'Romance of Fenianism' articles written for the *Irish Weekly Independent*. He endorsed the idea that the assassin had been carrying papers of importance, but in his version the policemen were sketched as sword-wielding bravados whose over-confidence became their own undoing:

> The constables closed in on him, cutlasses in hand. Then the hunted one wheeled around on his pursuers and there was the ominous flash of a revolver barrel in the flickering lamplight. 'If you follow me another step,' said a calm voice with an unmistaken American accent, 'I shall fill you full of lead.' The sergeant laughed at the threat and rushed in upon the stranger, the constable charging in upon his left flank. Two shots rang out and the passersby who had been attracted by the loud voices saw the two policemen topple over into the gutter.

Another man, Edmond O'Donovan, was not mentioned in any official correspondence, but there was a paper trail to suggest that he played a crucial role in the affair. Some years previously, he and his brother had been initiated into the IRB by Jeremiah O'Donovan Rossa at their home in Upper Buckingham Street. As far as the Brotherhood went, he was responsible for sourcing reliable weapons before the rising and also helped General William Halpin to make the maps they needed.[17] He had a fine collection of rifles which he displayed in the library of his house; on one occasion, he spent a whole evening explaining their various mechanisms to John Devoy. Later, he prepared a small handbook which he distributed among the circles and James Stephens, who valued his services, sent him into the country as one of several emissaries to teach the men how to make Enfield rifle cartridges. Despite the confidence invested in him by the IRB leader, his approach was occasionally foolhardy, however:

> I loaded the revolver with as much powder as the chambers would contain and fired it several times. On taking it asunder, I discovered a flaw reaching half way down one of the chambers which may eventually burst.[18]

Thomas Larcom had befriended O'Donovan's father John during the 1840s when they worked on the Ordnance Survey together. According to John Devoy and Irish Parliamentary Party MP, Timothy Michael Healy, he promised him on his deathbed to act as guardian to his sons. Thus, as soon as Larcom became aware of Edmond's involvement in the IRB, he tried to protect him by annexing him to Castle interests. Their relationship became strained when the young man refused to leave the Brotherhood and the under-secretary was left in a precarious position – torn between his bond to a dying man and his duty to the crown.[19]

When Edmond was arrested again in February 1867, Larcom was furious. Protesting that he had already used his influence to have him released on two prior occasions, he told him that this time he 'would leave him to rot in prison'.[20] Clearly, the young man's activities were beginning to compromise his position. Almost immediately, Maryanne O'Donovan wrote to beg for clemency for her son, but when no answer was forthcoming she contacted James Henthorn Todd, Regius Professor of Hebrew at Trinity College. Apparently Todd had also made a promise to the dying John O'Donovan. He acted as a benefactor to Edmond, paying his medical fees and employing him as a scribe on a salary of £50 a year. He felt that his participation in Fenianism was nothing less than criminality and that it nullified the oath he had made to his father. Nevertheless, he could not help feeling anxious about his young charge and asked, 'Is there any possible way of giving him another chance?'[21] Larcom relented.

In late October and with the rebellion seven months behind them, a small party of eight gathered in O'Donovan's home. Patrick Tynan was one of those present as they talked over the bones of what remained of the Brotherhood.[22] For the time being another rebellion was impossible, but there was a personal grievance to be settled.

Just a few days before, John Joseph Corydon had come to Dublin to give evidence at the trials of the men who were landed in Dungarvan by the ill-fated *Erin's Hope*. In March 1867, he had thwarted the projected attack on Chester Castle and caused the arrest of many of its organisers. Now the session at Green Street courthouse had commenced and Corydon, anxious to produce new revelations for his paymaster, Crown

Solicitor Robert Anderson, singled out Edmond O'Donovan as the agent who had assisted General Halpin.[23]

The men settled on a relatively simple plan. They knew that by night, Corydon was housed with John Devaney at Chancery Lane crown witness depot. Using Greek fire stored in a Ballybough safe house to create a diversion, they would find the hated informer and shoot him.

The layout of the Chancery Lane complex – a series of buildings that housed crown witnesses and a large police garrison – showed at once the ultimate folly of the protagonists' plan, as well as the extent of their desperation. The lane followed the course of a bent nail extending from Golden Lane at one end to Bride Street at the other. The station, whose entrance was on the corner, could only be entered through a gap in an 18-foot high boundary wall. Inside was a parade ground, to the right of which was another long wall, punctuated at regular intervals by four small iron-barred windows. These marked the location of the cells, access to which could only be gained from inside the station. The yard formed a tapered rectangle with its widest end nearest the laneway. At its narrowest end stood the station house – a ramshackle building with a pitched roof. The difficulty of approaching the complex from that side was the likelihood of discovery as one passed through the yard.

The only other possibility was to attack the complex from Ship Street, but that was not without its difficulties either. Such a strategy would have put the men in dangerous proximity to the nearby army barracks which was full of soldiers armed with the latest Snider-Enfield breech-loading rifles. There was one key advantage, however. The back of Clarke's Court station abutted the crown witness depot. The court formed a small yard of tenement houses beyond which a narrow, tortuous laneway led up into Chancery Lane. Once inside, a basement stairs led to a communal coal cellar which afforded access to the entire depot.[24]

From the outset, things did not go to schedule, however. According to Tynan, the wife of one of the men went into labour and as a consequence, he lost track of time and arrived at the rendezvous point before any of the others. Reaching Essex Bridge, he hesitated and was about to re-cross when he was suddenly noticed by a lone policeman, an incident which set off the chain of events that would lead to the shootings of Keena and Kelly. Suddenly O'Donovan's explanation to General Halpin about why he carried an unloaded revolver seemed tragically poignant:

> The average Dublin policeman has no wish to die for England and when he comes to arrest you and you point a revolver at him and say, 'begone', he will think twice before laying hands on you.[25]

When the remainder of the assassination party met, they were warned by a scout that some constables had been shot and, presuming that the crown witnesses would be long gone, they retreated quietly into the darkness.

Meanwhile, having anticipated the attack, Superintendent Ryan had relayed his fears to the commanding officer at Ship Street barracks.[26] Informer John Devaney was evidently aware of the same threat since he managed to steal a revolver from

Blackhorse police station in a hasty attempt to defend himself. The theft was discovered, however, and plans were made to move him and the other crown witnesses to another depot in Ballybough.[27] Corydon and a man named Gallagher refused to go – probably on the basis that an informer had almost been assassinated at Ballybough some years previously. Instead, they were sent to Kilmainham, while George Reilly and his family were taken to England. Later, Ryan's informant reported that if the assassination circle had done its duty, there 'would be small account … of Corydon'.[28]

Before returning to his lodgings, the gunman threw his bottle of Greek fire into a sewer where it burned away. Then he woke his landlady and asked for her daughter. Having handed over his weapon for safekeeping, he went to his room, took off his muddy shoes and undressed. A few minutes later, a police party arrived to carry out a routine search. They looked under beds and took particular care with the men's shoes and clothing but found nothing suspicious. The young lady's closet was another matter entirely, however:

> When they entered … the young woman felt very anxious. One of them, kicking against the steels of the hoop petticoat said, 'We had better not disturb the hoops anyway.' They retired after their unprofitable search to pay another midnight visit elsewhere.[29]

If Tynan was to be believed, the police had unwittingly come within a hair's breadth of solving the case. Later, Mrs Kirwan, whose husband John was on the run after his escape from the Meath Hospital, took the murder weapon from the landlady's daughter and gave it to Edmond O'Donovan for safe-keeping. He was arrested a week later as he alighted from a train in Limerick. He protested that he was on his way to Clare where he intended to spend the winter. The police found several photographs in his luggage, including one of himself, a scrap of newspaper concerning the escape of Kelly and Deasy, and a card with 'A' written on it. His possession of a revolver secured his arrest under the terms of the Arms Act and he was sent to Mountjoy. From there, he wrote several memorials requesting his release. One of these prompted a second letter from Professor Todd:

> I cannot say anything in his favour. He has been untruthful to me, although under considerable obligations to me, and I have not the smallest dependence upon him – his mother by his own account knows nothing of the Fenian doings of her sons and if so she must be a fool – she is (as I suppose you know) a sister of Curry's and from my regard for her husband, as well as for her brother, I feel bound to do whatever is possible for her – what a blessing we now see it to be that Curry is dead for if he had lived, I am certain he would have been in the midst of all this Fenianism.[30] I would be very much obliged to you if you could send Mrs O'Donovan's letter (enclosed) to some of the heads of the police and get them to write me such a reply to it, as I can send to her – as she has purchased or rather poor O'Donovan, before his death purchased a small farm in the County Clare. Her speculation was to get her son Edmond to work this farm for her but he was arrested as he was going down, I believe on the very platform of the railroad.[31]

O'Donovan continued to petition for his release, first on condition of his going to Buenos Aires, but later to North America. On 26 April, he finally received word that he would be freed and asked that he might be allowed some time at liberty on bail before leaving. For young Edmond there had been no special commission trial, no in-depth probe of the extent to which he had been involved in the IRB and no attempt to link him in any way with recent events. He had made regular contributions to the *Irish People* newspaper before its seizure, was identified by Pierce Nagle as one of James Stephens' most trusted friends and was arrested red-handed in a house in Nelson Street in 1866 with bullets, bullet-moulds and a Fenian memorial book. Surpassing all of this was his responsibility for ammunition prior to the rising and his subsequent role as organiser for the north of Ireland under Colonel Kelly.

As the police continued to round up the members of the shooting circle at home and abroad, the governor of Mountjoy gave O'Donovan 14s 2d and sent him on his way to Queenstown. The order was sanctioned by Crown Solicitor Samuel Lee Anderson.[32] Thus, one of the only people who probably knew the truth about who had shot the two policemen was permitted to disappear quietly and Thomas Larcom managed to avert a blemish on his distinguished career. As O'Donovan's ship passed ten miles west of Kinsale on the morning of 21 May 1868, it is possible to imagine him casting a glance back towards Ireland, thus calling to mind the words of O'Donovan Rossa's *Farewell to Dublin*:

Adieu my friends, in Dublin town,
I bid you all adieu;
I cannot yet appoint the day,

When I'll return to you.
I write these words aboard a ship,
Where stormy billows roar.
May the heavens save our Fenian boys,
Till I return on shore.[33]

APPENDIX 1

G DIVISION STAFF

G Division was established temporarily on 27 October 1842 and permanently on 17 March 1843. By 1867 it employed forty-four men, headed by Superintendent Daniel Ryan. In theory, the full complement comprised an inspector, thirteen acting inspectors, four sergeants, six acting sergeants and nineteen constables. Drawn overwhelmingly from rural, labouring backgrounds, the officers usually joined regular police divisions before being assigned to the detective branch at Exchange Court. In 1867, the average length of service was thirteen years and although one or two officers had seen prior service in the RIC, this was not the norm.

Following is a list of the detectives, sergeants and constables who were attached to the division in 1867. It is drawn from the *Report of the Central Committee for Relief of Distress in Ireland 1862–3, With Appendices* (Dublin, 1864), the *G Division Criminal Accounts* (NAI CSORP 1867, Cartons 1751–3) and cross-referenced with the *Dublin Metropolitan Police General Register 1838–1924* (DC).

N.B. Acting in G Division means the men were on temporary assignment.

Name	DMP no.	Year of birth	Place of origin	Former occupation	Initial division/Date of G Division enrolment
Constable John Bride	5681	1829	Clontarf, Co. Dublin	Labourer	C Division, 26 May 1865; Acting in G, 1 Nov. 1867; Disc. on pension, 22 June 1883
Acting Inspector Mathew Carey	5578	1836	Blackrock, Co. Dublin	Labourer	A Division, 13 Nov. 1857; Disc. on pension, 31 Mar. 1887
Acting Inspector Joseph Clarke	5060 (Previously 4350)	1831	Finnea, Co. Westmeath	Labourer	D Division, 17 Nov. 1854; G Division, 10 May 1861; Disc. 4 July 1868
Acting Inspector Patrick Clifford	4816	1834	Ballycarnew, Co. Wexford	Labourer	D Division, 10 Feb. 1854; G Division, 17 Feb. 1860; Disc. 31 Aug. 1867
Acting Sergeant John Cooke	7235 (Previously 5263)	1835	Borrisokane, Co. Tipperary	Labourer	A Division, 7 Sept. 1855; G Division, 23 Apr. 1869; Died 25 Mar. 1875, Suicide
Acting Sergeant Edward Cullen	4591	1831	Innistogue, Co. Kilkenny	Labourer	B Division, 11 Mar. 1853; G Division, 15 Nov. 1865; Disc. on pension, 20 Nov. 1872
Inspector Launcelot Dawson	4761	1834	Killincare, Virginia, Co. Cavan	Labourer	A Division, 28 Oct. 1853; G Division, 18 Jan. 1861; Disc. on pension for two years on 26 Sept. 1867

Name	DMP no.	Year of birth	Place of origin	Former occupation	Initial division/Date of G Division enrolment
Constable Patrick Doyle	5626	unknown	Crumlin, Co. Dublin	Labourer	G Division, 27 May 1864; Acting in G, 1 Nov. 1867; Disc. on pension, 15 April 1875
Acting Inspector William Doyle	6839	1843	Donnybrook, Dublin 4	Gardener	C Division, 1 Sept. 1865; Dismissed 4 April 1871
Acting Inspector John Egenton	5101	1834	Co. Meath	Labourer	D Division, 19 Jan. 1855. Disc. on pension 26 Mar. 1885
Inspector Edward Entwhistle	5482	1837	Williams' Place, Dublin 1	Clerk	A Division, 15 Aug. 1856; G Division, 18 Mar. 1859; Disc. on pension, 7 May 1885
Constable Patrick Ennis	3972	1828	Cadamstown, Co. Kildare	Labourer	G Division, 30 Oct. 1863; Acting in G, 1 Nov. 1867; Disc. on pension, 14 Oct. 1869
Acting Sergeant John Giles	4496	1830	Bray, Co. Wicklow	Labourer	D Division, 10 Dec. 1852; G Division, 18 Mar. 1859; Disc. on pension, 14 Aug. 1872
Sergeant Edward Hughes (Reinstated as Acting Inspector in Mar. 1868)	3179	1821	Leighlinbridge, Co. Carlow	Labourer	B Division, 3 Apr. 1846; G Division, 13 Apr. 1855; Disc. 22 Apr. 1869

Name	DMP no.	Year of birth	Place of origin	Former occupation	Initial division/Date of G Division enrolment
Constable Thomas Kavanagh	5715	1834	Paulstown, Co. Kilkenny	Farmer	Acting in G, 22 Sept. 1867; Permanent in G, 22 Nov. 1867; Disc. on pension, 10 Jan. 1888
Acting Sergeant John Kelly	4594	1832	Ashford, Co. Wicklow	Labourer	A Division, 11 Mar. 1853; G Division, 7 Jan. 1863; Disc. on pension, 14 Aug 1872
Acting Inspector Patrick King	4339	1831	Rogerstown, Co. Meath	Labourer	C Division, 28 May 1852; G Division, 18 Mar. 1859; Disc. on pension, 4 Aug. 1882
Acting Sergeant Thomas Magee	5280	1833	Drumcliffe, Co. Sligo	Labourer	B Division, 21 Sept. 1855; G Division, 15 Nov. 1861; Disc. 3 Nov. 1870
Acting Inspector John Mallon	5838	1838	Killeavy, Co. Armagh	Draper	F Division, 1 Dec. 1858; G Division, 7 Mar. 1862; Disc. on Commissioner's pension, 1 Jan. 1902
Sergeant Philip Matthews	4781	1832	Enniskeen, Co. Meath	Labourer	B Division, 2 Dec. 1853; G Division, 2 Jan. 1863; Disc. on pension, 13 July 1882
Acting Inspector Patrick J. Moclair	5492	1836	Bagenalstown, Co. Carlow	Stationer; then RIC for 8 months	F Division, 3 Sept. 1856; G Division, 22 Aug. 1862; Pensioned as superintendent, D Division, 31 Oct. 1894

Name	DMP no.	Year of birth	Place of origin	Former occupation	Initial division/Date of G Division enrolment
Acting Sergeant John McDermott	3726 (Previously 3298)	1823	Booterstown, Co. Dublin	Labourer	B Division, 30 Oct. 1846; G Division, 18 Mar. 1859; Disc. on pension, 31 Oct. 1867
Constable Andrew Morrow	6165	1838	Ballintra, Co. Donegal	Labourer	G Division, 4 Oct. 1867; Disc. on pension, 31 July 1890
Constable Peter Priestley	6104	1839	Navan, Co. Meath	Labourer	D Division, 19 Sept. 1862; G Division, 1 Nov. 1867; Disc. on pension, 27 May 1886
Inspector Thomas Rice	3359	1826	Borris-in-Ossory, Queen's County	Labourer	C Division, 19 Feb. 1847; Disc. on pension, 31 October 1867
Acting Inspector Thomas Rotheray	2821	1821	Rathfarnham, Co. Dublin	Labourer	D Division, 16 Oct. 1843; G Division on 10 Oct. 1863; Disc. 22 Apr. 1869
Superintendent Daniel Ryan	2607 (Previously 2187)	1818	Philipstown, King's County	Carpenter	F Division, 10 Apr. 1840; G Division, 17 Mar. 1843; Disc. 16 Sept. 1874
Acting Superintendent James Ryan	1460	1818	Philipstown, King's County	Labourer	B Division, 26 Oct. 1838; Acting in G, 30 Dec. 1851; Disc. on pension 30 May 1872

Name	DMP no.	Year of birth	Place of origin	Former occupation	Initial division/Date of G Division enrolment
Sergeant Charles Smith	3225	1827	Hillsborough, Co. Down	Labourer	C Division, 17 July 1846; G Division, 18 Mar. 1859; Disc. 23 July 1868
Acting Inspector John Smollen	3615	1827	Ferbane, King's County	Labourer	D Division, 12 May 1846; Disc. 12 Mar. 1868
Constable James Smyth	6564	1838	Scrabby, Co. Cavan	Teacher	A Division; G Division, 27 Sept. 1867; Disc. on pension, 1 June 1895
Constable Richard Woulfe	4437	1829	Athea, Co. Limerick	Labourer	G Division, 2 June 1865; Acting in G, 27 Sept. 1867; Disc. on pension, 1 June 1895

APPENDIX 2

Assassination Circle Suspects

The Irish Republican Brotherhood was based on the concept of secret cells. Each 'A' or head centre elected nine 'B's, who in turn elected nine 'C's. The 'C's elected nine 'D's each. In theory, this resulted in a total of 820 men. Most, if not all of the head centres selected to lead the assassination group were leaders of other circles. The same was true of the men who served under them. Like the IRB Supreme Council, the shooting circle only convened for specific purposes, thus giving rise (understandably) to disputes about its existence. Between 1858 and 1868, it was known variously as the 'Vigilance Committee', the rather Gallic-sounding 'Committee of Safety' and the 'Tontine Burial Society'. Some police reports also describe it as the 'Fenian police'. In consideration of the sometimes contradictory nature of government correspondence, this list does not purport to be conclusive. It is compiled primarily from Alfred Aylward's list found in the NAI's Fenian Briefs 3/714/Carton 10, but is cross-referenced with other CSORP sources.

Circle overseen by Directory (1867), composed of:

1. Feely, Michael (Dublin)
2. Murphy, John (Cork)
3. Walsh, John (Dublin)

Arms agents:
1. London   – Cooke, James (from mid 1867 as agent of President Roberts)
              – O'Sullivan Burke, Ricard (to unknown extent)
2. Dublin   – Downey, Denis (*c*.1866)

Paris paymaster:
O'Sullivan, Daniel, secretary for civil affairs (replaced by Dr Keenan in early 1868)

Centres (1865–1868)
1. Cody, James (*c*.1865 – convicted 1866; transported via *Hougoumont*)
2. Brady, Thomas (until May 1866)
3. Feely, Michael (from May 1866; arrested 15 November 1867). Also member of Directory
4. Lennon, Patrick (involved with assassination circle as 'B' after March 1867; then centre from 15 November 1867 to 8 Jan 1868)

Sub-centres (B)
1. Dondrell, James (alias Sweeney)
2. O'Loughlin, Jack Cade
3. Reilly, John

Rank and File
1. Brady, James (alias 'The D', porter in England)
2. Brophy, William; 2 Winetavern Street, carpenter. Six hundred men between him and David Gay. Well known to police
3. Dowling, John; arrested at Ryan's public house, later turned informer
4. Francis, Thomas; secretive centre and leader of sixty-five men
5. Hynes, Thomas; Mabbot Street, Dublin. Well known to police as a man who engaged in a scheme of 'shooting down or stabbing'

certain individuals; arrested 24 May 1866

6. Kearney, William; named by Alfred Aylward as an imposter or madman

7. Kevin, Sam; a carpenter, Aughrim Street. Sailed for America, wife followed him

8. Kingston, James (and brother); supposedly with Patrick Lennon when George Reilly was shot

9. McCann, John; bog oak carver, Abbey Street. Died of cholera, Sept. 1866

10. McDonnell, Peter; dog-handler whose work put him into contact with government officials

11. McGarry, Patrick; ropemaker who was prominent in National Brotherhood of St Patrick from 1861–3

12. Murray (McHale), Francis David; shoemaker who lived in a backroom opposite gate, Ship Street barrack. Led forty-five men

13. McNamara, Charles; bottle-glass works, supposed to have led seventy men

14. Monks, Michael; centre, seven hundred men. Lived for a time at Mrs Cooke's, Francis Street

15. Mullen, Peter; said to have been a painter, a native of Drogheda. Alleged by Alfred Aylward to have fired the fatal shot at George Clarke

16. O'Connell Considine, Daniel; may have worked with the assassination circle on its fringes. Arrested in November 1867 but released in February 1868

17. O'Shaughnessy, Garrett, alias 'The Doctor', a carpenter who worked on public works in Paris

18. Rooney, Thomas; brother to John Rooney who had taken part in the *Erin's Hope* expedition

NOTES

Abbreviations:
CP   Commissioners of Police
DC   Garda Síochána Museum and Archives, Dublin Castle
GL   Gilbert Library (Dublin)
LRO   Liverpool Record Office
MO   Meteorological Office of Ireland
NAI   National Archives of Ireland
NLI   National Library of Ireland
OPW   Office of Public Works (Dublin)
PRO   Public Record Office (London)
RCPI   Royal College of Physicians of Ireland Library
RCSI   Royal College of Surgeons of Ireland Library
SRO   Suffolk Record Office, Ipswich
TCD   Trinity College Dublin

Prologue

1   Acting Superintendent James Ryan to CP, 8 Oct. 1867 (NAI, Chief Secretary's Office Registered Papers – henceforth cited as CSORP – 1867/17683).

1   A Strange Errand

1   Superintendent Ryan to Thomas Larcom, 31 Oct. 1867 (NAI CSORP, 1867/19343).

2   Interview with Gerard Kennerk, 9 Oct. 2006. According to my family history, my great-great grandfather Cornelius (Con) Kennerk was the police assassin. I was given the same story by a number of distant relatives. There is evidence of the family's

IRB membership (see Superintendent Ryan to PC, 14 Oct. 1864, NAI Fenian Police Reports box 2/72), but as yet no direct link to their involvement in this case has been discovered. Con departed Ireland for New York on *The City of Washington* in June 1868 and did not return to Dublin for another eight years. Due to lack of evidence the gunman has been left unnamed.

3   *Saunders' Newsletter*, 9 Nov. 1867.

4   Crown Briefs 1865–1869, Patrick Lennon (NAI Fenian Papers, Crown Briefs No. 12).

2   **The DMP Man's Hospital**

1   *Freeman's Journal*, 9 Nov. 1867.

2   *Irish Medical Directory*, 1872 (RSCI).

3   Duties of the Resident Pupils of the Richmond Surgical Hospital, *c*.1868 (NAI Board of Governors' Minutes, House of Industry Hospitals, 9 Apr. 1868–22 Jun. 1871).

4   Cheyne Brady, 'The Dublin Hospitals' in *The Medical Press*, 17 May 1865 (NLI Larcom Papers MS 7646).

5   Larcom Papers, *Fenianism* (NLI MS 1867/7517), p. 332.

6   *Freeman's Journal*, 9 Nov. 1867.

7   Richard G.H. Butcher, *On Gunshot Wounds and Their Treatment* (Dublin, 1868), p. 5.

8   *Dublin Quarterly Journal of Medical Science*, 3 Nov. 1871.

9   *British Medical Journal*, 23 Dec. 1871 (RCSI), p. 717.

10 Thomas A. Longmore, *A Treatise on Gunshot Wounds* (Philadelphia, 1862), p. 54.

11 Acting Superintendent Ryan to Magistrate O'Donnel, 31 Oct. 1867 (NAI CSORP; 1867/19343).

12 Brian Griffin, 'The Irish Police, 1836–1914: A Social History' (unpublished PhD thesis, University of Chicago, 1991), pp. 759, 766, 771.

13 Meeting of the board of governors, 18 June 1868 (NAI Board of Governors' Minute Book; House of Industry Hospitals, 9 April 1868–22 June 1871).

3 First Round of Arrests

1 Acting Superintendent Ryan to Magistrate O'Donnel, 31 Oct. 1867 (NAI CSORP 1867/19343).
2 Superintendent Ryan to CP, 3 May 1868 (NAI CSORP 1866/8701).
3 *The Irish Times*, 16 Sept. 1867.
4 Robert Atkinson to Samuel Lee Anderson, 30 Oct. 1867 (NAI CSORP 1867/19031).
5 Frederick Moir Bussy, *Irish Conspiracies: Recollections of John Mallon, the Great Irish Detective and Other Reminiscences* (London, 1910), p. 14.
6 Description by himself of the career of Daniel Ryan, Detective in Dublin Castle Service 1842–1868 (NLI F.S. Bourke Collection, MS 10,744/3).
7 Frank Thorpe Porter, *Gleanings and Reminiscences* (Dublin, 1875), pp. 173–5.
8 Treason Felony Trial, Queen *v*. Halpin (NAI Fenian Briefs, 3/714/Carton 10).
9 Habeas Corpus Suspension Act (NAI Vol. I; 3).
10 *Weekly News*, 2 Nov. 1867.
11 *Freeman's Journal*, 9 Nov. 1867.
12 *Dublin Corporation Minute Book*, 31 Oct. 1867 (GL C2/A1/28).
13 Meeting of hospital governors, 20 Nov. 1867 (NAI Governors' Minute Book for Mercer's Hospital).
14 *Freeman's Journal*, 13 Nov. 1867.

4 Great Britain Street Raid

1 *Warder*, 2 Nov. 1867.
2 Desmond Ryan, *The Fenian Chief: A biography of James Stephens* (Dublin and Sydney, 1967), p. 213.
3 *Numerical Register of the Officers and Men of all Ranks of the Dublin Metropolitan Police* (DC).
4 *Saunders' Newsletter*, 1 Nov. 1867.

5   Alfred Aylward, 25 Oct. 1867 (NAI Fenian Briefs 3/714/Carton 10).

6   No further details are available as the original report is now available in précis form only (in the Chief Secretary's office index books). It is therefore impossible to determine the circumstances under which Ferguson believed he encountered the gunman.

7   G Division Criminal Account, 16 Oct.–3 Nov. 1867 (NAI CSORP/ 19305/in Carton 1751).

8   Description by himself of the career of Daniel Ryan, Detective in Dublin Castle Service 1842–1868 (NLI F.S. Bourke Collection, MS 10744/3).

9   Anon. to Sackville Place station, 10 Jan. 1866 (NAI CSORP 1866/5352).

10 Anon. to Superintendent Ryan, 12 Feb. 1866 (NAI CSORP 1866/ 5353).

11 Superintendent Ryan to CP, 3 May 1866 (NAI CSORP 1866/8701).

12 Ground Floor Plan, Head Police Office, Dublin Castle, c.1860 (OPW U16 7 misc. 2).

13 William T. Coleman, 'The San Francisco Vigilance Committees', *The Century Magazine* (1891) http://www.militarymuseum.org/ SFVC.html.

14 Superintendent Ryan to CP, 4 Nov. 1867 (NAI CSORP 1867/ 19348). For an excellent, albeit brief, examination of the subject of assassination on such ideological grounds, see T.W. Moody, 'The Fenian Movement in Irish History' in T.W. Moody (ed.) *The Fenian Movement: The Thomas Davis Lectures* (Cork, 1967), p. 110.

15 Larcom Papers, *Fenianism* (NLI MS 1867/7517), p. 355.

16 Richard Pigott, *Personal Recollections of an Irish National Journalist* (Dublin, 1883), p. 366.

17 *Trial and Conviction of American Citizens in Great Britain* (Washington, 1868), pp. 1174, 1192, 1198 & 1203.

18 Application for discharge of a prisoner in custody, 18 Dec. 1867 (NAI 18 1867/21086).

19 Alfred Aylward, *c.*25 Oct. 1867 (NAI Fenian Briefs, 3/714/ Carton 10).
20 John Dowling to governor of Mountjoy prison, 18 Jan. 1868 (NAI Fenian 'R' Files, 2207R).
21 Frederic Moir Bussy, *Irish Conspiracies*, p. 15.
22 Under-secretary of state to Earl of Mayo, 12 Nov. 1867 (NAI Marquis of Abercorn's Government Letters, CSO-LB-267, 19708).
23 R.V. Comerford, *The Fenians in Context: Irish Politics and Society, 1848–82* (Dublin, 2nd ed. 1998), p. 137.
24 Lord Gathorne Hardy to Earl of Mayo, 1 Nov. 1867 (NLI Papers of Richard Southwell Bourke; MS 11,118).
25 Marquis of Abercorn's Government Letters, 1 Nov. 1867 (NAI CSO-LB-267).
26 Superintendent Ryan to CP, 31 May 1866 (NAI CSORP 1866/10634).
27 *Daily Express*, 4 Nov. 1867.

5 Heroic Medicine
1 Richard G.H. Butcher, *On Gunshot Wounds*, p. 5.
2 T.A. Longmore, *Gunshot Wounds*, p. 100.
3 George H.B. MacLeod, *Notes on the Surgery of the War in the Crimea with Remarks on the Treatment of Gunshot Wounds* (London, 1862), p. 136.
4 Richard G.H. Butcher, *Casebook* (RCSI; Vol. X, cases 195, 219 and 259).
5 Minutes of Board of Governors, 21 May 1868 (NAI House of Industry Hospitals Minute Book; 9 Apr. 1868 to 22 Jun. 1871) and T.A. Longmore, *Gunshot Wounds*, p. 86.
6 *The Irish Times*, 29 Oct. 1867.

6 Jack Cade O'Loughlin
1 Superintendent Ryan to CP, 4 Nov. 1867 (NAI CSORP 1867/19343).

2   *Irishman*, 9 Nov. 1867.
3   Richard G. Butcher, *On Gunshot Wounds*, p. 6.
4   Superintendent Ryan to CP, 4 Nov 1867 (NAI CSORP, 1867/19348).
5   Richmond Bridewell Prison Register (NAI Reel 4535984/1031).

7   **Subscription Funds**
1   See T.D. Sullivan, *A.M. Sullivan: A Memoir* (Dublin, 1885), p. 66.
2   *The Irish Times*, 2 Nov. 1867.
3   T.D. Sullivan, *A.M. Sullivan*, p. 111.
4   *The Irish Times*, 2 Nov. 1867.
5   *Irishman*, 9 Nov. 1867.
6   Robert Atkinson to Samuel Lee Anderson, 21 Nov. 1867 (NAI CSORP, 1867/20410).
7   *Irishman*, 9 Nov. 1867.
8   James Fergusson to CP, 2 Nov. 1867(NAI CSORP 1867 19246/19218 on CSORP 19343).
9   *Meteorological Observatory Records, Phoenix Park Station*, Oct. 1867 (MO).
10 'G' division criminal account, 4 Nov.–13 Nov. 1867 (NAI CSORP 19967/1867/in Carton 1752).
11 Superintendent Ryan to CP, 4 Nov. 1867 (NAI CSORP 1867/19348).
12 *Ibid.*, 7 Nov. 1867 (NAI CSORP 1867/19361).
13 Superintendent Ryan to Marquis of Abercorn, 7 Nov. 1867 (NAI CSORP 1867/19343).

8   **The Net Tightens**
1   Lord Strathnairn to Earl of Mayo, 3 Nov. 1867 (NLI Papers of Hugh Rose Regarding Ireland POS 1,290).
2   Shin-ichi Takagami, 'The Dublin Fenians: 1858-1879' (unpublished PhD Thesis, Trinity College, Dublin, 1990), pp. 191–2.

3   Earl of Mayo to James Fergusson, 4 Nov. 1867 (NAI Marquis of Abercorn's Government Letters, CSO-LB-267/19274).
4   Superintendent Corr to CP, 13 Nov. 1867 (NAI CSORP 1867/19983).
5   *The Irish Times*, 4 Nov. 1867.
6   Superintendent Ryan to CP, 5 Nov. 1867 (NAI CSORP 1867/19361).
7   *Thom's Directory*, 1867.
8   Brian Griffin, 'The Irish Police, 1836–1914: A Social History' (unpublished PhD thesis, University of Chicago, 1991) pp. 750 and 763.
9   *London Post Office Directory*, 1862 and 1871. As a tragic postscript, Margaret Murphy, the woman who alerted Sergeant Dagg, was found murdered at her home in Bull Lane on 16 June 1870 (see: *The Irish Times*). The murder weapon, a razor, was left behind at the scene.

9   Lives in the Balance

1   Richard G.H. Butcher, *On Gunshot Wounds*, p. 5.
2   *Saunders' Newsletter*, 9 Nov. 1867.
3   Dublin City Council Minutes; 24 Mar. 1865; 29 Mar. 1866; 2 May 1870 (G.L. C1/A1/26, 27 and 31).
4   Shin-ichi Takagami, 'The Dublin Fenians', p. 185.
5   *Freeman's Journal*, 1 Nov. 1867.
6   Richard Pigott, *Personal Recollections*, p. 365. When another Fenian named Mullen was shot on Usher's Quay in 1870 he was also lured to his death on the pretext of helping to 'move boxes'.
7   *The Irish Times*, 31 Oct. 1867.
8   T.A. Longmore, *Gunshot Wounds*, p. 95.
9   *Freeman's Journal*, 9 Nov. 1867.
10 Richard G.H. Butcher, *On Gunshot Wounds*, p. 4.
11 Brian Jenkins, *The Fenian Problem: Insurgency and Terrorism in a Liberal State 1858–1874* (Montreal & Kingston, 2008), p. 119.
12 Chief Secretary's Office Registered Papers Abstract, 10 November

1864 (NAI CSORP 1864/20608).

13 T.A. Longmore, *Gunshot Wounds*, p. 24.

14 John Rutherford, *The Secret History of the Fenian Conspiracy: Its Origin, Objects and Ramifications* (Vol. I, Michigan, 1877), pp. 157–8.

15 Lord Gathorne Hardy, 8 Nov. 1867 (SRO Diary of Gathorne Hardy, First Earl of Cranbrook 1866–1870, HA43/T501/294).

16 George Black to anon, 1 Dec. 1867 (NAI Fenian Briefs 3/714/ Carton 10).

17 Superintendent Ryan to CP, 8 Nov. 1867 (NAI CSORP 1867/21155).

18 Alfred Aylward to Governor Price, 15 July 1867 (NAI Fenian Briefs, 3/714/Carton 10).

10 A Funeral Procession

1 A.M. Sullivan, *The Wearing of the Green or the Prosecuted Funeral Procession* (Dublin, 1868), p. 5.

2 During this period Catholics and Protestants were often buried together in the same cemetery (for more on this see: Margaret Franklin, *Tracing Your Limerick Ancestors* (Flyleaf Press, 2003) p. 67).

3 *Saunders' Newsletter*, 11 Nov. 1867.

11 International Connections

1 *Trial and Conviction of American Citizens*, p. 75.

2 Superintendent Corr to CP, 13 Nov. 1867 (NAI CSORP 1867/19983).

3 Thomas A. Larcom to Earl of Mayo, 7 Nov. 1867 (NLI Mayo Papers, MS 11,191).

4 Superintendent Ryan to CP, 9 Nov. 1867 (NAI CSORP 1867/19690 in Carton 1752).

5 *Chronological Index of Patents Applied for and Patents Granted* (London, 1868) www.googlebooksearch.com (accessed May 2009).

6   Earl of Mayo to Lord Gathorne Hardy, 11 Nov. 1867 (PRO Irish office Letter Book, CO 906/13).

7   Marquis of Abercorn's Government Letters, 11 Nov. 1867 (NLI CSO-LB-267, 270, 19794).

8   John A. MacDonald, *Troublous Times in Canada* (Toronto, 1910), p. 21.

9   Abstract of Habeas Corpus Suspension Act Cases 1866, Vol. II (NAI CSO-ICR-11).

10 Superintendent Ryan to CP, 11 Nov. 1867 (NAI CSORP, 1867/19361).

11 CP to Matthew Anderson, 16 Oct. 1867 (NAI CSORP 1867/18190).

12 Larcom Papers, Fenianism 1867 (NLI MS 7517/336).

13 Superintendent Ryan to CP, 11 Nov. 1867 (NAI CSORP 1867/19361).

14 R.V. Comerford, *Fenians in Context*, p. 157.

15 Report of the Trial of William G. Halpin for Treason-Felony at the County of Dublin Commission Court, November 1867 (NAI Fenian Briefs, 3/714/Carton 10), p. 73.

16 Superintendent Ryan to CP, 11 Nov. 1867 (NAI CSORP, 1867/19361).

17 Superintendent Ryan to CP, 9 Nov. 1867 (NAI CSORP, 1867/19690 in Carton 1752).

18 Larcom Papers, Fenianism, 1867 (NLI MS7517/357).

19 Superintendent Ryan to CP, 11 Nov. 1867 (NAI CSORP 1868/20374).

20 R.V. Comerford, *Fenians in Context*, p. 126. The context here was the short-lived National Brotherhood of Saint Patrick which commandeered Terence Bellew McManus' funeral in Dublin. It signalled the strength of ordinary IRB rank and file members.

21 Edward Archibald to Lord Stanley, 22 Nov. 1867 (PRO FO 5/1342).

22 *Ibid.*, 27 Nov. 1867 (PRO FO 5/1342).

12 Rattled Nerves

1 Acting Inspector Entwhistle to Superintendent Ryan, 14 Nov. 1867 (NAI CSORP 1867/19896).
2 *The Times*, 15 Nov. 1867.
3 Acting Inspector Entwhistle to Superintendent Ryan, 14 Nov. 1867 (NAI CSORP 1867/19896).
4 *Daily Express*, 15 Nov. 1867.
5 Royal Archives, Queen Victoria Journal, 18 Nov. 1867 in James H. Murphy, *Abject Loyalty: Nationalism and Monarchy in Ireland during the Reign of Queen Victoria* (Cork, 2001), p. 157.
6 Alfred E. Gathorne Hardy, *Gathorne Hardy, 1st Earl of Cranbrook: A Memoir* (London, 1910), p. 234.
7 Earl of Derby, Address to Her Majesty on the Lords Commissioner's speech; 19 Nov. 1867 Hansard 3, i (1868).

13 Brandy and Scalpels

1 Richard G.H. Butcher, *On Gunshot Wounds*, p. 14.
2 William Doolin in J.B. Lyons (ed.), *Dublin's Surgeon Anatomists and Other Essays: A Centenary Tribute* (Dublin, 1987), p. 105.
3 Richard G.H. Butcher, *On Gunshot Wounds*, p. 17.
4 J.B. Lyons, *The Quality of Mercer's: The Story of Mercer's Hospital, 1734–1991* (Dublin, 1991), p. 90.
5 T.A. Longmore, *Gunshot Wounds*, p. 15.

14 Raid on the Coombe

1 Superintendent Ryan to CP, 19 Dec. 1867 (NAI CSORP 1867/22145 in Carton 1753).
2 *Ibid.*, 15 Nov. 1867 (NAI CSORP 1867/19977).
3 Superintendent Ryan to Colonel Lake, 16 Nov. 1867 (NAI CSORP 1867/19343).
4 Superintendent Ryan to CP, 5 Jan. 1866 (NAI CSORP 1866/260).
5 Acting Superintendent Ryan to CP, 16 Nov. 1867 (NAI CSORP 1867/20036).

6   SC to Alfred Aylward, 17 Nov. 1867 (NAI Fenian Briefs, 3/714/ Carton 10).
7   Transcript of Abstracts of Cases under Habeas Corpus Suspension Act 1866 (NAI CSO-ICR-10).
8   *Numerical Register of the Officers and Men of all Ranks of the Dublin Metropolitan Police* (DC).
9   John O'Leary, *Recollections of Fenians and Fenianism* (London, 1896) p. 231.
10 Alfred Aylward, 25 Oct. 1867 (NAI Fenian Briefs, 3/714/Carton 10).
11 Inspector William Campbell to CP, 18 Nov. 1867 (NAI CSORP 1867/20102).
12 *Numerical Register of the Officers and Men* (DC).
13 Superintendent Ryan to CP, 22 Nov. 1867 (NAI CSORP, 307/20374).
14 Fenianism, Index to Names 1867 (NAI CSO-ICR-15).
15 Superintendent Ryan to CP, 11 Apr. 1866 (NAI CSORP 1866/7131).
16 *Ibid.*, 22 Nov. 1867 (NAI CSORP 1871/307/20374).
17 Superintendent Ryan to CP, 19 Nov. 1867 (NAI CSORP 1867/20362).

15 The Felon's Track

1   'A' division report to Superintendent Ryan, 20 Nov. 1867 (NAI CSORP 1867/20521).
2   Telegraph, 21 Nov. 1867 and Superintendent Ryan to Colonel Lake, 25 Nov. 1867 (NAI CSORP 1871/20521).
3   Robert Atkinson to Samuel Lee Anderson, 21 Nov. 1867 (NAI CSORP 1867/20410).
4   *The Times* (London), 25 Nov. 1867.
5   C.J. O'Donnel to Superintendent Ryan, 22 Nov. 1867 (NAI CSORP, 1871/307/20374).
6   A.M. Sullivan, *The Dock and the Scaffold: The Manchester Tragedy and the Cruise of the Jacknell* (Dublin, 1868), pp. 59–62.

7   'B' division report to Superintendent Ryan, 23 Nov. 1867 (NAI CSORP 1867/20521).

8   Alfred Aylward *c*.25 Oct. 1867 (NAI Fenian Briefs 3/714/Carton 10).

9   Superintendent Ryan to CP, 25 Nov. 1867 (NAI CSORP 1867/10478 in Carton 1752).

10 Superintendent Ryan to Colonel Lake, 25 Nov. 1867 (NAI CSORP, 1867/19361).

11 Superintendent Ryan to CP, 25 Nov. 1867 (NAI CSORP 1867/20478 in Carton 1752).

12 Acting Superintendent Ryan to CP, 24 Nov. 1867 (NAI CSORP, 1867/20446/1867 in Carton 1752).

13 *The Irish Times*, 25 Nov. 1867.

14 Superintendent Ryan to CP, 3 May 1866 (NAI CSORP 1866/8701).

15 This may well have been James 'Skin the Goat' Fitzharris, who achieved public notoriety as getaway driver for the 'Invincibles' in 1881.

16 A Mock Funeral Procession

1   A.M. Sullivan, *Wearing of the Green*, p. 165.

2   Lord Strathnairn to Captain Wesley (NLI Papers of Hugh Rose, 17 Dec. 1867, POS 1,290).

3   For an excellent commentary on this, see R.V. Comerford, *Fenians in Context*, p. 137.

4   *The Irish Times*, 10 Dec. 1867.

5   A.M. Sullivan, *Wearing of the Green*, p. 165.

6   *The Irish Times,* 11 Mar. 1868.

7   Strathnairn to G. Lambert, 10 Dec. 1867 (NLI Papers of Hugh Rose POS 1,290).

8   A.M. Sullivan, *Wearing of the Green*, p. 19.

9   Lord Strathnairn to Marquis of Abercorn, 8 Dec. 1867 (NLI Papers of Hugh Rose, POS 1,290).

10 Superintendent Ryan to CP, 17 Dec. 1867 (NAI CSORP

1867/21915 on Fenian Briefs 3/714/Carton 10).

11 *Freeman's Journal*, 14 Feb. 1868.

17 Desperado

1 Report of the Trial of William G. Halpin for Treason-Felony at the County of Dublin Commission Court, November 1867 (NAI Fenian Briefs, 3/714/Carton 10), p. 73.

2 Joseph I.C. Clarke, *My Life and Memories*, p. 45.

3 Superintendent Ryan to CP, 24 Feb. 1868 (NAI Abstract of Cases under Habeas Corpus Suspension Act, 1866, CSO-ICR-12 Vol. 3/49).

4 Larcom Papers, Fenianism, 1867 (NLI MS 7517/332-333).

5 Superintendent Ryan to CP, 13 Sept. 1867 (NAI CSORP 1867/16135). Judging by the frequency with which the police mention the presence of youths in association with shootings or incendiary attacks, it would seem that the assassination circle used them as scouts and messengers.

6 George Black to Superintendent Ryan, 21 Sept. 1867 (NAI Fenian Briefs, 3/714/Carton 10).

7 Alfred Aylward, 4 Dec. 1865 'Republicanism in Ireland: A Political Pamphlet', 4 Dec. 1865 and anon. to Alfred Aylward 17 Nov. 1867 (NAI Fenian Briefs 3/714/Carton 10).

8 Superintendent Ryan to CP, 29 Nov. 1867 (NAI CSORP 1867/21842).

9 *Ibid.*, 15 Jan. 1868 (NAI Abstract of Cases Under Habeas Corpus Suspension Act, 1866, CSO-ICR-12, Vol. 3/25).

10 Edward Archibald to Lord Stanley, 12 Nov. 1867 (PRO FO 5/1342).

11 Lord Gathorne Hardy, 25 Nov. 1867 (SRO Diary of Gathorne Hardy, 1st Earl of Cranbrook, 1866–1870 HA43/T501/294).

12 Robert Anderson to CP *c.* 1 Dec. 1867 (NAI CSORP 1867/21842 on 1871/320).

13 Larcom Papers, Fenianism (NLI MS 7517/333).

14 Anon. to Alfred Aylward, 17 Nov. 1867 (NAI Fenian Briefs

3/714/Carton 10).

15 Queen *v.* Lennon, Confidential, Liverpool, 5 Dec. 1867 (NAI F4851/ 4715). In 1865, Anderson had employed the services of the famous photographer William Mervyn Lawrence but the prison soon acquired its own photographers.

16 Transcript of Abstracts of Cases under Habeas Corpus Suspension Act 1866 (NAI CSO ICR 10).

17 Superintendent Ryan to CP, 17 May 1867 (NAI CSORP 1867/456 on Fenian Briefs 3/714/Carton 10) and reports of Superintendent Ryan and Surgeon Ross, 17 May 1867 (NAI CSORP 1867/8764).

18 Alfred Aylward, 25 Oct. 1867 and *c.*1 Dec. 1867 (NAI Fenian Briefs, 3/714/Carton 10).

19 Thomas Larcom (Irish Office) to Superintendent Ryan, 5 Dec. 1867 (NAI CSORP 1867/16135).

20 Adolphus Liddell to Earl of Mayo, 7 Dec. 1867 (PRO; HO 122/23/65).

21 Robert Anderson, *Sidelights on the Home Rule Movement* (London, 1907), p. 37.

22 Shin-ichi Takagami, 'The Dublin Fenians', p. 187.

23 Larcom Papers, Fenianism 1867 (NLI MS 7517/366).

24 Joseph I.C. Clarke, *My Life and Memories*, pp. 46–49; Brian Jenkins, *The Fenian Problem*, pp. 152–155.

25 *British Medical Journal*, Vol. 2, 1867.

26 Anon. to Alfred Aylward 17 Nov. 1867 (NAI Fenian Briefs 3/714/Carton 10) and Matthew Anderson to CP, 12 Dec. 1867 (NAI CSORP 1867/21574).

27 Superintendent Ryan to CP, 19 Dec. 1867 (NAI CSORP 1867/19343).

28 Earl of Mayo to Thomas Larcom, 27 Nov. 1867 (NAI CSORP, 1867/20844).

29 *Trial and Conviction of American Citizens*, p. 1452.

30 William McLoughlin to John Devoy, Mar. 1919 in William O'Brien and Desmond Ryan (eds), *Devoy's Postbag 1871–1928*

(Dublin, 1948), p. 526.

31 Superintendent Ryan to Colonel Lake, 9 Jan. 1868 (NAI CSORP, 1871/320 on 20374).

32 Habeas Corpus Suspension Act, Vol. I (3) (NAI 22298).

33 Shin-ichi Takagami, 'The Dublin Fenians', pp. 191–2.

18 Home for Christmas

1 CP to William Lane Joynt, 23 Dec. 1867 (GL Dublin Corporation Minute Book).

2 Description by himself of the career of Daniel Ryan, Detective in Dublin Castle Service 1842–1868 (NLI F.S. Bourke Collection, MS 10744/13).

3 Anon. to Thomas Larcom, 10 Dec. 1867 (NLI Larcom Papers Ms 7,593).

4 James H. Murphy, *Abject Loyalty*, p. 160.

5 Lord Strathnairn to Colonel McKenzie, 29 Dec. 1867 (NLI Papers of Hugh Rose POS 1,290).

6 Joseph I.C. Clarke, *My Life and Memories*, p. 55–6.

7 M.J. Kelly, *The Fenian Ideal and Irish Nationalism, 1882–1916* (New York, 2006), p. 20.

8 Anon. to Lord Gathorne Hardy, 14 Dec. 1867 (SRO, Correspondence between Lord Mayo and Gathorne Hardy, HA43/T501/270).

9 Adolphus Liddell to Robert Anderson (Irish Office), 27 Feb. 1868 (PRO HO 122/23).

10 Superintendent Ryan to CP, 19 Dec. 1867 (NAI CSORP 1867/22145 in Carton 1753).

11 *The Irish Times*, 15 Jan. 1868.

12 F.F. Millen to Col John O'Mahony, 1 Aug. 1868 (The American Catholic History Research Centre and University Archives, *Fenian Brotherhood Collection*, www.aladin.wlrc.org).

13 Anon. *c.*Dec. 1867 (*Fenian Brotherhood Collection*, www.aladin. wlrc.org).

14 *The Irish Times*, 15 Jan. 1868.

15 Edward Archibald to Lord Stanley, 11 Dec. 1867 (PRO FO 5/1342).

16 James Stephens to his wife, 30 Dec. 1867 (TCD Davitt Papers 9659/17).

19 A Discreet Arrest

1 Corporation Minute Books, 3 Jan. 1868 (GL).

2 *Cork Constitution*, 1 Jan. 1868.

3 Chief Superintendent's report, 8 May 1868 (NAI CSORP 1868/6345).

4 Fenianism, Index of Names, 1862–1865 (NAI CSO-ICR-14).

5 A.F. Foster to home secretary, 9 Jan. 1868 (NAI CSORP 376/on 457R).

6 Samuel Lee Anderson, 7 Jan 1868 (NLI, Crown Solicitor's Diary, MSS 5965–5969).

7 W.W. Hunter, *A Life of the Earl of Mayo* (London, 1875), p. 358.

8 Description by himself of the career of Daniel Ryan (NLI F.S. Bourke Collection, MS 10744/4-5).

9 Superintendent Ryan to CP, 9 Jan. 1868 (NAI CSORP 1871/320 in 20374).

10 *Abstract of Cases under Habeas Corpus Suspension Act 1866, Vol. II* (NAI CSO-ICR-11).

11 Superintendent Ryan to Colonel Lake, 9 Jan. 1868 (NAI CSORP 1871/320 on 20374). Rather than unavoidably, the oath should probably read inviolably.

12 Description by himself of the career of Daniel Ryan (NLI F.S. Bourke Collection, MS 10744/3).

13 Superintendent Ryan to Colonel Lake, 9 Jan. 1868 (NAI CSORP 1871/320 on 20374).

14 Earl of Mayo to Earl of Derby, 9 Jan. 1868 (LRO Derby Papers, 1868 155/3).

15 Colonel Lake to Earl of Mayo, 9 Jan. 1868 (NLI Papers of Richard Southwell Bourke, MS 7,950).

16 Superintendent Ryan to CP, 15 Jan. 1868, Abstract of Cases

Under Habeas Corpus Suspension Act (NAI, 1866, CSO-ICR-12, Vol. 3/25).

17 Lord Gathorne Hardy to Earl of Mayo, 10 Jan. 1868 (NLI Papers of Richard Southwell Bourke, MS 7,950).

18 Lord Strathnairn to Earl of Mayo, 12 Jan. 1868 (NLI Papers of Hugh Rose, POS 1,290/244).

19 *Irishman*, 18 Jan. 1868.

20 Lord Mayo to Secretary of the Treasury, 18 Jan. 1868 (NAI Marquis of Abercorn's Government Letters, CSO-LB-267/915).

21 *Trial and Conviction of American Citizens*, p. 592.

22 Larcom Papers, Fenianism, 1867 (NLI 7517).

23 *Belfast Newsletter*, 25 Jan. 1868; Superintendent Ryan report, 24 Jan. 1868 (NAI 3105R).

24 Samuel Lee Anderson, 16 and 19 Jan. 1868 (NLI Crown Solicitor's Diary MSS 5965-5969).

20 Sergeant Kelly has a Visitor

1   Samuel Lee Anderson, 15 Jan. 1868 (NLI Crown Solicitor's Diary, MSS 5965-5969).

2   Annexed report from Matthew Anderson; Samuel Lee Anderson to CP, 18 Jan. 1868 (NAI CSORP 1871/320 on 20374).

3   Superintendent Ryan to Colonel Lake, 17 Jan. 1868 (NAI CSORP 1868/10160/460).

4   Strathnairn to Lieutenant Colonel Feilding, 18 Jan 1868 (NLI Papers of Hugh Rose, POS 1,290).

5   Ciphered telegram to Earl of Mayo, 18 Dec. 1867 (NLI Papers of Richard Southwell Bourke, MS 11,201/4) and papers of Adolphus Liddell to Earl of Mayo, 11 Jan. 1868 (NAI CSORP 376 on 457R).

6   Letters to Charles McNamara, 14 and 15 Jan. 1868 (NAI Fenian 'R' Files/3105R).

7   Superintendent Ryan to CP, 24 Jan. 1868 (NAI Abstract of Cases Under Habeas Corpus Suspension Act, 1866, CSO-ICR-12, Vol. 3/25).

8   *Londonderry Standard*, 18 Jan. 1868.
9   Richard G.H. Butcher, *On Gunshot Wounds*, p. 23.
10 *Daily Express*, 21 Jan. 1868.

21 A Belated Confession
1   Superintendent Ryan to Colonel Lake, 28 Jan. 1868 (NAI CSORP 1868/829).
2   *Rules for Crown Solicitors and Sessional Crown Solicitors* (2nd ed.) (Dublin, 1868), p. 8.
3   Superintendent Ryan to CP, 21 Jan. 1868 (NAI CSORP 570R 2983 on 20374).
4   Kilmainham prison register, 1867–1871 (NAI, MFGS 51/044).
5   Application for discharge of prisoner in custody, 19 Dec. 1867; Superintendent Ryan to CP, 17 Dec. 1867 (NAI CSORP 1867/21916).
6   Thomas Reynolds to Governor of Mountjoy, 3 Jan. 1868 (NAI Fenian 'R' Files, 2207R).
7   Mountjoy prison register, 1867 (NAI MFGS 51/152).
8   *Bristol Daily Post*, 7 Jan. 1868 (PRO HO45/7799).
9   Superintendent Ryan to CP, 29 Feb. 1868 (NAI Fenian 'R' Files, 2136R).
10 Thomas Larcom to military secretary, 5 Feb. 1868 (NLI Kilmainham Papers, MS 1061).
11 'D' division report, Liverpool to CP, 7 Feb. 1868 (NAI CSORP 1868/5746).
12 Crown solicitor's diary (NLI Samuel Lee Anderson Collection, MSS 5965–5969).
13 Thomas Larcom to Lord Gathorne Hardy, 9 Feb. 1868 (NAI Marquis of Abercorn's Government Letters CSO-LB-267).

22 Commission of 'Oyer and Terminer'
1   Earl of Mayo to secretary of the treasury, 5 Nov. 1867 (NAI Marquis of Abercorn's Government Letters CSO-LB-

    267/19330).
2 Superintendent Ryan to CP, 15 Nov. 1865 (NAI Fenian Police Reports 345/1).
3 *Ibid.*, 26 Nov. 1867 (NAI CSORP, 1867/20521).
4 Edward Archibald, 12 Nov. 1867 (NAI Fenian A Files, Box 3/A295). Some years later, Lomasney participated in an ill-fated London bombing attack which resulted in his death.
5 A.M. Sullivan, *Wearing of the Green*, p. 82.
6 Superintendent Masterson to Colonel Lake, 31 Oct. 1867 (NAI CSORP, 1867/19343).
7 *Irishman*, 15 Feb. 1868.
8 There was a marked distinction between the aims of the Fenians and the Reform League which had been formed to press for male suffrage. The latter believed in constitutional reform rather than in insurrection. During this period however, the newspapers blithely disregarded such nuances.

23 Trial

1 Military secretary to CP, 11 Nov. 1867 (NAI CSORP 1867/19725).
2 David Jeffrey Bentley, *English Criminal Justice in the Nineteenth Century* (London, 1998), p. 113.
3 A.M. Sullivan, *Wearing of the Green*, p. 75.
4 J.A. Curran, *Reminiscences of John Ayde Curran* (London, 1915), p. 10.
5 *The Irish Times*, 21 Dec. 1867.
6 Charles Francis Adams to William H. Seward, 1 Nov. 1867, *Trial and Conviction of American Citizens*, p. 79.
7 John Denvir, *The Life Story of an Old Rebel* (Dublin, 1910), p. 67.
8 Captain Hall to military secretary, 12 Feb. 1868 (NLI Kilmainham Papers, 1868/MS 1061).
9 Samuel Lee Anderson (NLI Crown Solicitor's Diary, MSS 5965–5969).
10 J.A. Curran, *Reminiscences of John Ayde Curran* (London, 1915),

pp. 29–30.

11 *Tomahawk*, 22 Feb. 1868.

12 *Rules for Crown Solicitors and Sessional Crown Solicitors* (2nd ed. Dublin, 1868), pp. 7, 10.

13 'G' division criminal account, 15 Nov. 1867 (NAI CSORP 1867/20619 in Carton 1752).

14 Eva Ó Cathaoir, 'Patrick Lennon (1841–1901): Dublin Fenian Leader' in *Dublin Historical Record* (Vol. XLIV No. 2, Autumn 1991), p. 43.

15 Ulick O'Connor, *The Gresham Hotel, 1865–1965* (Cork, 1966), p. 14.

24 Alibi

1 *Irish Weekly Independent*, 20 Oct. 1894.

2 James Cooke to Daniel O'Connell, 28 Aug. 1868 (PRO HO 45/7799).

3 In 1868, phrenology was still some years from reaching its peak and would culminate in Cesare Lombroso's 1876 work, *L'uomo delinquente* ('The Criminal Man'). It was later discredited as a 'pseudo science'. Alfred Aylward took a personal interest in it as evidenced by a letter in the NAI's Fenian Briefs 3/714/Carton 10.

4 Crown Briefs 1865–1869 (NAI No. 12).

5 Military secretary to Colonel Lake, 15 Feb. 1868 (NLI Kilmainham Papers, MS 1061).

6 Lord Naas, 12 Apr. 1867 Hansard 3, i (1867).

7 Earl of Mayo, First Reading of Habeas Corpus Suspension (Ireland) Act Continuance Bill; 14 Feb. 1868 Hansard 3, i (1868).

25 A Plot Unmasked

1 *The Nation*, 15 Feb. 1868 and under-secretary to governor of Mountjoy, 25 Feb 1868 (NAI Irish Department Book CSO-LB-

170/167 1235R).

2 Criminal warrant book, 15 Feb. 1868 (PRO HO 15/7).

3 Superintendent Ryan to CP, 18 Feb. 1868 (NAI CSORP R3259).

4 Earl of Mayo to secretary of the admiralty (NAI Convict Letter Book, CONLB5/193).

5 M. Murphy to Captain Barlow, telegram, 26 Feb. 1868 (NAI CSORP 1868/20374).

6 Eva Ó Cathaoir, 'Patrick Lennon (1841–1901): Dublin Fenian Leader' in *Dublin Historical Record* (Vol. XLIV No. 2, Autumn 1991), p. 46.

7 Report of Superintendent Ryan, 18 Mar. 1868 (NAI Abstract of Cases under Habeas Corpus Suspension Act 1866, Vol. III, CSO ICR 12/61). In the years the followed, hundreds if not thousands of such weapons were dismantled and hidden. In some cases, they were deemed to be unrecoverable by the IRB (Owen McGee, *The IRB*).

8 Larcom Papers, Fenianism 1867 (NLI MS 7517/362-3).

9 Samuel Lee Anderson, 11 July 1868 (NAI Crown Solicitor's Diary, MS 5965–5969).

10 James Cooke to Daniel O'Connell and Daniel O'Sullivan (alias Davis), 28 Aug. 1868 (PRO HO 45/7799).

11 Commissioners of police to secretary of the treasury, 16 Jun. 1868 (NAI CSORP 1868/7814). From a pecuniary standpoint, this was not a bad outcome. Police pensions had been halved with the passing of the Dublin Metropolitan Police Pensions Act on 12 August 1867 (30 & 31, Vic., C.95) but those who joined before this date were not affected.

12 Larcom Papers, 6 Aug. 1868 (NLI Constabulary Organisation and Duties, MS 7619).

13 Richard Pigott, *Personal Recollections*, p. 366.

14 Superintendent Mallon to CP, 20 May 1882 (NAI CBS, boxes a and b).

15 Larcom Papers – Fenianism, 1867 (NLI MS 7517/360 & 357).

For a direct comparison, see NAI CSORP 1867/19343.

16 Patrick J.P. Tynan, *The Irish National Invincibles and Their Times* (New York, 1894), p. 168.

17 John Denvir, *Life Story of an Old Rebel*, p. 77.

18 Edmond O'Donovan to James Stephens, 4 Aug. *c*.1866 (TCD Davitt Papers 9659/374).

19 Timothy Michael Healy, *Letters and Leaders of my Day, Vol. I* (London, 1929), p. 117.

20 John Devoy, *Recollections of an Irish Rebel*, p. 364.

21 Professor Dodd to Thomas Larcom, 22 Feb. 1867 (NLI Larcom Papers, MS 7,593).

22 Tynan, a small Kingstown shopkeeper, was identified by some witnesses as the possible 'No. 1' after the Phoenix Park murders; see also Malcom Brown, *The Politics of Irish Literature: From Thomas Davis to W.B. Yeats* (Washington, 1973). Owen McGee further identifies him as a 'militia soldier and member of the London IRB' in *The IRB*, p. 89. He was eventually arrested at Boulogne in September 1896. The French refused to extradite him and he was later released. See also, *Annual Register*, 1897), p. 58.

23 Larcom Papers, Fenianism (NLI MS 7517/359).

24 Chancery Lane/Clarke's Court, Dublin: site map, tracing from lease dated 23 Sept 1861, Scale 20ft to 1 inch (OPW; L10 11/ Drawing 112439).

25 John Devoy, *Recollections of an Irish Rebel*, p. 365.

26 Superintendent Ryan to CP, 4 Nov. 1867 (NAI CSORP 1867/19348).

27 Police commissioners' report, 24 Oct. 1867 (NAI CSOR 1867/161817).

28 Superintendent Ryan to CP, 4 Nov. 1867 (NAI CSORP 1867/19322).

29 Patrick J.P.Tynan, *Irish National Invincibles*, p. 169.

30 This was Eugene O'Curry (20 Nov. 1794–30 July 1862), an Irish scholar of some repute. He was born in Carrigaholt, County Clare

and employed in 1835–1842 in the topographical section of the Ordnance Survey. He was married to Anne Broughton, sister of Maryanne. This made him a brother-in-law to John O'Donovan.

31 Professor Todd to Thomas Larcom, 24 Jan. 1868 (NLI Larcom Papers, MS 7593).

32 Director of convict prisons to chief secretary, 10 Jun. 1868 (CSORP 1868/7529).

33 Georges Denis Zimmermann, *Songs of Irish Rebellion: Political Street Ballads and Rebel Songs, 1780–1900* (Michigan, 1967), p. 261.

BIBLIOGRAPHY

MANUSCRIPTS AND NEWSPAPERS

National Library of Ireland

Address of Gen. John O'Neill, President, F.B., to the Officers and Members of the Fenian Brotherhood, on the State of the Organisation, and Its Intended Disruption (New York, 1868)

Description by himself of the career of Daniel Ryan, Detective in Dublin Castle Service, 1842–1868 (MS 10744)

General F.F. Millen Papers (POS 740)

Journal of the Statistical and Social Enquiry Society of Ireland (Vol. III, Jan. 1861)

Kilmainham Papers, Letter Book 1868 (MS 1061)

Larcom Papers, Fenianism, 1867 (MS 7517)

Larcom Papers, the Dublin Hospitals (MS 7646)

Larcom Papers, Letters and Papers, Constabulary Organisation and Duties (MS 7619)

Papers of Sir Hugh Rose (Baron Strathnairn) regarding Ireland (POS, 1290)

Proceedings of the Senate and House of Representatives of the Fenian Brotherhood in Joint Convention at Philadelphia, P.A. (New York, 1868)

Richard Southwell Bourke papers (MS 11118 and MS 7950)

Samuel Lee Anderson Collection: Reports, Minutes etc. Relating to the work of the Crown Solicitor's Office, 1867–1885 (MS 5970)

Official diary kept in the Crown Solicitor's Office, Dublin Castle, 1868–1871 and 1874 (MSS 5965–5969)

Thom's Street Directory – various years

Royal College of Surgeons Library

Butcher, Richard G.H., *On Gunshot Wounds and Their Treatment* (Dublin, 1868)

Butcher, Richard G.H., *Manuscript Casebook* (Volume X, 1859)

Card catalogue of physicians and surgeons (Kildare Street Repository)
Irish Medical Directories for 1867, 1872 and 1873 (Kildare Street Repository)
Stokes, Dr William, 'An Account of Constable Talbot's Treatment' in *British Medical Journal*, 23 Dec. 1871 (Kildare Street Repository)

Liverpool Record Office

Lord Derby Papers (Correspondence of Lord Mayo 1868/155/3)

National Archives of Ireland

Chief Secretary's Office Registered Papers (1867 and 1868)
Convict Letter Book (1 Jan. 1864–31 May 1869, CON LB 5)
Crown Briefs 1865–1869, No. 12 1868; Dublin Commission Court Indictment – Queen *v*. Patrick Lennon, February 1868
Crown solicitor's Book, 1 Jan. 1867–10 Oct. 1870 (CSO-LB-400)
Fenian Briefs, Carton 10 (City Commission 25 Oct. 1867, Manuscript Brief No. 8 – Incomplete)
Fenian Photographs (FP 89–194; 195–360; 361–509)
Habeas Corpus Act (Abstracts), Volume I (II)
Habeas Corpus Suspension Act, Volume I (III)
Abstracts from Habeas Corpus Suspension Act (Volume II)
Fenianism, Index of Names 1862–1865 (CSO-ICR-14)
Irish Department Book, 16 Nov. 1867–6 Oct. 1868 (CSO-LB-170)
Kilmainham Gaol Prison Reel, 1867–1871 (MFGS 51/044)
List of Warrants Issued on the Grounds of Detention Habeas Corpus Suspension Act, 1866 (CSO/ICR 13)
Minutes from the Board of Governors' Meeting of Mercer's Hospital, Various, Nov. 1867 (Form no. 6936)
Mountjoy Gaol Prison Reel (MFGS 51/152)
Police Letter Book, 1864–1869 (CSO LB 456 3/745)
Richmond Bridewell Prison Reel (MFGS 51/073)
The Marquis of Abercorn's Government Letters 1867 (CSO-LB-267)
Will Abstract Book (Last Will of Daniel Ryan, 1887/316)

National University of Ireland, Maynooth

Griffin, Brian, *The Irish Police, 1836–1914: A Social History* (Chicago, 1991)

Office of Public Works

5a College Street, Dublin: site map, 5 June 1915 (U8 9 'C'/Drawing 12)
Head Police Office, Dublin Castle: ground plan c.1867 (U16 7/ Misc. 2)
Chancery Lane/Clarke's Court, Dublin: site map, tracing from lease dated 23 Sept 1861 (L10 11/Drawing 112439)

Registry of Births, Deaths And Marriages

Death Register for 1867

Gilbert Library

Dublin City Council Minutes; Mar. 1867–Mar. 1868
Dublin Corporation Reports 1869
Kane, Edward, P. Beryl Phair and Thomas U. Sadlier (eds), *King's Inns Admission Papers, 1607–1867* (Dublin, 1982)
Shaw's New Pictorial City Directory (Dublin, 1850)

Harvard Library, USA

Trial and Conviction of American Citizens in Great Britain (Washington, 1868)

Public Records Office (London)

Foreign Office Letter Book, Fenianism (5/1342)
Home Office Letter Book (HO 45/7799)
Home Office Letter Book (HO 122/23)
Home Office Letter Book (HO 123/32)
Irish Office Letter Book (CO 906)

Garda Síochána Museum and Archives

Numerical Register of the Officers and Men of all Ranks of the Dublin Metropolitan Police

Meterological Office Archive (Dublin)

Meteorological Observatory Records, Phoenix Park Station, October 1867–February 1868

Suffolk Record Office, Ipswich

Diaries of Gathorne Hardy, 1st Earl of Cranbrook 1866–70 (HA43/T501/294)

Correspondence between Lord Derby and Gathorne Hardy 1867–8 (HA43/T501/259)

Trinity College Dublin

Hansard's Parliamentary Debates, third series, 1830-91 (Vols i–ccclvi, London, 1831–91)

Takagami, Shin-ichi, 'The Dublin Fenians: 1858–1879' (unpublished PhD thesis, Trinity College, Dublin, 1990)

— 'The Dublin Fenians after the Rising: 1867–1879' (unpublished PhD thesis, Trinity College, chapter revision, Dublin, 1992)

Newspapers

Belfast Newsletter
Cleveland Leader
Cork Constitution
Commercial Journal and Family Herald
Daily Express
Freeman's Journal and Daily Commercial Advertiser
Londonderry Standard
Irish Catholic Chronicle and People's News of the Week
Irishman
Irish Weekly Independent (series of articles entitled: 'Romance of Fenianism')
New York Tribune
Penny Dispatch and Irish Weekly Newspaper
Police Gazette – Hue and Cry
Saunders' Newsletter and Daily Advertiser
The Irish Times

The Times (London)
Tomahawk: A Saturday Journal of Satire (London)
Warder
Weekly News (Dublin)
Westmeath Guardian and Longford Newsletter

BOOKS AND ARTICLES

Anderson, A.P. Moore, *Sir Robert Anderson and Lady Agnes Anderson* (London, 1947)

Anderson, Robert, *Sidelights on the Home Rule Movement* (London, 1906)

Bentley, David Jeffrey, *English Criminal Justice in the Nineteenth Century* (London, 1998)

Bussy, Frederick Moir, *Irish Conspiracies: Recollections of John Mallon, the Great Irish Detective and other reminiscences* (London, 1910)

Brown, Malcolm Johnston, *The Politics of Irish Literature: From Thomas Davis to W.B. Yeats* (Washington, 1973)

Campbell, Christy, *Fenian Fire* (London, 2003)

Clarke, Joseph I.C., *My Life and Memories* (New York, 1925)

Comerford, R.V., *The Fenians in Context: Irish Politics and Society 1848–82* (2nd ed.) (Dublin, 1998)

Curran, John Ayde, *Reminiscences of John Ayde Curran, KC – Late County Court Judge and Chairman of the Quarter Sessions* (London, 1915)

D'Arcy, William, *The Fenian Movement in the USA* (Washington, 1947)

Denieffe, Joseph, *A personal narrative of the Irish Revolutionary Brotherhood, giving a faithful report of the principal events from 1855 to 1867, written at the request of friends* (New York, 1906)

Denvir, John, *The Life Story of an Old Rebel* (Dublin, 1910)

Devoy, John, *Recollections of an Irish Rebel* (New York, 1929)

Dillon, William, *Life of John Mitchel* (Vol. II) (London, 1888)

Doolin, William, *Dublin's Surgeon Anatomists and Other Essay: a Centenary Tribute*, ed. J.B. Lyons (Dublin, 1987)

Gathorne Hardy, Alfred E., *Gathorne Hardy, 1st Earl of Cranbrook: A Memoir* (London, 1910)

Herlihy, Jim, *The Dublin Metropolitan Police: a Short History and Genealogical Guide* (Dublin, 2001)

— *The Royal Irish Constabulary: a Complete Alphabetical List of Officers and Men, 1816–1922* (Dublin, 1999)

— *The Dublin Metropolitan Police: a Complete Alphabetical List of Officers and Men, 1836–1925* (Dublin, 2001)

Hunter, W.W., *A Life of The Earl of Mayo* (London, 1875)

James Stephens, chief organizer of the Irish Republic: embracing an account of the origin and progress of the Fenian Brotherhood: being a semi-biographical sketch of James Stephens, with the story of his arrest and imprisonment, also his escape from the British authorities (New York, 1866)

Jenkins, Brian, *The Fenian Problem: Insurgency and Terrorism in a Liberal State 1858–1874* (Montreal & Kingston, 2008)

Kelly, M.J., *The Fenian Ideal and Irish Nationalism, 1882–1916* (New York, 2006)

Liddy, Pat, *Temple Bar: An Illustrated History* (Dublin, 1992)

Lyons, J.B., *The Quality of Mercer's: The Story of Mercer's Hospital, 1734–1991* (Dublin, 1991)

MacDonald, John, *Troublous Times in Canada* (Toronto, 1910)

McGee, Owen, *The IRB: The Irish Republican Brotherhood from the Land League to Sinn Féin* (Dublin, 2005)

MacLeod, George H.B., *Notes on the Surgery of the War in the Crimea with Remarks on the Treatment of Gunshot Wounds* (London, 1862)

Meenan, F.O.C., *St Vincent's Hospital, 1834–1994: an Historical and Social Portrait* (Dublin, 1995)

Moody, T.W., 'The Fenian Movement in Irish History' in T.W. Moody (ed.) *The Fenian Movement: The Thomas Davis Lectures* (Cork, 1967)

Murphy, James H., *Abject Loyalty: Nationalism and Monarchy in Ireland during the Reign of Queen Victoria* (Cork, 2001)

Neidhardt, W.S., *Fenianism in North America* (Pittsburgh, 1975)

O'Brien, William and Ryan, Desmond (eds), *Devoy's Postbag 1871–1928* (Dublin, 1948)

Ó Broin, Leon, *Fenian Fever: an Anglo-American Dilemma* (London, 1971)

Ó Cathaoir, Eva, 'Patrick Lennon (1841–1901): Dublin Fenian Leader' in *Dublin Historical Record* (Vol. XLIV No. 2, autumn 1991), pp. 38–50

O'Connor, Ulick, *The Gresham Hotel 1865–1965* (Cork, 1966)

O'Leary, John, *Recollections of Fenians and Fenianism* (London, 1896)

Ó Lúing, Seán, *Ó Donnabháin Rossa*, Vol. I (Dublin, 1969)

Pigott, Richard, *Personal Recollections of an Irish National Journalist* (Dublin, 1883)

Porter, Frank Thorpe, *Gleanings and Reminiscences* (Dublin, 1875)

Prunty, Jacinta, *Dublin Slums 1800–1925: A Study in Urban Geography* (Dublin, 1998)

Report of the Central Committee for Relief of Distress in Ireland 1862-3 with Appendices (Dublin, 1864)

Rules for Crown Solicitors and Sessional Crown Solicitors (2nd ed. Dublin, 1868)

Rutherford, John, *The Secret History of the Fenian Conspiracy: Its Origin, Objects & Ramifications* (London, 1877)

Ryan, Desmond, *The Fenian Chief: a Biography of James Stephens* (Dublin, 1967)

Ryan, Dr Mark F., *Fenian Memories* (Dublin, 1945)

Savage, John, *Fenian Heroes and Martyrs* (Boston, 1868)

Sullivan, A.M., *The Dock and the Scaffold: The Manchester Tragedy and the Cruise of the Jacknell* (Dublin, 1868)

— *Report of the Trials of Alexander M. Sullivan and Richard Pigott for Seditious Libels on the Government at the County of Dublin Commission* (Dublin, 1868)

— *The Wearing of the Green or The Prosecuted Funeral Procession* (Dublin, 1868)

Sullivan, T.D., *A.M. Sullivan: A Memoir* (Dublin, 1885)

— *Recollections of Troubled Times in Irish Politics* (Dublin, 1905)

Tynan, Patrick, *The Irish National Invincibles and Their Times* (New York, 1894)

Walker, Mabel Gregory, *The Fenian Movement* (Colorado Springs, 1969)

Zimmermann, Georges Denis, *Songs of Irish Rebellion: Political Street Ballads and Rebel Songs, 1780–1900* (Michigan, 1967)

INTERNET SOURCES

Brooklyn Eagle, New York, 1867 and 1868, http://www.brooklynpubliclibrary.org/eagle/index.htm, accessed Sept. 2007

Chronological Index of Patents Applied for and Patents Granted (London, 1868), http://books.google.com, accessed May 2009

Confederate States Medical and Surgical Journal, Vol. 1, No. 2 (Feb. 1864). Richmond: J.B. McCaw (ed.), pp. 22–23, http://www.mdgorman.com/Hospitals/CSMSJ_Vol._I,_No._2.htm, accessed Dec. 2007

The American Catholic History Research Center and University Archives

(Fenian Brotherhood Records), www.aladin.wrlc.org, accessed May 2008

Return of Judicial Statistics of Ireland, 1866 (1867, Volume 66), www.eppi. ac.uk, accessed Mar. 2008

Leavenworth Medical Herald, June 1867; Vol. 1; No. 1, p. 317, http://books. google.com, accessed Jan. 2008

Longmore, Thomas, *A Treatise on Gunshot Wounds* (Philadelphia, 1862), www.biomedcentral.com/content/download/xml/1749-7922-2-28.xml, accessed Dec. 2007

Coleman, William T., 'The San Francisco Vigilance Committees' in *The Century Magazine* (1891), www.militarymuseum.org/SFVC.html, accessed Apr. 2008

Marx, Karl and Engels, Friedrich, *Marx/Engels: Selected Correspondence*, George Hanna (trans.), Robert Daglish (ed.) (Moscow, 1955), www2. cddc.vt.edu/marxists/archive/marx/works/1867/letters/67_11_02-abs. html, accessed Jun. 2007

INDEX

A

Abercorn, Marquis of (lord lieutenant) 71
Allen, William (magistrate) 133, 179, 238
Allen, William O'Meara 165, 168, 169, 172
Anderson, Matthew 122, 137, 199, 236
Anderson, Robert 189, 198, 199, 292, 293, 300
Anderson, Samuel Lee 94, 167, 191, 194, 195, 229, 231, 232, 239, 241, 245, 248, 251, 259, 264, 270, 276, 292, 295, 304
Arms Act 42, 59, 85, 131, 132, 175, 303
Army surgeons 75, 148, 154
Assassination circle 60, 63, 64, 71, 101, 102, 106, 130, 135, 139–141, 155, 157, 159, 161, 163, 173, 182, 188, 193, 205, 246, 261, 286, 288, 290, 291, 293, 302, 312–314
Atkinson, Robert 33, 41, 42, 72, 94, 141, 167, 186, 187, 194, 232
Aylward, Alfred 32, 55, 56, 68, 80, 108, 113, 122, 157, 159, 171, 187, 188, 191–193, 218, 280, 291, 312, 314

B

Ball, John Thomas (MP) 259, 264, 280
Ballybough 300, 302
Bermingham, John (ex army sergeant) 166, 167
Black, George 122, 187
Bolton, George (crown solicitor) 56, 122, 192
Boltonites (street gang) 174
Brady, Thomas 60, 313
Breslin, Michael 158

Brophy, William 139, 140, 164, 188, 219, 225, 236, 313
Burke, Inspector William 64, 79, 80, 84, 101, 131, 172, 174, 175
Butcher, Richard G.H. 15, 30, 32–36, 38, 39, 49, 75–77, 83, 109, 110, 113–116, 118, 119, 128, 148–154, 203, 204, 239, 269, 270

C

Capel Street 56, 79, 80–83, 106, 130, 131, 135, 157, 164–166, 172, 174, 180, 217, 264, 276
Carey, Acting Inspector Mathew 87, 179, 180, 201, 218–220, 230, 246, 263, 307
Carey, Sergeant 160
Chancery Lane 21, 30, 32, 33, 37, 51, 103, 116, 157, 163, 166, 221, 222, 295, 296, 300, 301
Clarke, Ann 28, 46, 49, 81, 108, 240, 256, 273, 278, 283
Clarke, George 58, 112, 113, 171, 251, 295
Clarke, Inspector Joseph 32, 48, 54, 102, 105, 106, 161, 185, 193, 219, 307
Clerkenwell House of Detention 14, 196, 199, 210, 211, 285, 292
Cody, James 32, 220, 261, 286, 290, 313
College Street station 25, 45, 46, 48, 49, 54, 108, 160, 206, 207, 216
Cooke, James 135, 136, 139, 140, 160, 164, 188–190, 196, 210, 221, 280, 292, 293, 313
Coombe 155, 160, 161, 165, 166, 168, 201
Corr, Superintendent Richard 64, 66, 67, 84, 101, 124, 125, 131

Corydon, John Joseph 65, 103, 104, 186, 189, 194, 249, 261–263, 295, 299, 300, 302

Curran, John Ayde 258, 259, 264, 270, 272, 273, 275, 276, 278, 282, 284, 285

D

Dawson, Inspector Launcelot 58, 307

Deasy, Baron Rickard 245, 250, 254, 260, 263, 270, 286

Deasy, Timothy 14, 19, 61, 63, 168, 303

Derby, Earl of 145, 146, 195, 208, 224, 225

Devaney, John 194, 195, 232, 295, 296, 300, 301

Devoy, John 41, 45, 56, 199, 201, 298

Directory (IRB) 139, 140, 164, 186, 202, 312, 313

Dix, Edward Spencer (magistrate) 164, 166, 229–231, 251

Dondrell, James (alias 'Sweeney') 97, 102–104, 130, 132–134, 167, 249, 313

Donnelly, Mary 27, 28, 46, 49, 56, 81, 108, 233, 234, 239, 241, 244, 256, 272, 275

Donnelly, Constable James 28, 29, 35, 46, 243–245, 273, 278, 283

Doran, Inspector William 32, 34, 36, 37, 39, 102–104, 116, 118, 124, 157, 160, 162, 165, 171, 201, 245, 256

Dowling, John 66, 69, 70, 81, 86, 88, 98, 130, 246, 247, 313

Downey, Denis 140, 218–221, 224, 232, 313

Doyle, Acting Inspector William, 48, 54, 60, 81, 102, 105, 106, 188, 308

Doyle, Acting Sergeant Patrick 54, 161

Drumcondra 47

Dublin Castle 17, 18, 45, 48, 56, 57, 72, 73, 75, 100, 105, 125, 132, 144, 178, 187, 195, 199, 209, 214, 217, 228, 246, 248, 280

Dublin Corporation 22, 26, 50, 89, 90, 92–94, 97, 111, 163

E

Egenton, Acting Inspector John 54, 160, 201, 202, 218–220, 230, 232, 234, 244, 263, 268, 274, 308

Eustace Street 27, 28, 82, 102, 204, 252

Exchange Court 40, 45, 46, 52, 58, 60, 67, 158, 223, 234, 243, 306

F

Feely, Michael 138–141, 159, 187, 188, 190, 202, 312, 313

Feilding, Lt Col Percy 100, 199, 213, 214, 234, 235

Fenian rising (1867) 13, 15, 17, 18, 21, 61, 120, 136, 138, 140, 162, 164, 179, 180, 184, 185, 191, 194, 200, 208, 222, 229, 239, 253, 262, 263, 286, 296, 297, 304

Fergusson, James 95, 101

Fire brigade 55

Fitzgerald, Charles 130–132, 174, 175

Fitzgerald, John David 250, 252, 254–256, 265, 266, 267, 269, 270, 275, 282, 283, 284

Fitzgerald, Richard 254

Forrester, Arthur 17–19, 37, 48, 52, 95, 101, 104, 143, 193, 279, 289, 296, 297

Francis, Thomas 97, 139, 140, 171, 248

Frith, Tom 155

G

Garvey, John 279, 281

G Division 23, 37, 40, 41, 43, 44, 86, 125, 157, 171, 201, 202, 232, 251, 292, 306–311

Georgians (Street Gang) 174

Gibney, Luke 183, 279, 280, 284

Gray, Sir John 50, 89

Great Britain Street 53, 64, 84, 96, 131

Green Street courthouse 46, 142, 143, 144, 230, 241, 252, 253, 257, 260, 265, 287, 289, 299

Guilfoyle, John 244, 273

H

Habeas Corpus Suspension (Ireland) Act 14, 43, 49, 132, 247, 287
Hardy, Lord Gathorne 72, 73, 95, 121, 145, 188, 192, 218, 226, 235
Harrison, Michael 245, 254, 259, 267–269, 273, 276, 282
Hayburne, Patrick J. 17, 48, 49, 97, 139, 180, 202, 247, 292
Hemingway, Thomas Alexander 107, 108
Henrick, Stephen John 161–165, 254
Hickey, Constable John 23–25, 27, 30, 36, 37, 117, 233, 238, 240, 271
Hill, William James 134, 190
Holbrook, Christopher 36, 83, 281
Hopper, William 106, 161–165, 254
Hughes, Acting Inspector Edward 59, 60, 135, 155, 308

J

Jordan, Constable Michael 28, 35, 46, 271
Jordan, Michael 51, 108
Joynt, William Lane 78, 90, 92, 124
Jurisprudence (medical) 270

K

Keena, Constable Patrick 15, 21–25, 27, 30, 32, 34–36, 39, 49, 50, 63, 70, 75, 77, 78, 83, 90, 94, 95, 110, 112, 113, 115, 116, 118, 119, 123–127, 130, 133, 148, 153, 168, 182, 194, 201, 205, 215, 252, 255, 265, 266, 271, 274, 282, 285, 293, 295, 296, 301
Keena, John 109, 129, 153
Kelly, Colonel Thomas J. 14, 15, 19, 61, 63, 121, 122, 135, 155, 168, 184, 188, 189, 193, 208, 214, 227, 303, 304
Kelly, Sergeant Stephen 15, 25–28, 35, 36, 39, 49, 68, 70, 77, 78, 82, 83, 90, 94, 95, 110, 113, 120, 148–152, 154, 168, 182, 194, 201, 203–205, 215,

232–234, 236, 238–241, 244, 245, 252, 255, 265, 267–271, 274, 278, 281–286, 288, 293, 296, 301
Kilmainham Gaol 17, 23, 48, 224, 228, 275
Kirwan, John 287, 302

L

Lake, Henry Atwell 70, 71, 86, 98, 124, 135, 140, 157, 167, 200, 205, 206, 217, 223, 225, 243–245, 270
Larcom, Thomas Aiskew 70, 71, 73, 109, 133, 140, 143, 167, 186, 194, 208, 248, 249, 270, 295, 296, 298, 299, 304
Ledwich, Dr Edward 114, 150
Lennon, Patrick J. 122, 140, 159, 182–194, 200–202, 215–219, 222–241, 243, 244, 248, 251, 254–263, 265–268, 272–291, 293–295, 313, 314
Liddell, Adolphus 73, 134, 194, 199
Longmore, Dr Thomas 36, 76, 77, 116, 152, 153
Luby, Thomas Clarke 91, 170

M

Mallon, Acting Inspector John 61, 70, 181, 224, 272, 295, 309
Manchester Martyrs 170, 183, 202, 223, 254, 280
Mayne, Sir Richard 177, 194, 196, 199, 214, 249
Mayo, Earl of 46, 71, 72, 99–101, 121, 127, 133, 143, 145, 166, 168, 182, 189, 198, 217, 218, 224–226, 228, 235, 250, 259, 287, 290, 296
McDonnell, Patrick 22, 278
McDonnell, Peter 65, 66, 68, 69, 80, 81, 88, 97, 98, 104, 130–132, 247, 314
McGarry, Patrick 139, 140, 141, 159, 202
McGrath, James 192, 259, 279, 291
McNamara, Charles 225, 236–238, 246, 314

Mercer's Hospital 15, 29, 30–32, 38, 49, 76, 83, 89, 90, 92, 109, 112, 114, 118, 123, 127, 149–151, 168, 191, 204, 281

Monks, Michael 185, 279, 280, 281, 293, 314

Moore, Dr William 77, 114, 150

Morgan, Dr John 50, 51, 151

Mountjoy Gaol 23, 49, 136, 180, 202, 246, 247, 290, 303, 304

Mulholland, Acting Inspector 64–67, 131, 132

Mullen, Peter 106, 108, 314

Mullingar 22, 55, 109, 125–127, 293

Murphy, John 138–140, 164

Murphy, Margaret 106

Murphy, Patrick John (crown solicitor) 229, 231, 239, 241, 248, 249

Murray, Francis (McHale) 66–69, 80–84, 86, 88, 97, 98, 130, 132, 134, 200, 246, 314

N

Nugent, John Francis 233, 275

O

O'Connell, Daniel 280, 293

O'Connell Considine, Daniel 80, 81, 87, 88, 130, 132, 314

O'Donnel, Charles Joseph (magistrate) 39, 56, 81, 83, 117, 130, 168, 174, 268, 269

O'Donnell, Joseph William (magistrate) 43, 130

O'Donoghue, Maurice 136, 190

O'Donovan, Edmond 297–301, 303, 304

O'Donovan, John 298, 299, 303

O'Ferrall, Commissioner John Lewis 124, 294

O'Loughlin, Jack Cade 79– 81, 83–85, 87, 88, 97, 104, 122, 130–132, 200, 201, 218, 291, 295, 296, 313

O'Mahony, John (James) 13, 48, 135, 212

O'Neill, Constable Charles 25, 41, 51, 93, 112, 116, 219, 295

O'Neill, John 211, 292

O'Sullivan, Daniel 48, 136–139, 188, 210, 213, 214, 291–293, 313

O'Sullivan Burke, Ricard 120, 134, 195–197, 210, 313

Opium 37, 66, 75, 109, 110, 148, 149, 154

P

Penal servitude 286

Police Magistrates 44, 133, 196, 251, 268

Power, John 214

Price, Governor 233

Prison vans 61, 72, 122, 145, 234, 264, 276, 286

Purcell, Theobald Andrew 258–263, 266–269, 274, 278, 279, 281, 282, 285

R

Reilly, George 33, 97, 137, 140, 188, 254, 284, 302, 314

Reilly, John 60

Roberts, William Randall 15, 122, 135–139, 141, 155, 156, 164, 184–188, 193, 208–214, 218–220, 280, 291, 292, 313

Rooney, Thomas 65–67, 69, 80–84, 88, 97, 98, 130–132, 246, 292, 314

Rotheray, Acting Inspector Thomas 54, 95, 108, 200, 310

Ryan, Acting Superintendent James 18, 23, 37, 40–42, 46, 95, 171, 207, 223, 225, 229, 310

Ryan, Constable John 32, 33

Ryan, Superintendent Daniel 14, 43–45, 47, 52, 57–61, 63, 64, 68–70, 73, 75, 80, 81, 86, 87, 95, 96, 98, 100–102, 125, 132–135, 137, 139, 140, 143, 146, 148, 156–159, 163–168, 170, 171, 178, 182, 187–189, 193, 196, 200, 201, 205,

206, 216–219, 221–226, 234–236,
243, 244, 246, 248, 265, 274, 290,
291, 296, 301, 302, 306, 310

S

Sackville Place station 58, 69, 70, 80,
  106, 172, 174
Scanlon, Michael 277, 279, 281
Senate wing (FB) 15, 122, 135, 138,
  139, 188, 208, 211, 214
Seward, William H. (Secretary of State)
  130, 260
Shaw, Charles (law advisor) 248, 254,
  259, 271, 281
Shaw, Dr James (apothecary) 30, 35
Smith, Sergeant Charles 36, 48, 310
Smollen, Inspector John 41, 311
Special commission, (administration of)
  17, 200, 222, 304
Stephens, James 13, 54, 60, 87, 90, 91,
  135, 139, 141, 144, 156, 158, 183,
  212, 214, 220, 251, 298, 304
Stokes, Dr William 36, 38, 119
Strathnairn, Baron (Sir Hugh Rose) 99,
  100, 145, 177, 180, 182, 209, 226,
  234, 235, 270, 274, 296
Stronge, John Calvert (police magis-
  trate) 251
Sullivan, Alexander Martin 90–92, 126,
  176, 178, 252, 254

T

Talbot, Head Constable Thomas 33,
  141, 159, 186
Thompson, Phearson 190, 193, 194
Tisdall, Dr 36, 204
Todd, James Henthorn 299, 303
Tontine Burial Society 159, 193, 312
Tynan, P.J. 295, 296, 299, 301, 302

W

Walsh, John 137–140, 157, 160, 161,
  163, 164, 170, 184, 186, 202, 232,
  251, 254, 281, 284, 291, 312

Warren, Colonel John 65, 260
Warren, Robert 125, 245, 259, 266, 267
Waters, John 176, 223, 225, 236
Westmoreland Street 124, 170, 280
White, Denton 104–106
White, Dr William (Coroner) 112,
  118, 119
White, William Frederick 105, 106

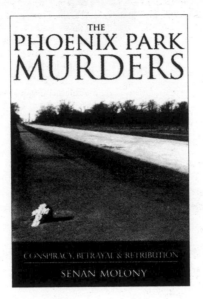

THE PHOENIX PARK MURDERS
Senan Molony
ISBN: 978 1 85635 511 7

A gripping true story of conspiracy, bloodletting, intrigue, execution and revenge, *The Phoenix Park Murders* tells the story of the most infamous crime of nineteenth-century Ireland, when assassins wielding deadly surgical knives killed two men walking in the Phoenix Park on 6 May 1882.

One of the dead is the new chief secretary for Ireland, Lord Frederick Cavendish. The other is Thomas Henry Burke, head of the Irish Civil Service. The government and police must solve this crime. But there are no clues and city detectives do not know where to begin. Forensic evidence is non-existent, and they must attempt to penetrate the dangerous Fenian underworld. But even here no one knows anything because the audacious crime has been carried out by an entirely new group, one styling itself the 'Irish Invincibles'.

www.mercierpress.ie

MERCIER PRESS

IRISH PUBLISHER - IRISH STORY

We hope you enjoyed this book.

Since 1944, Mercier Press has published books that have been critically important to Irish life and culture. Books that dealt with subjects that informed readers about Irish scholars, Irish writers, Irish history and Ireland's rich heritage.

We believe in the importance of providing accessible histories and cultural books for all readers and all who are interested in Irish cultural life.

Our website is the best place to find out more information about Mercier, our books, authors, news and the best deals on a wide variety of books. Mercier track the best prices for our books online and we seek to offer the best value to our customers, offering free delivery within Ireland.

Sign up on our website or complete and return the form below to receive updates and special offers.

www.mercierpress.ie
www.facebook.com/mercier.press
www.twitter.com/irishpublisher

Name:

Email:

Address:

Mercier Press, Unit 3b, Oak House, Bessboro Rd, Blackrock, Cork, Ireland